THE AUTOBIOGRAPHY OF
A SUPER-TRAMP

PARTHIAN
LIBRARY OF WALES

William Henry Davies was born in a pub and learnt early in life to rely on his wits and his fists—and to drink. Around the turn of the century, when he was twenty-two, his restless spirit of adventure led him to set off for America, and he worked around the country taking casual jobs where he could, thieving and begging where he couldn't. His experiences were richly coloured by the bullies, tricksters, and fellow-adventurers he encountered—New Haven Baldy, Wee Shorty, The Indian Kid, and English Harry, to name but a few. He was thrown into prison in Michigan, beaten up in New Orleans, witnessed a lynching in Tennessee, and got drunk pretty well everywhere. A harrowing accident forced him to return to England and the seedy world of doss-houses and down-and-outs like Boozy Bob and Irish Tim.

When Shaw first read the *Autobiography* in manuscript, he was stunned by the raw power of its unvarnished narrative. It was his enthusiasm, expressed in the Preface, that ensured the initial success of a book now regarded as a classic.

THE
AUTOBIOGRAPHY
OF A SUPER-TRAMP

W.H. DAVIES

PARTHIAN
LIBRARY OF WALES

Parthian, Cardigan SA43 1ED
www.parthianbooks.com
The Library of Wales is a Welsh Government initiative which
highlights and celebrates Wales' literary heritage in the English language.
Published with the financial support of the Books Council of Wales.
www.thelibraryofwales.com
Series Editor: Dai Smith
Autobiography of a Super-tramp first published in 1908
© Library of Wales edition 2013
Reprinted 2020
ISBN: 978-1908946072
Cover design by Marc Jennings
Typeset by Elaine Sharples
Printed by 4edge Limited

CONTENTS

FOREWORD

BY TREVOR FISHLOCK

The critical event in the extraordinary life of William Henry Davies was his fall from a freight train in Canada. As a hobo he was an old hand at stowing away on the railway. The trick was to run alongside the train as it started to move, grasp a handle, swing onto a step and settle down to a free ride. In 1899 Davies and his companion Three Fingered Jack were heading for the Klondike gold rush in Alaska. As their chosen train rumbled from the station Davies made an allowance for 3FJ's missing digits and told him to jump aboard first. But as the train gathered speed 3FJ 'stood thoughtlessly irresolute' on the step. Davies ran to keep up until, too late, he leapt and fell.

The wheels severed his right foot. He lay in the snow in the dark calling for help. Good people found him. With impressive sang-froid he lit his pipe. 'I bore this accident with an outward fortitude that was far from the true state of my feelings. I managed to impress all comers with a false indifference.' Good doctors saved him.

He forged his catastrophe into redemption. Had he reached the Klondike he would have continued his rackety ways and spent his gold on more binges and prostitutes. He had sometimes worried about his wandering and squandering. 'The waste of time appalled me, for I still had the conviction that I was born to a different life.' Contemplating his wooden leg in Wales he vowed that since he was denied a Klondike fortune he would strike it rich in writing. 'I pictured myself returning home, not with gold nuggets ... but with literary fame, wrested from no less a place than the mighty London.'

W.H. was born in 1871 at Newport in Gwent. He and his brother and sister were under five when their father died. Their grandparents adopted them and their mother remarried. William read and wrote poetry at school and left at fourteen to be a frame-maker's apprentice. At twenty-two he sailed for New York with adventure in mind. In a park he met a man called Brum who introduced him to the free beggar's life and off they went to look for America.

They rode the buffers of trains, begged for food and wangled winter overnights in warm jails. They fell in with such vagrant buddies as New Haven Baldy, Australian Red, Washington Shorty, Oklahoma Sam and Indian Kid, men who scorned Davies for breaching the beggar's code by taking a job like fruit-picking. He also worked aboard ships carrying cattle to Britain. And then he heard the Klondike call.

All of this is the stuff of *The Autobiography of a Super-Tramp*. Davies did not write it, however, until he had endured years of purgatorial transition from poverty to poethood. He was not entirely penniless when he started on this road: his grandmother in Wales had left him a slender legacy and this he eked in sixpence-a-night lodgings in London as he struggled with writing and rhyming.

He was humiliatingly hopeless at begging and pavement peddling; and his sense of uselessness detonated volcanic rages. After five years of writing and doss houses he felt consigned to despair. Yet his only way out of the swamp was to cling to the fantasy and persevere with the scribbling.

The sudden change in his fortunes was an Edwardian melodrama. You couldn't make it up. He assembled forty of his poems in a thin volume he called The Soul's Destroyer. A printer took a chance on him on condition that Davies himself sold the books. Davies invested in postage stamps and sent the book to people listed in the Who's Who at his local library. A begging letter asked those who liked his work to send him half a crown.

This was a measure as desperate as that of a shipwrecked sailor putting a note in a bottle and throwing it into the ocean. But one of Davies's bottles washed up on the desk of a journalist on the popular *Daily Mail*. With an unerring instinct he wrote a human interest story of the doss house poet with a shining talent. It just so happened that the reading public was ready for such a curiosity. Plus ca change. Other newspapers ran positive reviews of the tramp who could write. *The Tatler*, for heaven's sake, sent a photographer.

There was a second astonishment. Another of Davies's bottles floated to the home of George Bernard Shaw. The great playwright later recalled that he noted Davies's 'remarkably delicate' handwriting and then turned to the poems. 'Before I had read three lines I perceived that the author was a real poet. His work was not in the least strenuous or modern. There was no sign of his ever having read anything otherwise than as a child reads. The result was a freedom from literary vulgarity which was like a draught of clear water in a desert.'

The practical Shaw sent Davies a pound and a list of writers and critics who might help him. One was the Anglo-Welsh poet Edward Thomas who played a crucial part in Davies's fortunes. First of all he sympathized with his struggle, liked his poetry and wrote a handsome review of The Soul's Destroyer in the *Daily Chronicle*. Later, he and his wife, by no means well off, found Davies a cottage in Kent where he could work; and Thomas tactfully arranged a whipround to buy Davies a new wooden leg. He also entertained him to beer and tobacco at the family fireside where Davies told the Thomas children stories of his travels. The children dubbed him 'Sweet William'. A cottage and a cosy fire glowed in Davies's dream of writing success.

Edward Thomas also shepherded him into London's literary gathering places where he met Walter de la Mare, Hilaire Belloc, John Masefield, Joseph Conrad and others. Thomas wrote: 'I have often wondered idly how I should meet the apparition of a new poet ... and now all that I can do is to help lay the cloak of journalist's words over which he may walk a little more easily to his just fame.'

To his dismay Thomas found that some of the poems Davies wrote for a second volume in 1906 were 'painfully mediocre' and 'shabby'. 'It is distressing,' he said, 'and I have to tell him what I think.' Meanwhile Davies started work on his autobiography. As Thomas and his critic friend Edward Garnett read through the first draft they saw it was unpublishable.

The background story, of how Thomas and Garnett midwifed the book into print, was remarkable. Davies had no idea of the difficulties inherent in autobiography and needed their skilled help. His first version was a batch of lurid tales of drink and sex. Thomas and Garnett cut this rubbish and encouraged him to develop the book's laconic prose, the spare, undramatic and straightforward sentences of simple storytelling.

Thomas looked for a literary star to write the preface. Davies wrote to Shaw who said he deemed the task a privilege. His first sentence praised 'this amazing book'. He also composed the title. Shrewd and entertaining, the preface is a significant element of the book. Shaw had his fun, writing that Davies 'had mislaid one of his feet somewhere on his trampings', but was struck by his matter of fact way of dealing with a disaster that most writers would have headlined. Shaw was impressed generally by the 'extraordinary quietness' and 'very curious quality' of the narrative; and declared the book 'worth reading by literary experts for its style alone'. Davies's reaction to the lynching he witnessed in the Deep South retains the power to shock.

The Autobiography of a Super-Tramp was published in 1908 and has been in print ever since. Lawrence Normand, who wrote a searching and admirable biography, *W. H. Davies* (Seren 2003), noted that Shaw's title was a label Davies later resented. He saw himself as a poet and not a tramp. But this most readable book was the bridge that delivered him from his agony and into the life he desired. He was a tramp transformed into a celebrity. For his lyrical and traditional nature verse, in his case sometimes banal, he became with John Masefield, Edmund Blunden, John Drinkwater, Edward Thomas and others one of the group of early twentieth-century Georgian poets. Jacob Epstein sculpted his head, Augustus John and William Nicholson painted his portrait. At fifty he ended a life of temporary relationships with women and found domestic happiness with a young wife, Helen Payne, in a Gloucestershire cottage. His story of this relationship, *Young Emma*, was published in 1980, the year after her death.

In his preface to *Super-Tramp* Shaw wrote of the 'terrible destinies and crushing burdens' that Fortune might award a poet. Davies was a difficult and restless man with a steely view of personal freedom. He derived much in his life from the kindness of strangers and the help of his friends. Among other benefits they secured him a Civil List pension. 'I've never worked in my life,' he said once, 'that is what your friends do for you.'

Trevor Fishlock

PREFACE

BY G. BERNARD SHAW

I Hasten to protest at the outset that I have no personal
knowledge of the incorrigible Super-tramp who wrote this
amazing book. If he is to be encouraged and approved, then
British morality is a mockery, British respectability an
imposture, and British industry a vice. Perhaps they are: I
have always kept an open mind on the subject; but still one
may ask some better ground for pitching them out of window
than the caprice of a tramp.

I hope these expressions will not excite unreasonable
expectations of a thrilling realistic romance, or a scandalous
chronicle, to follow. Mr. Davies' autobiography is not a bit
sensational: it might be the Post Office Directory for the
matter of that. A less simple minded super-tramp would
not have thought it worth writing at all; for it mentions
nothing that might not have happened to any of us. As to
scandal, I, though a most respectable author, have never
written half so proper a book. These pudent pages are

unstained with the frightful language, the debased dialect, of the fictitious proletarians of Mr. Rudyard Kipling and other genteel writers. In them the patrons of the casual ward and the doss-house argue with the decorum of Socrates, and narrate in the style of Tacitus. They have that pleasant combination of childish freshness with scrupulous literary consciousness only possible to people for whom speech, spoken or written, but especially written, is still a feat to be admired and shown off for its own sake. Not for the life of me could I capture that boyish charm and combine it with the *savoir vivre* of an experienced man of the world, much less of an experienced tramp. The innocence of the author's manner and the perfection of his delicacy is such, that you might read his book aloud in an almshouse without shocking the squeamishness of old age. As for the young, nothing shocks the young. The immorality of the matter is stupendous; but it is purely an industrial immorality. As to the sort of immorality that is most dreaded by school mistresses and duennas, there is not a word in the book to suggest that tramps know even what it means. On the contrary, I can quite believe that the author would die of shame if he were asked to write such books as *Adam Bede* or *David Copperfield*.

The manuscript came into my hands under the following circumstances. In the year 1905 I received by post a volume of poems by one William H. Davies, whose address was The Farm House, Kennington, S.E. I was surprised to learn that there was still a farmhouse left in Kennington; for I did not then suspect that the Farmhouse, like the Shepherdess Walks and Nightingale Lanes and Whetstone Parks of Bethnal Green and Holborn, is so called nowadays in irony, and is, in fact, a doss-house, or hostelry where single men can have a night's lodging for, at most, sixpence.

I was not surprised at getting the poems. I get a gift of minor poetry once a week or so; and yet, hardened as I am to it, I still, knowing how much these little books mean to their authors, can seldom throw them aside without a twinge of compunction which I allay by a glance at one of the pages in the faint but inextinguishable hope of finding something valuable there. Sometimes a letter accompanies the book; and then I get a rapid impression, from the handwriting and notepaper as well as from the binding and type in the book, or even from the reputation of the publisher, of the class and type of the author. Thus I guess Cambridge or Oxford or Maida Vale or West Kensington or Exeter or the lakes or the east coast; or a Newdigate prizeman, a romantic Jew, a maiden lady, a shy country parson or whom not, what not, where not. When Mr. Davies' book came to hand my imagination failed me. I could not place him. There were no author's compliments, no publisher's compliments, indeed no publisher in the ordinary channel of the trade in minor poetry. The author, as far as I could guess, had walked into a printer's or stationer's shop; handed in his manuscript; and ordered his book as he might have ordered a pair of boots. It was marked "price half a crown". An accompanying letter asked me very civilly if I required a half-crown book of verses; and if so, would I please send the author the half-crown: if not, would I return the book. This was attractively simple and sensible. Further, the handwriting was remarkably delicate and individual: the sort of handwriting one might expect from Shelley or George Meredith. I opened the book, and was more puzzled than ever; for before I had read three lines I perceived that the author was a real poet. His work was not in the least strenuous or modern: there was in it no sign that he had ever read anything later than Cowper or Crabbe, not even Byron, Shelley or Keats, much less Morris, Swinburne, Tennyson, or Henley and Kipling. There was indeed no sign of his ever having read anything otherwise than as a child reads. The result was a freedom from literary vulgarity which was like a draught of clear water in a desert. Here, I saw, was a genuine innocent, writing odds and ends of verse about odds and ends of things, living quite out of the world in which such things are usually done, and knowing no better (or rather no worse) than to get his book made by the appropriate craftsman and hawk it round like any other ware.

Evidently, then, a poor man. It horrified me to think of a poor man spending his savings in printing something that nobody buys: poetry, to wit. I thought of Browning threatening to leave the country when the Surveyor of Taxes fantastically assessed him for an imaginary income derived from his poems. I thought of Morris, who, even after *The Earthly Paradise*, estimated his income as a poet at a hundred a year. I saw that this man might well be simple enough to suppose that he could go into the verse business and make a living at it as one makes a living by auctioneering or shopkeeping. So instead of throwing the book away as I have thrown so many, I wrote him a letter telling him that he could not live by poetry. Also, I bought some spare copies, and told him to send them to such critics and verse fanciers as he knew of, wondering whether they would recognise a poet when they met one.

And they actually did. I presently saw in a London

newspaper an enthusiastic notice of the poems, and an account of an interview with the author, from which I learnt that he was a tramp; that 'the farm house' was a doss-house; and that he was cut off from ordinary industrial pursuits by two circumstances: first, that he had mislaid one of his feet somewhere on his trampings, and now had to make shift as best he could with the other; second, that he was a man of independent means—a *rentier*—in short, a gentleman.

The exact amount of his independent income was ten shillings a week. Finding this too much for his needs, he devoted twenty per cent of it to pensioning necessitous friends in his native place; saved a further percentage to print verses with; and lived modestly on the remainder. My purchase of eight copies of the book enabled him, I gathered, to discard all economy for about three months. It also moved him to offer me the privilege (for such I quite sincerely deem it) of reading his autobiography in manuscript. The following pages will enable the world at large to read it in print.

All I have to say by way of recommendation of the book is that I have read it through from beginning to end, and would have read more of it had there been any more to read. It is a placid narrative, unexciting in matter and unvarnished in manner, of the commonplaces of a tramp's life. It is of a very curious quality. Were not the author an approved poet of remarkable sensibility and delicacy I should put down the extraordinary quietness of his narrative to a monstrous callousness. Even as it is, I ask myself with some indignation whether a man should lose a limb with no more to-do than a lobster loses a claw or a lizard his tail, as if he could grow a new one at his next halting place! If such a thing happened to me, I should begin the chapter describing it with 'I now come to the event which altered the whole course of my life, and blighted etc. etc.' In Mr. Davies' pages the thing happens as unexpectedly as it did in real life, and with an effect on the reader as appalling as if he were an actual spectator. Fortunately it only happened once: half a dozen such shocks would make any book unbearable by a sensitive soul.

I do not know whether I should describe our super-tramp as a lucky man or an unlucky one. In making him a poet, Fortune gave him her supremest gift; but such high gifts are hardly personal assets: they are often terrible destinies and crushing burdens. Also, he chanced upon an independent income: enough to give him reasonable courage, and not enough to bring him under the hoof of suburban convention, lure him into a premature marriage, or deliver him into the hands of the doctors. Still, not quite enough to keep his teeth in proper repair and his feet dry in all weathers.

Some flat bad luck he has had. I suppose every imaginative boy is a criminal, stealing and destroying for the sake of being great in the sense in which greatness is presented to him in the romance of history. But very few get caught. Mr. Davies unfortunately was seized by the police; haled before the magistrate; and made to expiate by stripes the bygone crimes of myself and some millions of other respectable citizens. That was hard luck, certainly. It gives me a feeling of moral superiority to him; for I never fell into the hands of the police—at least they did not go on with the case (one of incendiarism), because the gentleman whose property I burnt had a strong sense of humour and a kindly nature, and let me off when I made him a precocious speech—the first I ever delivered—on the thoughtlessness of youth. It is remarkable what a difference it makes, this matter of the police; though it is obviously quite beside the ethical question. Mr. Davies tells us, with his inimitable quiet modesty, that he begged, stole, and drank. Now I have begged and stolen; and if I never drank, that was only an application of the principle of division of labour to the Shaw clan; for several members of it drank enough for ten. But I have always managed to keep out of the casual ward and the police court; and this gives me an ineffable sense of superior respectability when I read the deplorable confessions of Mr. Davies, who is a true poet in his disregard for appearances, and is quite at home in tramp wards.

Another effect of this book on me is to make me realise what a slave of convention I have been all my life. When I think of the way I worked tamely for my living during all those years when Mr. Davies, a free knight of the highway, lived like a pet bird on titbits, I feel that I have been duped out of my natural liberty. Why had I not the luck, at the outset of my career, to meet that tramp who came to Mr. Davies, like Evangelist to Christian, on the first day of his American pilgrim's progress, and saved him on the very brink of looking for a job, by bidding him to take no thought for the morrow; to ask and it should be given to him; to knock and it should be opened to him; and to free himself from the middle-class assumption that only through taking a ticket can one take a train. Let every youth into whose hands this book falls ponder its lesson well, and, when next his parents and guardians attempt to drive him into some inhuman imprisonment and drudgery under the pretext that he should earn his own living, think of the hospitable countrysides of America, with their farmhouses overflowing with milk and honey for the tramp, and their offers of adoption for an every day labourer with a dash of poetry in him.

And then, how much did I know about hotels until I read this book! I have often wondered how the poor travel; for it is plain that the Ritzes and Metropoles, and even the hotels noted by Baedeker as 'unpretending', are not for them. Where does the man with sixpence in his pocket stay? Mr. Davies knows. Read and learn.

It is to be noted that Mr. Davies is no propagandist of the illusions of the middle-class tramp fancier. You never suspect him of having read *Lavengro*, or got his notions of nomads from Mr. Theodore Watts Dunton. He does not tell you that there is honour among tramps: on the contrary, he makes it clear that only by being too destitute to be worth robbing and murdering can a tramp insure himself against being robbed and murdered by his comrade of the road. The tramp is fastidious and accomplished, audacious and self-possessed; but he is free from divine exploitation: he has no orbit: he has the endless trouble of doing what he likes with himself, and the endless discountenance of being passed by as useless by the Life Force that finds superselfish work for other men. That, I suppose, is why Mr. Davies tramps no more, but writes verses and saves money to print them out of eight shillings a week. And this, too, at a moment when the loss of a limb has placed within his reach such success in begging as he had never before dared to dream of!

Mr. Davies is now a poet of established reputation. He no longer prints his verses and hawks them: he is regularly published and reviewed. Whether he finds the change a lucrative one I venture to doubt. That the verse in *The Soul's Destroyer* and in his *New Poems* will live is beyond question; but whether Mr. Davies can live if anything happens to his eight shillings a week (unless he takes to the road again) is another matter. That is perhaps why he has advised himself to write and print his autobiography, and try his luck with it as Man of Letters in a more general sense. Though it is only in verse that he writes exquisitely, yet this book, which is printed as it was written, without any academic corrections from the point of view of the Perfect Commercial Letter Writer, is worth reading by literary experts for its style alone. And since his manner is so quiet, it has been thought well by his friends and his publishers to send a trumpeter before him the more effectually to call attention to him before he begins. I have volunteered for that job for the sake of his poems. Having now done it after my well-known manner, I retire and leave the stage to him.

G. B. S.
Ayot St. Lawrence. 1907.

CHAPTER I

CHILDHOOD

I was born thirty-five years ago, in a public house called the Church House, in the town of Newport, in the county of Monmouthshire.

It was kept by my grandfather, native of Cornwall, a retired sea captain, whose pride it was, drunk or sober, to inform all strangers that he had been master of his own ship, the said ship being a small schooner. In those days there was a steam packet, called the *Welsh Prince*, trading regularly between Newport and Bristol, and in the latter town we had relatives on my grandmother's side. The fact of the matter was that my grandmother belonged to Somerset, and she often paid a visit to three maiden sisters, first cousins of hers, living, I believe, near Glastonbury, who had a doting relative that had gone on the stage, and was causing some stir under a different name from his own, which was Brodribb. My grandmother held very strong opinions about the stage, and when these first cousins met, no doubt the young man in those early days, was most severely discussed, and, had he not been a blood relation, would have been considered a sinner too far advanced for prayer.

My earliest recollection is of being taken as a small boy with an elder brother to Bristol on the *Welsh Prince* by my grandfather. I believe the frequency of these trips was mainly owing to the friendship existing between the two captains, as my grandfather seldom left the bridge, taking a practical part in the navigation of the ship and channel—except at times to visit the saloon cabin for a little refreshment.

On one trip we had a very stormy passage, and on that occasion the winds and the waves made such a fool of the *Welsh Prince* that she—to use the feminine gender, as is the custom of every true mariner, of one of whom I am a proud descendant—often threatened to dive into the bowels of the deep for peace. It was on this occasion that my grandfather assisted the captain of the *Welsh Prince* to such purpose that people aboard acclaimed him as the saviour of their lives, and blessed him for the safety of the ship. It is not therefore to be wondered at when the old man ashore, returning at midnight from this rough voyage with me and my brother, would frequently pause and startle the silent hour with a stentorian voice addressed to indifferent sleepers—'Do you know who I am? Captain Davies, master of his own ship.' Whether the police were awed by this announcement, or knew him to be an honest, respectable man with a few idiosyncrasies, I cannot say; but it was apparent to me in those young days that they assisted him home with much gentleness, and he was passed on carefully from beat to beat, as though he were a case of new-laid eggs.

Alas! the *Welsh Prince* became childish in her old age. She would often loiter so long in the channel as to deceive the tide that expected her, and to disappoint a hundred people who assembled on the bridge—under which she moored—to welcome her. What with her missing of tides, her wandering into strange courses, her sudden appearance in the river after rumours of loss, her name soon became the common talk of the town. Her erratic behaviour became at last so usual that people lost all interest as to her whereabouts, or whither she had wandered, and were contented to know that she arrived safe, though late. They were not curious to know if she had been dozing in a fog or had rested for a day or two on a bank of mud; whatever she had done, she had been too wary to collide, and, being too slow to dash through the waves, had allowed them to roll her over with very little power of resistance. These things happened until she was condemned and sold, and her mooring place to this day is unoccupied by a successor. When I now cross the bridge and look down on her accustomed place, I think with a tender emotion of the past. After the *Welsh Prince* had been deposed in her old age, accused of disobeying captain and crew, charged with being indifferent to her duties, and forgetful of her responsibilities—her captain, losing his beloved ship, idled a few months ashore and died. No doubt he had grown to love her, but she had gone beyond the control of living man, and a score of the best seamen breathing could not have made her punctual to her duties; therefore he could not reasonably answer the charges made against her. Some other company, it was rumoured, had chartered her for the Mediterranean, which would certainly be much better for her time of life; the Mediterranean being

3

so large a body of water as compared with the Bristol Channel, would allow her more scope for manoeuvres. But all this was idle talk, probably a profane sneer at her old age, for it was told me by an eye-witness, that she was run ashore in an isolated pool, at the mouth of the river, stripped unceremoniously of her iron, and her wood-work burned. It is only a few years ago since the river was hers, but her name is seldom mentioned at the present day.

It was through being born in a public house that I became acquainted with the taste of drink at a very early age, receiving sups of mulled beer at bed time, in lieu of cocoa or tea, as is the custom in more domestic houses. So that, after my school days were over, I required but very little inducement to drink.

At last the old people, being tired of business and having a little property, retired into private life; my father, whom I cannot remember, being dead, and my mother marrying the second time, much to the old folks' annoyance. Their own children having all died, they kindly offered to adopt us three children, the only grandchildren they had; and mother, knowing that such would be to our future benefit, at once agreed. When we were sealed in private life our home consisted of grandfather, grandmother, an imbecile brother, a sister, myself, a maidservant, a dog, a cat, a parrot, a dove, and a canary bird. I remember those happy days, and often wish I could speak into the ears of the dead the gratitude which was due to them in life, and so ill returned.

My school days began, but I played truant day after day, and the maidservant had to lead me as a prisoner to school. Although small of figure I was a good athlete, and so often fighting that some of my relatives thought that prize fighting

4

was of a certainty to be my future vocation. Mother's father and brothers all took great interest in pugilism, and they knew the game well from much practice of their own. They were never so much delighted as when I visited them with a black eye or bloody nose, at which time they would be at the trouble to give cunning points as to how to meet an opponent according to his weight and height. 'He certainly has the one thing essential,' they affirmed, one to the other, 'and that is the heart. Without that experience would be of no account, but with that it will be the making of him.' If I took off my coat to battle in the streets, the shirt itself came off in the lanes and fields. When attending school I would accompany a dozen or more boys 'following the leader'. Needless to say, I was the leader; and, being a good jumper, would leap over ditches that would try every nerve in my body. Two or three would follow a little less successfully, and then we would bully and threaten the less active to make the attempt. Often we had to drag them out by the hair of the head, and it was in this condition that they were led back to school late— always late. The dirtiest boy, who had had the most pressure put upon him, and was truly the most gentle and least guilty of us all—would be punished the most severely for these escapades, owing to his dirtier condition, and most likely receive more punishment afterwards at home. Strange that I was not a bad scholar, and that I passed all my standards with ease. In the last year of my school days I became captain of the school's football team, and was honoured and trusted by being allowed to take charge of the ball, but owing to making private use of the same, and practising in secret with boys of other schools, I was requested by the Committee to forfeit my trust, although I might still continue captain as aforesaid. If I had been contented with these innocent honours, and had not been so ambitious to excel in other and more infamous parts all would have been well, and my schooldays would have been something of a credit to me. But unfortunately, at this time, I organised a band of robbers, six in number, and all of good families and comfortable homes. It was our wont to enter busy stores, knowing that small boys would not be attended to until the grown people had finished their purchases. Then we would slyly take things up for a curious examination, at the same time watching a favourable opportunity to surreptitiously appropriate them. When accosted by the shopman as to our wants we would innocently ask the price of some article we had agreed on, and receiving answer, would quietly leave the premises. This went on for some time, and I had nefariously profited by a large assortment of miscellaneous articles, such as paints, brushes, books, bottles of scent and various other items that could not be preserved, such as sweets and confectionery. How this continued for six weeks speaks well for our well-laid plans and our dexterity in the performance of them. My girl, Maggie, who had, during our early acquaintance, received only presents of wild flowers and birds' eggs, and occasionally a handful of nuts, was now the happy possessor of valuable presents in the shape of purses, pocket-books, bottles of scents, pencils of silver, not to mention having received a hundred different sorts of sweets and cake that was superior to her mother's. Time after time she promised not to betray me; or any of my confederates. The latter often warned me against reposing confidence in the other sex. One produced a book, at that very moment, which told how a woman betrayed a gang of robbers; and it was his firm opinion that the other sex could not be trusted farther than they could be seen.

At home I was cured of thieving by what I thought at that time to be a very remarkable incident—no more or less than the result of witchcraft. One day my grandmother happened to be standing before the fire cooking, and above the fireplace was a large mirror, towards which her eyes were turned. Thinking this a favourable opportunity to rifle the sugar basin, I lost no time in making the attempt; but my fingers had scarcely closed on a large lump when the old lady, without in the least turning her head, cried in a shrill voice, 'You dare!' For my life I could not account for this discovery, and it sent such a shock through me that I never again attempted in the old lady's presence to be other than honest. She could close her eyes in the arm chair and even breathe audibly, but I never had the confidence to make another attempt. But this incident at home had no detrimental effect on my courage abroad.

One day I and my lieutenant played truant from school, and making our way up town, began to execute various little plans that had been concocted the night before. After several desperate sorties on confectionery, with our usual success, we began to meditate on higher game. We blundered at a cigar case in a chemist shop, and had to leave our spoils behind. Although fearful, we entered a large grocery store, and were having great success, when my lieutenant dropped a bottle of scent, and not having the presence of mind to stand his ground and make it appear an accident, made a guilty rush through the open door. I followed him at once, and catching him up, got clear ahead. But the hue and cry was out, and every one shouted, 'Stop thieves!' This terrible

7

cry, taken up by one and another, took all the strength out of our legs, and our own sheer terror brought us to a halt. In five minutes we were captured and crying over our ill luck in a prison cell. We made a confession of everything, and the rest of the gang were soon under arrest. Our houses were visited by detectives and searched, and different articles were found in cupboards, drawers, desks, and chests which were soon identified by the shopkeepers. Maggie, at the instigation of her mother, gave several articles to the police, with information, proving to me, even in those early days, how little her sex was to be trusted. The unfortunate part of this was that we all had good homes. My grandfather would most certainly have paid a fine of twenty or thirty pounds to save me from punishment, and offered, I believe, to do the same. Alas! the magistrates were inexorable, and I and my lieutenant were sentenced each to twelve strokes with the birch rod, whilst the other four, not being caught red-handed, received six strokes each. I do not at present feel much remorse for those desperate times, but often think of the disgrace to parents. The kindly admonishment of my schoolmaster made me shed the real tears of repentance, not being forced from me by any thought of punishment. This ended my schooldays; and after the breaking up of our gang, I was not allowed much liberty, our elders being afraid of a reorganisation. When I was allowed out for an hour's play, strict injunctions were given me not to leave our own door, and this was not much to my liking. In the dark winter evenings I would sit with my grandfather, my brother and sister, painting ships or reading before a large fire that was never allowed to burn below its highest bar. My grandfather, with his old habits, would pace slowly up and down the half dark passage, shutting himself out in the cold. Every now and then he would open the front door to look at the stars or to inform himself from what latitude the wind blew. The wind never changed without his knowledge; for this wary mariner invariably surprised it in the act of doing so. Three or four times in the evening he would open the kitchen door to see that his family were comfortable, as though he had just made his way from the hurricane deck to enquire after the welfare of passengers in the cabin. When this was done, the old lady would sometimes say, rather peevishly, 'Francis, do sit down for a minute or two.' Then he would answer gruffly, but not unkindly—'Avast there, Lydia,' closing the door to begin again his steady pacing to and fro.

At this time I had a boy companion, named Dave, who was a great reader, had enough self-confidence to recite in public, and was a wonderful raconteur of tales. Great things were expected of him in after years. I have heard since that intemperance prevented their fulfilment, but we were too innocent in those days to think that such would be the case. Through him I became a reader, in the first place, with an idea of emulating his cleverness, which led to a love of literature for its own self. Of course I began with the common penny novel of the worst type, but acquired a taste for better work in a shorter time than boys usually do.

CHAPTER II

YOUTH

Life was very irksome to me at this period, being led to chapel morning and evening on Sundays, and led back; having the mortification of seeing other boys of the same age enjoying their liberty. The only way to alter these conditions was to apply for work. This was soon done, hiring myself out to an ironmonger, at a weekly wage of five shillings. The old people now began to take a pride in me, advising me to study my master's interests, and without doubt succeed to his business at his decease. My brother, two years my senior, who, as I have said before, was odd in his behaviour, took example by me, and succeeded in being employed at a large clothing establishment. It was there and then that he began and finished his life's work in half a day. Having been sent to the dock with a large parcel valued at two pounds ten shillings, he found on arrival that the *Betsy Jane* was moored in the middle of the dock. My brother, seeing this, and not being blessed with inventive faculties, placed the parcel on the quay and returned to his master. Naturally the shopkeeper thought it was safely delivered, until the captain of the *Betsy Jane*, coming straight from his ship, entered the shop to make enquiries about his goods. My brother, having a clear conscience, explained matters in his simple way to the open eyed astonishment of his hearers. The result was a summary dismissal, and a letter to my grandfather requesting him to make good the loss of the parcel; which was duly done, my grandfather being extremely afraid of the law. The old people would never admit that my brother was different from other boys, although it was apparent not only to grown folk, but to the smallest child in the street. Some days before the affair just mentioned my grandmother, having to answer the door, ordered my brother to watch some fish, which was being prepared for dinner. When she returned, the cat was enjoying a good meal under the sofa. To the old lady's cry of 'Francis, did I not tell you to watch the fish,' my brother answered truthfully: for he always told the truth and did what he was told—'So I did, grandmother, and the cat took it.' If she had explained to him properly why she wanted the fish watched, at the same time making special mention of a cat's partiality for fish, no doubt he would have watched to better purpose.

Nothing could have happened better than this instance of the loss of the ship's goods to undeceive my grandfather as to my brother's state of mind. A sudden blaze of intelligence broke in on the old man's mind, which was not of the most brilliant kind. 'Lydia,' said he to his wife, 'there's something wrong with the boy; to think he did not have sense enough to shout, ship ahoy.' I ventured to say, to show my cleverness, that there might have been several ships in the middle of the dock, and they would have all answered to ship ahoy. Would it not have been better to cry, *Betsy Jane*, ahoy? The old man paused thunderstruck. 'Avast there,' he cried, 'drop anchor: will ye have more pudding?'

In our street almost every woman had some one connected with the sea, and it was my grandfather's pleasure by day to parade the street and inform the women as to what winds and tides were favourable to their husbands or sons. One woman had a husband that had sailed away in a barque, which was never sighted or hailed after leaving port, and was now three months overdue. My grandfather feared to meet this sailor's wife, and would often peep around his door, trying to escape consultation from her, knowing well his own forebodings as to the fate of the barque and her crew.

I have mentioned Dave, who was a very studious lad, and who became my one companion and the sharer of my dreams. He had received an old copy of Byron, and we both became fascinated by the personality of that poet. His influence on Dave was so great that it was publicly shown to all the boys and girls in the chapel's schoolroom, where we had gathered for childish games, under the supervision of the elders. While we were playing kiss in the ring, singing and laughing, dancing with merriment, when small white teeth, red lips and bright eyes were all the rage—Dave would lean his figure (not so tall as he would like it) against a pillar, biting his lips and frowning at our merry-making. None but myself knew that his troubles and sorrows were purely imaginary, but they certainly succeeded in causing some sensation, even the notice of the elders being drawn to him. Some time after this we had more trouble with Dave, when we went for a day's trip to the seaside. On this occasion he took his own path across the sands, a solitary figure, with his head bowed down, and when we called him he would not heed us. That night, when it was time to return Dave stood perilously near the edge of the pier, gazing with melancholy eyes on the water. Several women hastened towards him, and drawing him gently away, enquired as to his trouble. On which Dave stood erect, was motionless, frowned, bit his lip, and stalked away into the darkness, without uttering a word. He came back in time to catch the boat. Dave soon got tired of these doings, but the influence of Byron was more lasting on me. It was the first time for me to read verse with enjoyment. I read Shelley, Marlowe, and Shakespeare, indifferent to Wordsworth, but giving him since the attention of wiser days.

My grandmother had only read one novel in her life, called *The Children of the Abbey*, and had been severely punished by her mother for doing so. She therefore continually warned me against reading such works, but strongly recommended Milton's *Paradise Lost* and Young's *Night Thoughts*; her favourite quotation being from the latter—'Procrastination is the thief of time'. It pleased her to tears when a friend saw a likeness between John Bunyan and myself, and she regretted that she saw no prospect of ever tracing a resemblance between our hearts.

I was now bound apprentice to the picture frame trade, but owing to my passion for reading, could not apply myself sufficiently to that business so as to become a good workman. The fact of the matter was that I was reading deep into the night and having to be up early for work, was encroaching on Nature's allowance of sleep. Owing to being

13

young and conceited and not being satisfied at having knowledge concealed, I, showed at this time some parts that made older and wiser people of both sexes prophesy good results in manhood. Having no knowledge of metre and very little of harmony I composed and caused to be printed a poem describing a storm at night, which a young friend recited at a mutual improvement class, making after mention of the author's name, when I was publicly congratulated. Some time after this I—having surreptitiously visited the playhouse on more than one occasion—boldly read out an article to the same class entitled—'In defence of the Stage'. This daring performance caused some commotion among the full grown sheep, who thought they detected a wolf in lamb's clothing; but the young lambs—my companions— bleated for pride and joy. My grandmother was told of this, and as she did not take the trouble to enquire the subject of my address, and it was not told unto her, she was satisfied to know that I had surprised several members of the congregation and in particular a deacon, for whom she had great respect.

It has always been a wonder to me where my conversational power has gone: at the present time I cannot impress the most ordinary men. It must be through associating so many years with companions uncongenial to my taste, a preference for indulging in my own thoughts, and forcing myself to comment on subjects uninteresting to me. I remember at one time being in a lodging house where one man stood out as an authority on books, disease, politics, military tactics, and more especially the meaning and right pronunciation of words. Several times different men have said to me, 'That man is a scholar; he is not an ignoramus,

14

as the likes of you and me.' It was a secret satisfaction to know that this gentleman to whom they referred, often paid me the compliment of knowing more than himself by asking information, which, on my part, was imparted with much secrecy, as I did not wish to appear in any way superior to those with whom I was forced by circumstances to associate. Yet, in those happy days of my apprenticeship, I rarely visited a house but what a second invitation was assured, although a painful shyness marred the beginning. We enjoyed ourselves so much one evening at a friend's house, where the lady had been all day indisposed, that her husband said, on leaving, 'My wife has been laughed out of her sickness, and you have certainly saved me an item on the doctor's bill.' Instead of this giving more confidence and overcoming my shyness, when I received from them an invitation for a second party I became so overpowered at the thought of what would be expected of me, that for the life of me I could not accept it, knowing I would have made an ass of myself. It is not altogether shyness that now makes me unsuccessful in company. Sometimes it is a state of mind that is three parts meditation that will not free the thoughts until their attendant trains are prepared to follow them. Again, having heard so much slang my thoughts often clothe themselves in that stuff from their first nakedness. That being the case, shame and confusion in good company make me take so long to undress and clothe them better, in more seemly garments, that other people grow tired of waiting and take upon themselves the honour of entertainers. It was in the second year of my apprenticeship that I met a young woman living in a small village adjoining this town of my birth, who was very clever, a great reader of fine literature;

and it was to her hands, after I had enjoyed her conversation on several occasions, that I submitted a small composition of my own. Her encouragement at that early time has been the star on which these eyes have seldom closed, by which I have successfully navigated the deeps of misery, pushing aside Drink, my first officer, who many a day and many a night endeavoured to founder me. She was the first to recognise in my spirit something different from mere cleverness, something she had seen and recognised in her books, but had never before met in a living person. I had known her only six months which she died, but her words of encouragement have been ringing in my ears ever since they were uttered.

My grandfather had also died; a straightforward honest, simple man, with a mortal dread of being in debt, and always well prepared to pay his rates and taxes. He had a horror of being a principal in the police courts, but appeared there three times for no offence of his own. Called upon once to examine a rope supposed to be stolen from a ship he proved the rope was of the land, and different from a ship's rope—discharge of the prisoner. On another occasion, Sunday morning, and grandfather being in bed, a detective, disguised as a poor working man that was almost dying for a drink, wheedled the old man's daughter to sell him some liquor over the back wall—the result being a summons for supplying drink during closed hours, followed by a heavy fine, which was at once paid. The third time was at my trial with five other desperados, as described in the preceding chapter. There was nothing false about this man, and he had the heart of a lion. He claimed to have beaten the champion of Portsmouth, but undoubtedly this was some drunken fellow who had taken on himself this much coveted title. Grandfather's pet yarn, which I have heard him recount a hundred times, took place in a public house, where a thin partition divided him from another person who was loudly extolling himself to the admiration of others. Grandfather allowed this man to continue for some time, but at last, losing patience, he looked around the partition and cried in a stern voice, 'Avast there, Captain Jones: I knew thee when thou wert glad to eat barley bread without butter.' Captain Jones looked disconcerted at this remark and then, quickly putting his own head around the partition, whispered: 'Hush, hush, Captain Davies; there's nothing like making one's self look big in a strange place.'

I was now in the last year of my apprenticeship, and was running a bit wild, taking no interest in my trade, and determined in a few months to throw off all restraint. When my time had expired, my master wanted me to continue working for him, which I did for a short time; and, for one who had not yet reached his twenty-first year, received a very fair wage. In three or four months I found some excuse for leaving. I was eager to start for the new world; but my grandmother would not, on any account, supply money for that purpose; so I applied for work at Bristol, was accepted, and worked there six months, being then called home through the death of the good old lady. The licence indulged in during these six months, being in a strange town and unknown, was sufficient to wreck the brains and health of any man beyond recovery, and for the time being deadened all literary ambition. It could not have continued this way much longer, and no doubt it was her death that prevented the collapse of my life, by a change of circumstances. Her estate was in the hands of a trustee, and its profits were to be divided weekly among her three grandchildren. She was a good old soul, and I have lived long enough to cherish every hair of her head. She was a Baptist, stoutly opposed to other creeds—called the stage the Devil's Playground—abhorred second marriages—and thought as much of me in life as I think of her in death. Many of the little kindnesses that were given to her in life were done more out of a sense of duty than from the gratitude of which she was so worthy. But the good old soul died without suspecting any other than gratitude. Mine is the shame and sorrow that she did not receive it, as I am even now thirteen years after her death, living on her bounty. When my grandmother died, I joined home with mother and her second family, but after a month or two of restlessness, I sought the trustee, got an advance from him of some fifteen pounds, and full of hope and expectation embarked for America.

CHAPTER III

MANHOOD

On arriving at Liverpool, I made the acquaintance of a man who had been in America some years previously, and not having his hopes realised at that time, had returned desperate to England, taken in a fresh cargo of hopes, and was now making a second attempt with as much enthusiasm, if not more, than others in making their first. In him I placed implicit confidence, and received such an extraordinary description of that country, the number of stories of some of its highest buildings which were called skyscrapers; the houses of wood which could be moved from one street to another without in any way interfering with the comfort of the people within, cooking, sweeping and washing going on without hindrance; the loneliness of its prairies and deserts; engineering triumphs over high mountains; and how the glorious South was flushed with roses what time the North could not save a blade of green from the snow; all this happening under the one wide spreading flag; this made such an impression on me that I at once went to the steerage cabin and wrote a full description of the country, that very first evening aboard; telling of my arrival in America, and the difference between the old and the new world. This letter was given to the steward at Queenstown, and was written to save me the trouble of writing on my arrival, so that I might have more time to enjoy myself. Several years elapsed before it occurred to me how foolish and thoughtless I had been. The postmark itself would prove that I had not landed in America, and they would also receive the letter several days before it would be due from those distant shores. I can certainly not boast a large amount of common sense.

It was in the month of June, when we made this voyage, and the great Atlantic was as smooth as an inland river. Everyone sought to escape the thoughts of home, and to do so, we often worked ourselves into a frenzy of singing and dancing. Sometimes our attention would be drawn to an iceberg on the port side, very innocent and beautiful to the eyes of passengers, but feared by mariners, who saw into its depths. And then a ship full sail; or another great Atlantic liner on the starboard bow. There was a total lack of ceremony aboard, strangers familiar with strangers, and the sexes doing each other little kindnesses, who had never met before and probably would never meet again, parting without even enquiring or giving each other a name. As we neared the coast we had a thunderstorm, and I was surprised and somewhat awed at the sound of its peals, and at the slower and larger flashes of lightning. Nature, it seemed, used a freer and more powerful hand in this country of great things than is her wont among our pretty little dales, and our small green hills. I thought the world was coming to an end, and in no way felt reassured when an American, noting my expression, said that it was nothing to what I would see and hear if I remained long in God's own country of free and law abiding citizens.

My impression of Americans from the beginning is of the best, and I have never since had cause to alter my mind. They are a kind, sympathetic race of people and naturally proud of their country. The Irish-American is inclined to be the most bitter, remembering from his youth the complaints of his parents, who were driven through unjust laws from their own beloved land; and such a man is not to be idly aggravated, especially under the consideration that our conscience is not too clean in this respect, and that we are apt to be very slow in making that open confession which is good for the soul. The most pleasing trait in Americans, which cannot for long escape us, is their respect for women and the way in which the latter do their utmost to deserve it. No sight of a woman behind the saloon bar listening to the ribald jests of drunken men, and no woman at the bar's front drinking glass for glass with her associates. However weak in this respect a woman may be in private, she is certainly too strong to make a public exhibition of her weakness. Husband and wife may be unhappy, but you seldom hear of a woman carrying the marks of a man's brutality as witness against him which is common in the police courts of old England. A man in a fit of ungovernable passion may kill his wife; and better so, I should say, than to leave her half killed at the foot of the stairs every Saturday night and holidays for twenty or thirty years, and blacken her eyes before they can recover their natural colour, the brutality that shamed me so much in after years in the slums of London, hearing it so often recorded as a jest.

I was so anxious to see the different states of America that I did not stay long in New York before I succumbed to the persuasion of my Liverpool acquaintance to visit with him some friends in a small town in the state of Connecticut, at which place we soon arrived, with something like ten dollars between us. America, at this time, was suffering from a depression in trade, and people were daily returning to the old country, most of them with the intention of returning again to America at a more favourable time. Not being able to get employment at once, and resolved to be independent of the bounty of strangers, I walked out alone, and sat on a seat in the park, trying to conceive some plans for the future. My box, full of clothes, books, brushes, etc., would amply compensate, I thought, for the week's lodging which I had had. Yes, I would see Chicago: and, suddenly becoming aware of a man occupying the other end of the seat, I enquired of him the way to Chicago, as though the distance was a paltry ten miles, instead of a hundred times greater. This man looked at me in astonishment, and at last asked me if I intended to beat my way. Seeing my lack of understanding, he enquired as to my financial resources. On shaking my head in the negative, implying that I had no money, he said: 'No more have I: and if you are agreeable we will both beat our way to Chicago.'

This was Brum, a notorious beggar, who made himself at home in all parts of the country, from the Atlantic to the Pacific coast, and from the northern provinces of Canada to the Gulf of Mexico. The easy and sumptuous way of his catering made me indifferent to all manual labour. In that country, where food was to be had for the asking, where it often went begging to be received, and people were not likely to suffer for their generosity, I became, under Brum's tutorage, a lazy wretch with but little inclination for work. Cockneys make good beggars. They are held in high esteem by the fraternity in America. Their resource, originality and invention, and a never faltering tongue, enable them to often attain their ends where others fail, and they succeed where the natives starve. But my friend Brum held them in great scorn, for their methods were not his methods. Brum was a genuine beggar, who did not make flashes in the dark, having one day plenty and nothing on the next day. What he required he proceeded to beg, every morning making an inventory of his wants. Rather than wash a good handkerchief he would beg an old one that was clean, and he would without compunction discard a good shirt altogether rather than sew a button on—thus keeping up the dignity of his profession to the extreme. He scorned to carry soap, but went to a house like a Christian, and asked to be allowed to wash, with a request for warm water if the morning was cold. Begging was to him a fine art, indeed, and a delight of which he never seemed to tire. I have known him, when surfeited with an abundance of common food, such as steak, chops, etc.—to beg lozenges and sweets, complaining I suppose of throat troubles. Even in a new country like America, there are quite a number of hostile towns, owing to their lying on the main roads between large cities that are not far apart; but Brum never seemed to fail, and would certainly never lower his dignity by complaining of difficulty. In every street, he said, there lived a good Samaritan, and seeing that a good beggar knocks at every door, he must ultimately succeed. She may live in the last house, and therefore the unsuccessful beggar, having no patience and perseverance, fails in his calling. Brum was a slow man in action and went about his business in a dogged way. And that reminds me of how this slowness of action once saved his life. We had built a campfire in the woods, within a mile or more of a small town. Now, it was Brum's habit, before lying down for the night to wind his handkerchief around his neck, and this he had done. Next morning I was the first to rise, and Brum, deliberately following my example, began in his own easy way to slowly unwind this handkerchief, when to my horror a large tarantula fell from its folds. Now, had Brum been an impulsive man, no doubt the spider would have been squeezed, and would have then fastened on his neck and poisoned his blood mortally.

I was soon initiated into the mysteries of beating my way by train, which is so necessary in parts of that country, seeing the great distances between towns. Sometimes we were fortunate enough to get an empty car; sometimes we had to ride the bumpers; and often, when travelling through a hostile country, we rode on the roof of a car, so as not to give the brakesman an opportunity of striking us off the bumpers unawares. It is nothing unusual in some parts to find a man, always a stranger, lying dead on the track, often cut in many pieces. At the inquest they invariably bring in a verdict of accidental death, but we know different. Therefore we rode the car's top, so as to be at no disadvantage in a struggle. The brakesman, knowing well that our fall would be his own, would not be too eager to commence hostilities. Sometimes we were desperate enough to ride the narrow iron rods, which were under the car, and only a few feet from the track. This required some nerve, for it was not only uncomfortable, but the train, being so near the line, seemed to be running at a reckless and uncontrollable speed, whereas, when riding on the car's top, a much faster train seems to be running much slower and far more smooth and safe. Sometimes we were forced to jump off a moving train at the point of a revolver. At other times the brakesmen were friendly, and even offered assistance in the way of food, drink or tobacco. Again, when no firearm was in evidence, we had to threaten the brakesman with death if he interfered with us. In this way Brum and myself travelled the States of America, sleeping at night by camp fires, and taking temporary possession of empty houses.

One night, when darkness had overtaken us, before we could find a fit and comfortable place for camping, we spied a house, and seeing no light in the window, presumed it to be unoccupied. We knocked at the door, and the hollow sound which followed convinced us that no living person was then on the premises. When we lifted the latch and entered we were surprised to see chairs, a table and various articles of domestic utility scattered in confusion on the floor. In spite of this we proceeded to make ourselves easy for the night, and coming out again began to feel in the darkness for wood. Being successful in our search we returned and made a fire, and there we slept until morning. As usual, I was the first to rise on the following day, and went forth in quest of water to make our breakfast coffee. This I soon found, and was bearing it along, when my attention was drawn to a board nailed to the front of the house. There I saw the letters 'Haunted', painted large, and ragged, as though by a hand that had shaken with fear. If we had seen this board on the night previous, no doubt we would have hurried on in dread of our lives, but as it was, we made our coffee and laughed heartily in the daylight. At this time I took a notion to work for a few days, but Brum showed his grinning face so often that I grew ashamed of him, and discharged myself. He seemed to have taken a strange liking to me, and would not leave me, but swore that not even for my sake would he become a working man.

CHAPTER IV

BRUM

Brum was a man of an original turn of mind and his ideas were often at variance with others. For instance, all tramps in America travel on the railroad, whether they walk or take free rides. Therefore it seems reasonable to infer that the people who live on the outskirts of a town, being farthest from the track, would be more in sympathy with tramps, for they would see and hear less of them. But Brum laughed at this idea, and claimed that his own success was through being of a different mind. 'For,' said he, 'as all tramps are of that opinion, therefore the outskirts are begged too much and the centre of the town too little. For instance,' he continued, 'here is the railroad depot, with its restaurant; now, not one tramp in a hundred would visit such a place, for it is on their direct road, and they believe that it receives far too many appeals. This opinion, being so common, must prove it to be false. However, we will test it and see.' Saying which Brum boldly entered the restaurant, leaving me to wait outside. It was a considerable time before he reappeared, and I began to think he was being supplied with a meal on the premises, but at last he came, carrying in his hand a large paper parcel. 'The place is as good as gold,' said he, 'for here we have a day's provisions for two. Take it down the track to that clump of woods, said he, 'for the waiter promised that did I bring a jug or can he would supply me with hot coffee.' I started at once towards the woods with this bag, the weight of which proved the presence of either much meat or pudding; while Brum made his way to a small house near the railroad to see if he could borrow a can. It was not long after this when we were seated in the shady green wood with the contents of this parcel before us, which were found to consist of a number of chops, bread and butter, some potatoes and cake. These, with a quart or more of good hot coffee, made such a meal as a working man could only reasonably expect once a week—the day being Sunday.

One of Brum's peculiarities was, on approaching a town, to look out for a church steeple with a cross, which denoted a Catholic church, and therefore a Catholic community. Making his way in the direction of that cross he would begin operations in its surrounding streets, 'and,' said he, 'if I fail in that portion of the town, I shall certainly not succeed elsewhere.'

I shall never forget the happy summer months I spent with Brum at the seaside. Some of the rich merchants there could not spare more than a month or six weeks from business, but, thanks be to Providence, the whole summer was at our disposal. If we grew tired of one town or, as more often the case, the town grew tired of us, we would saunter leisurely to the next one and again pitch our camp; so on, from place to place, during the summer months. We moved freely among the visitors, who apparently held us in great respect, for they did not address us familiarly, but contented themselves with staring at a distance. We lay across their runs on the sands and their paths in the woods; we monopolised their nooks in the rocks and took possession of caves, and not a murmur heard, except from the sea, which of a certainty could not be laid to our account. No doubt detectives were in these places, but they were on the look out for pickpockets, burglars and swindlers; and, seeing that neither the visitors nor the boarding house keepers made any complaint, these detectives did not think it worth while to arrest tramps; for there was no promotion to he had by doing so. 'Ah,' I said to Brum, as we sat in a shady place, eating a large custard pudding from a boarding house, using for the purpose two self-made spoons of wood—'Ah, we would not be so pleasantly occupied as tramps in England. We would there receive tickets for soup; soup that could be taken without spoons; no pleasant picking of the teeth after eating; no sign of a pea, onion or carrot; no sign of anything except flies.' Two-thirds of a large custard pudding between two of us, and if there was one fault to be found with it, it was its being made with too many eggs. Even Brum was surprised at his success on this occasion. 'Although,' as he said, 'she being a fat lady, I expected something unusual.' Brum had a great admiration for fat women; not so much, I believe, as his particular type of beauty, but for the good natured qualities he claimed corpulence denoted. 'How can you expect those skinny creatures to sympathise with another when they half starve

29

their own bodies?' he asked. He often descanted on the excellencies of the fat, to the detriment of the thin, and I never yet heard another beggar disagree with him.

After seeing Brum wash the dish, and wipe it with his pocket handkerchief, with a care that almost amounted to reverence, and trusting in my own mind that the good lady would have the thought and precaution to wash it again—I settled to a short nap, till Brum's return. For there was no knowing how long he might be away; he might take a notion to beg a shirt, a pair of trousers or shoes, or anything else that came to his mind.

Now, when Brum left, he had on a dark shirt, but I was so accustomed to seeing him change his appearance with a fresh coat, or a different shaped hat, that I was not at all surprised on waking to see him sitting before me in a clean white shirt with a starched front. I said nothing about this change, and he was too good a beggar to give unsolicited information, which would look too much like boasting of his own exploits. That he had met another of his favourite fat ladies, or perhaps the same one had added to her kindness-there was not the least doubt.

Brum's first words rather startled me, for he continued the conversation from the place I left off previous to my sleep. 'When I was in England,' he began, 'I did not experience such hardship as is commonly supposed to exist. Beggars there, as here, choose the wrong places, and not one in three knows which are the best.' 'Surely,' I said, 'a good clean street of houses with respectable fronts, of moderate size, and kept by the better class mechanics, are the best?' 'And so they would be,' he answered, 'if every beggar did not think so. But let me tell you, for your benefit if ever stranded in England, the best places for beggars to operate.' How I learned the truth of his wise teaching, in after days! Every fine looking street you chance upon, pass it; but every little court or blind alley you come across, take possession without delay, especially if its entrance is under an arch, which hides the approach to the houses, making them invisible from the street. Such little out of the way places are not only more profitable than good streets, but are comparatively safe where the police are unusually severe. Then again you should avoid every town that has not either a mill, a factory, or a brewery; old fashioned towns, quiet and without working people—except a few gardeners, coachmen, domestic servants etc.; such places where you see a sign at the free libraries warning tramps not to enter, and every plot of land has its sign—'Beware of the Dog'. In towns where working men are numerous, and the idle rich are few, such signs are not to be seen. 'Of course,' he continued, 'your object in England must be money, for you cannot expect to get meat, cake and custard pudding in a land where even the rich live poorer, with regards to diet, than the labouring classes of this country.' I remembered these wise thoughts of Brum, uttered on the shores of the Atlantic, and if I did not profit much by them in my own experience in England, I certainly made enough attempts to test their truth. I always kept a keen eye for blind alleys, and quiet courts under arches, and I invariably came out of one richer than I went in. And what nice quiet places they are for drinking cups of tea on a doorstep, with only a neighbour or two to see you, and perhaps thousands of people passing to and fro in the street at the other side of the arch. There is no thoroughfare for horses and carts; no short cut for business men, and the truth of the matter is that a number of the inhabitants themselves, born and bred in the town, know not of the existence of such places; and others, knowing them, would be ashamed to confess their acquaintance with them. But Brum knew where to find the kindest hearts in England, not in the fine streets and new villas, but in the poor little white-washed houses in courts and alleys.

CHAPTER V

A TRAMP'S
SUMMER VACATION

We were determined to be in the fashion, and to visit the various delightful watering-places on Long Island Sound. Of course it would be necessary to combine business with pleasure, and pursue our calling as beggars. With the exception of begging our food, which would not be difficult, seeing that the boarding houses were full, and that large quantities of good stuff were being made, there was no reason why we should not get as much enjoyment out of life as the summer visitors. We would share with them the same sun and breeze; we could dip in the surf at our own pleasure, and during the heat of the day we could stretch our limbs in the green shade, or in the shadow of some large rock that overlooked the Sound. However, we could no longer stand the sultry heat of New York, where we had been for several days, during which time we had been groaning and gasping for air. So I and Brum started out of the city, on the way towards Hartford, Connecticut, with the intention of walking no more than six miles a day along the sea coast. What a glorious time we had; the people catered for us as though we were the only tramps in the whole world, and as if they considered it providential that we should call at their houses for assistance. The usual order of things changed considerably. Cake—which we had hitherto considered as a luxury—became at this time our common food, and we were at last compelled to install plain bread and butter as the luxury, preferring it before the finest sponge-cake flavoured with spices and eggs. Fresh water springs were numerous, gushing joyously out of the rocks, or lying quiet in shady nooks; and there was many a tramp's camp, with tin cans ready to hand, where we could make our coffee and consume the contents of paper bags. This part of the country was also exceptionally good for clothes. Summer boarders often left clothes behind, and of what use were they to the landladies, for no rag-and-bone man ever called at their houses. The truth of the matter was that in less than a week I was well dressed from head to foot, all of these things being voluntary offerings, when in quest of eatables. Brum, of course, had fared likewise, but still retained the same pair of dungarees, which he swore he would not discard except at the instance of a brand new pair of tweeds. It was this pair of working man's trousers which had caused a most regrettable mistake. We had just finished begging at one of these small watering-places and, loaded with booty, were on our way in the direction of the camp which Brum informed me, was half a mile north of the town. When we reached this camp we found it occupied by one man, who had just then made his coffee and was about to eat. On which Brum asked this man's permission

34

to use his fire, which would save us the trouble of making one of our own. The stranger gave a reluctant consent, and at the same time moved some distance away, as though he did not wish further intimacy. While we were gathering wood and filling our cans at the spring, I could not help but see this stranger glaring hatefully at my companion's trousers, and expected every moment to hear some insulting remark. At last we were ready and Brum proceeded to unload himself. He had eight or nine parcels of food distributed about his clothes, but in such a way that no one could be the wiser. It was then that I noted a change come over the stranger's face, who seeing the parcels, seemed to be smitten with remorse. In another moment he was on his feet and coming towards us, said impulsively—'Excuse me, boys, for not giving you a more hearty welcome, but really'—glancing again at my companion's trousers—'I thought you were working men, but I now see that you are true beggars.' Brum laughed at this, and mentioned that others had also been deceived. He explained that the said trousers had been given him against his wish, but on seeing that they were good, and were likely to outlast several pairs of cloth, he had resolved to stick to them for another month or two. 'I regret having had such an opinion of you,' said the stranger, in a choking voice, 'and trust, boys, that you will forgive me.' Thus ended in a friendly spirit what promised at first to become very unpleasant.

This stranger turned out to be New Haven Baldy. We had never had the pleasure of meeting him before, but had often heard of him. He had a great reputation in the State of Connecticut, which he never left—except for an annual trip through Massachusetts to the city of Boston. There was not one good house in the former State that was not known to Baldy. This was put to the test in our presence, that very day. A man came to the camp who, poor fellow, claimed to be a hard-working man. He had lost his job and had been robbed of his savings, now being forced to walk home to Meridan. He had never begged in his life, and had now been without food for two days, and was almost too weak to continue his journey. 'Yes' said Baldy, 'and when you are settled at home, and the wrinkles are taken out of you, what sympathy will you have with us? You will tell us to go and work for our living, the same as yourself.' The poor fellow protested, saying that he had never known his mother to refuse any man food. At this Baldy pricked up his ears and enquired of the stranger his mother's address. On hearing the name of the street Baldy at once proceeded to describe the one—and only one—good house to be found there. 'That is our house,' said the stranger. Baldy, not yet convinced, asked for a description of the old lady and her husband. This was given, to Baldy's satisfaction. 'Well,' said he, 'I have had many a meal at your house, and you shall now have one with me.' Saying which he gave the stranger a parcel which, being spread on the grass, was seen to contain several meat sandwiches and a number of small cakes. After eating these, and others from Brum, the stranger left, saying that he would not again feel hungry until he reached home.

After the stranger had gone Baldy laughed immoderately. 'That man's father,' said he, 'was a railroad man, who became a boss, and at last retired on a comfortable little sum. In the kitchen, where the old people have often fed me, the old man has hung on the wall the shovel which he had used in his early days. There it is to be seen tasselled and kept shining bright, and treated reverently as a family heirloom. How I have laughed,' continued Baldy, 'to see that shovel, to think what a simple old fellow he must be to take a pride in showing how he toiled in his early life. Every time I go there the old man points at the shovel with pride, and I have as much as I can do to keep a calm face in listening to its history. But in spite of all that the old man is a good sort, and I am glad to have been able to assist his son.'

Alas, what a disastrous end was ours! When we reached the town of New Haven, we began to beg from passers-by in the open streets and in less than an hour were in jail. On being brought up next morning before the judge, we were each sentenced to thirty days. But what hurt our feelings most was the personal comment of the judge that we were two brawny scoundrels who would not work if we had the chance. However true this might be as applied to us in a moral sense, it certainly was not a literal fact, for we were both small men. People who, not seeing us, would read this remark in the local paper, would be misled as to our personal appearance. I am doubtful whether any judge is justified in using such a term. At any rate, thirty days had to be served.

We were in a far better position than an Italian who was waiting to be tried for murder, and whose cell was not far distant from ours.

At this jail we had to perform the light labour of caning chairs, and were well treated in the way of food and sleeping accommodation and, in addition, received a liberal supply of chewing tobacco.

Being interested in the Italian, the first thing we did on regaining our liberty was to enquire as to his fate. We were told that he had received a life sentence; or, as our alien informant strangely expressed it - 'Antonia, he didn't get some of de time, but he got all of de time.'

Thus what promised to be a summer's outing full of enjoyment, came to a disastrous close sooner than we expected. And, when we were again free, the summer season was practically over, the visitors were gradually leaving for their town houses; which meant that our treatment at the boarding houses would become colder and colder in accordance with the number of boarders.

At this time I accepted employment as a wood-chopper, but unfortunately the work did not last; and just as I began to feel the inclination for this more respectable life, I was discharged, much to Brum's delight, who was apparently disgusted with this new innovation called work, and could not understand any man's desire for it.

CHAPTER VI

A NIGHT'S RIDE

Although I had at this time become lazy, losing almost all sense of respectability, I often reproached Brum for the aimlessness of this existence; telling him we must seek work and attend to other wants than those of the body. I would tell him of the arts, and how the cultivation of them was lost to us through a continual lack of funds. I told him of the pleasures of reading, visiting picture galleries, museums and theatres, and of the wonders of instrumental music, and of the human voice. Once when we were passing through a street in New Orleans, I paused to listen to a woman singing. Brum, like the faithful companion he was, waited my pleasure, until he too seemed to become impressed by some unusual feeling. The song ended, and as we went our way, I said—'There, Brum, what do you think of that?' 'O lor,' he answered, awestruck, 'wasn't she a blooming cat!' making me laugh heartily at such a strange expression of praise, knowing that it was meant to be truthful and sincere.

Having done a few days' work, as mentioned in the preceding chapter, I resolved to come to an understanding with Brum at once as to our future plans. With this end in view, I invited him to a drink, and thus began: 'What do you intend doing? Your life is not mine. We often go for days without reading matter, and we know not what the world is saying; nor what the world is doing. The beauty of nature is for ever before my eyes, but I am certainly not enriching my mind, for who can contemplate Nature with any profit in the presence of others. I have no leisure to make notes in hopes of future use, and am so over-packing my memory with all these scenes, that when their time comes for use, they will not then take definite shape. I must go to work for some months, so that I may live sparingly on my savings in some large city, where I can cultivate my mind.' Now, Brum's method of begging was different in large cities from what it was in the country. In the latter he found no use for money, except for hair cutting or shaving; and when this became necessary he never failed to get the requisite amount for his purpose. When he was ready to have this office performed, it was his custom to interview the Catholic priest of the community, and beg the use of his razor, knowing it was part of that person's creed to shave continually. Of course, the priest would not think of lending his razor to an entire stranger, but seldom refused the ten cents that were necessary for that operation. But in the large cities, Brum scorned private houses, and begged money in the streets, and in their various stores; purchased his meals at a restaurant, and paid his lodgings like an honest working man. Therefore, thinking my discontent was mainly owing to the lack of funds, he said—'All this haste from

40

place to place is not at all to my liking. If you wish to settle in a large city, I can guarantee two dollars a day, at the least, between us, for a visit to the theatre, music hall, for books, papers, or an occasional glass of grog.' 'No, no,' I said, 'we must either work or part. There are three dollars, half of my earnings, so please yourself whether we work or part, whether you go or stay; for I have already decided my own course. What is it to be?' 'Well,' said he, after a long pause, 'we are now near to the hop country, and they start picking some time next week; that is about the only work to be had at this time of the year.'

Upon this we had several drinks, for I was so pleased at Brum's decision, that I ordered drink after drink with bewildering succession. Brum informed me of a freight train that was to leave the yards at midnight, on which we could beat our way to a small town on the borders of the hop country. Not knowing what to do with ourselves until that time arrived, we continued to drink until we were not in a fit condition for this hazardous undertaking—except we were fortunate to get an empty car, so as to lie down and sleep upon the journey. At last we made our way towards the yards, where we saw the men making up the train. We kept out of sight until that was done and then in the darkness Brum inspected one side of the train and I the other, in quest of an empty car. In vain we sought for that comfort. There was nothing to do but to ride the bumpers or the top of the car, exposed to the cold night air. We jumped the bumpers, the engine whistled twice, toot! toot! and we felt ourselves slowly moving out of the yards. Brum was on one car and I was on the next facing him. Never shall I forget the horrors of that ride. He had taken fast hold on the handle bar of his car, and I had done likewise with mine. We had been riding for some fifteen minutes, and the train was going at its full speed when, to my horror, I saw Brum lurch forward, and then quickly pull himself straight and erect. Several times he did this, and I shouted to him. It was no use, for the man was drunk and fighting against the overpowering effects, and it was a mystery to me how he kept his hold. At last he became motionless for so long that I knew the next time he lurched forward his weight of body must break his hold, and he would fall under the wheels, and be cut to pieces. I worked myself carefully towards him and woke him. Although I had great difficulty in waking him, he swore that he was not asleep. I had scarcely done this when a lantern was shown from the top of the car, and a brakesman's voice hailed us. 'Hallo, where are you two going?' 'To the hop fields,' I answered. 'Well,' he sneered I guess you won't get to them on this train, so jump off, at once. Jump! d'ye hear?' he cried, using a great oath, as he saw we were little inclined to obey. Brum was now wide awake. 'If you don't jump at once, shouted this irate brakesman, you will be thrown off.' 'To jump,' said Brum quietly, 'will be sure death and to be thrown off will mean no more.' 'Wait until I come back,' cried the brakesman, 'and we will see whether you ride this train or not,' on which he left us, making his way towards the caboose. 'Now,' said Brum, 'when he returns we must be on the top of the car, for he will probably bring with him a coupling pin to strike us off the bumpers, making us fall under the wheels.' We quickly clambered on top and in a few minutes could see a light approaching us, moving along the top of the cars. We were now lying flat, so that he

42

might not see us until he stood on the same car. He was very near to us, when we sprang to our feet, and unexpectedly gripped him, one on each side, and before he could recover from his first astonishment. In all my life I have never seen so much fear on a human face. He must have seen our half drunken condition and at once gave up all hopes of mercy from such men, for he stood helpless, not knowing what to do. If he struggled it would mean the fall and death of the three, and did he remain helpless in our hands, it might mean being thrown from that height from a car going at the rate of thirty miles an hour. 'Now,' said Brum to him, 'what is it to be? Shall we ride this train without interference, or shall we have a wrestling bout up here, when the first fall must be our last? Speak?' 'Boys,' said he, affecting a short laugh, 'you have the drop on me; you can ride.' We watched him making his way back to the caboose, which he entered, but every moment I expected to see him reappear assisted by others. It might have been that there was some friction among them, and that they would not ask assistance from one another. For instance, an engineer has to take orders from the conductor, but the former is as well paid, if not better, than the latter, and the most responsibility is on his shoulders, and this often makes ill blood between them. At any rate, American tramps know well that neither the engineer nor the fireman, his faithful attendant, will inform the conductor or brakesman of their presence on a train. Perhaps the man was ashamed of his ill-success, and did not care to own his defeat to the conductor and fellow brakesmen; but whatever was the matter, we rode that train to its destination and without any more interference.

As we neared the town we saw a large campfire in a small dingle near the track, at which a man lay asleep. Seeing this comfortable sight, and being cold and tired, we made up our minds to jump off the train as soon as possible, and to return to that fire for a few hours' comfort. The whistle blew for the station, and the train began gradually to slacken speed, when we jumped from the bumpers; and our limbs being stiff, we staggered and fell, but received no hurt. It must have been a mile or more back to that place, but we arrived there in due time, and without waking its solitary occupant, were soon stretched out fast asleep on the other side of the fire. When we awoke the stranger had already been to town, had returned with food, and was now making coffee in a tomato can, all of which he generously offered to share with us. This I gladly accepted, but Brum declined with thanks, saying that he was always capable of getting his own meals, and if needs be, could beg enough for half a dozen others. I gave this stranger my entire confidence, and soon learnt that he had come to these parts for the same purpose. 'We three,' said he, 'will work together on the same land, and under the one master. I am a moulder by trade,' he continued, 'and a week ago I had a hundred dollars saved, but went on the spree, and am now probably without a cent.' To my surprise, at this stage of the narrative, he unlaced his right boot and began to feel in its toes, at the same time shaking his head despondently. After which he put it on again and laced it. 'Yes,' he said, taking off his coat and feeling the lining, 'a week ago I had a hundred dollars saved.'

Brum, having now returned from town laden with sandwiches, cakes, etc., and he having had a hot dinner from a convent we packed those necessaries for future use, and started on foot for the hopfields. Every now and then the stranger—whom Brum at once called Australian Red, owing to his being born in that country, and his having a florid complexion—would try our patience extremely by sitting on fallen timber and taking off his boot, sometimes the two; and after feeling in them, replacing them on his feet, with a sigh of disappointment. Often he would take off his hat and minutely examine the lining, to our unfeigned astonishment. At one time we lost all patience with him. He had seen a low stack of timber, and requested a few moments' delay. On this being granted, Australian Red began to take off his garments one by one, and to examine them. Not one article was placed aside without having undergone a thorough scrutiny, until nothing but his shirt remained. All this waste of time was very trying to our patience, and when he was again dressed, we requested him at once and for all to put a stop to such manoeuvres. We walked on in silence, but had scarcely covered a short mile, when Red was seen to be preparing to strip for another investigation. On seeing which Brum, losing a little patience, said—'Look here, old fellow, if such is going to be your conduct, you can't, on no account, travel any further with us.' For a time Australian Red looked undecided, and then let his coat slip back to its position. 'It is like this,' he said, 'I am a moulder by trade: a week ago I had a hundred dollars saved, but where are they now? It is always my custom,' he continued, 'when I go on the spree, to secrete my money in some safe place. Although I have no recollection of doing so, I am positively assured that such has been the case; and would not be surprised at any moment to discover a twenty dollar bill in the lining of my clothes; but, with regards to the boots, I am now thoroughly satisfied.' When I became better acquainted with Australian Red, this peculiarity was often made apparent to me. Perhaps he did secrete money, for I have often wondered as to where it had vanished. Whether or not, it was certainly never to be found on his person, and must have been slipped under the mat in strange places, dropped into vases, or hidden behind looking-glasses.

In a day or two we reached the hop-fields and all three succeeded in being hired by the same farmer. This could not have been very well different, as neither one would have otherwise worked. The season, if I remember right, lasted between three and four weeks, which we began and finished, but were not very well satisfied with the financial result. Our total earnings were, clear of all expenses, about forty dollars, and with that amount we walked to the nearest large town intending to beat our way to New York. The sight of a flask of whiskey in the hands of Australian Red, enlightened us considerably as to the time of trains, their qualification for carrying human freight, and the cruel or kind disposition of their attendant crews. We made choice of a train leaving about dusk, and finding an empty car on a sidetrack, we entered it, to wait as patiently as possible until that time came. We were not so quiet as we should have been, considering that we were trespassing on the railroad; and that is why we were soon startled by a voice crying: 'What are you doing there? Do you know that you are trespassing on the railroad?' With that the marshal of the town stood before the open door, showing the star of his authority on his dark clothes. 'I can't get any sleep day or night, through you fellows,' he said; 'consider yourselves

under arrest.' Saying this, he marched us off at the point of
a revolver, and began seeking the judge for our trial at that
strange hour of the night.

CHAPTER VII

LAW IN AMERICA

As he marched us along, he made several enquiries as to our finances, to know if we were prepared to pay a fine. Being assured of this he took a very despondent view of our case.

Brum explained afterwards, when it was too late, that trespassing on the railroad was always considered a very serious offence during this month of the year, when men were returning with their small earnings from the hop-fields, which were not sufficient to enable them to travel as passengers. He explained that trespassing on the railroad was not only overlooked, but was openly encouraged when men had to pick hops to fill their pockets; but as soon as those pockets were filled by picking hops, the local magistrates lost no time in giving the police strict orders to fall to, arrest and detain, so that a picker's pocket might be picked by them of his little earnings.

The marshal stopped several citizens, enquiring as to the whereabouts of a person named Stevens. To my surprise, we were not lodged for the night in the common jail, but were led into a public house, which in that country is referred to as a saloon. As we entered this place, and stood in front of its bar, we did not look much like prisoners. Brum called for four drinks, and the marshal drank his respect for us in a very friendly manner indeed. After which he took the landlord aside for a short consultation, in which I heard the man Stevens mentioned more than once. Then he came back and had another drink, this time at the expense of Australian Red. Some customers now arrived, followed by a lean, solemn looking person, whom the marshal took no time in accosting as Judge Stevens. This gentleman at once called for whiskey, then looked from the marshal to us, and from us to the marshal, at the same time nodding his head approvingly to the latter. The marshal cleared his throat and began: 'I found these men trespassing on the railroad, and at once arrested them.' The judge again nodded his head in approval to this red, burly individual, who had made a claim of being robbed of his sleep day and night, and turning to us said: 'Boys, we have to put a stop to these things, drink and follow me.' He led the way into a small back room, and we followed with the marshal, the citizens bringing up the rear. The marshal gave evidence of our arrest, making special mention of our possession of money. The judge wished to be informed of the exact amount, and being told that it was something like ten dollars each, summed up the case at once. 'Boys,' he said, 'I fine you each five dollars, in default of which you must go to Syracuse for thirty days'—at which place was the county jail. Now, I was always outspoken, and was never forced by fear, under any circumstances, to conceal my thoughts, which if I saw real injustice or

49

hypocrisy, would be blurted out in a more dignified court than this. This mock trial, which at first had been highly amusing, exasperated when it came to paying half of my hard earnings, so I told this judge plainly that my friends might please themselves, but that he would not get one cent out of me. Brum supported me in this, but Australian Red began to finger his dollars, whereat the marshal quickly snatched them out of his hand, deducted five dollars, which he gave to the judge, and returned the rest. Judge Stevens looked at us steadily for a time, and then asked this astounding question: 'Boys, how much are you prepared to pay?' Brum, who had very little sense of justice, and being such a good beggar, set very little value on money, asked the judge if he would accept three dollars from each of us. If I had been alone at this time I would have paid nothing, but to save Brum from going to prison, who I knew would support me through all, I satisfied myself that, if the judge approved of this amount, I would pay it without further comment. The judge appeared to weigh the matter seriously, and then cried, with a magnanimity that was irresistible— 'Pass over the dollars, boys; you shall have a chance this time.'

The trial was not here ended, as most of us believed. A citizen, who had been an interested spectator of this scene, and who had been fidgeting in his seat for some time, now rose to his feet, and said—'Where is the justice of this? These men are all guilty of the same offence, and yet one is fined five dollars, and the other two get off more leniently, with the loss of three dollars each; this certainly cannot be called justice.' At this the judge showed the first signs of passion. 'Sir,' he shouted in wrath, 'who is the judge, I or you? If you ever again interfere with our proceedings, in this manner, I shall fine you for contempt of court—contempt of court, sir, contempt of court.' This citizen and lover of justice, collapsed stricken with awe, bluffed and discouraged. 'Come, boys,' said the judge, and he led the way back to the bar. There, he produced a two dollar bill, which was part of our fine, and called for drinks for the house. We followed his example, late prisoners and citizens, and were all happy together until a late hour.

The marshal who seemed to have a little respect for me, for having shown the spirit of free speech before the judge, took me aside and asked whether we intended to take advantage of the invitation given by the citizen who had been threatened for contempt of court—to spend the night at his house. 'I don't think so,' I said; 'we have had enough of this town, and intend leaving it tonight.' Shortly after these words we left the saloon, but had scarcely reached the street end, when I heard steps following, and to my surprise, the marshal was soon at our side. Now comes the most extraordinary part of this story, which I have often been diffident in relating, thinking it would not be credited. 'Boys,' said this burly fellow, who could not get any sleep day or night, 'get you to the railroad, and if any one interferes with you, tell them that the marshal sent you; I shall be with you in about twenty minutes.' We were soon at the railroad, were not interfered with, and the marshal followed in a short time. 'Listen,' he said to us, who were again trespassers on the railroad, at his pleasure and instigation: 'There is a train already made up to start in five minutes time; get into this empty car, and by heavens, no man shall interfere with you.' Which we did, and when the train started, the marshal was there, beside the car, wishing us a pleasant goodbye. 'Why,' said Brum, when I commented in astonishment at all this, 'it is nothing unusual. One day,' he began, 'I was in a small town in Ohio. Seeing a freight train leaving the station, I leaped into an empty car, just as the train started. When safe inside, I turned and stood in the open doorway, and looking out, saw the marshal standing on the platform, looking after me, so I waved him a sarcastic farewell. But the train, instead of increasing in speed, began to slow, and coming to a standstill, began at once to back towards the station. Before I could decide on my course of action, we were again standing in front of the station, with my car facing the marshal, who seemed to have waited, expecting this to happen. "Hallo," he cried, "come out of that for you are under arrest." I was lodged in the jail, and was next morning brought up for trial. The marshal gave evidence as to seeing me jump the train, and I was charged with that offence. Having no money, I was about to be sent to jail when the judge asked the marshal to examine my hands which, although I had done no work for a number of years, were still hard and horny. I said that I was a seafaring man, and exhibited pictures of boats and anchors tattooed on my arms, at the same time offering to show the *Polly Jane* in full sail across my breast. My strange calling, in that inland town more than a thousand miles from the coast, appeared to greatly interest the judge, who, after several friendly questions, discharged me with a caution. Instead of at once taking advantage of my freedom, I sat down, waiting the end of the court. Another prisoner was then brought up who had been seen loafing on the station platform all the previous day. This prisoner pleaded guilty, and said that he had waited in vain for hours for a freight train to carry him to his destination, he having no money to pay his fare as a passenger. "Hold," cried the marshal, that is a lie, for I myself saw a train steaming out when you were loafing indifferently on the platform." "Ten dollars, or sixty days," said the judge. This will show you how one prisoner was charged for stealing a ride on a freight train, and another prisoner was charged for not doing so as the opportunity occurred, happening in the same court, and under the same judge. Again,' continued Brum, 'I know a prisoner, in an adjoining state, who was sentenced to ten years for embezzlement. The money was never recovered, and he probably has it safe until his time expires. This prisoner is receiving a salary of ten dollars a week for keeping the prison books, is allowed to converse with anyone, and is entrusted to go the rounds of the turnkey. He is the one man allowed to wear private clothes, and is even allowed at night the liberty of a stroll in the open air, and unattended, with the one stipulation that he returns before a certain hour at night. And,' continued Brum, 'what with the money he has concealed—held probably by a relative—and his weekly salary of ten dollars as the book keeper of the prison, he will never need work more, after his sentence is served. But, listen to me,' continued Brum more earnestly, 'some of these queer laws are to a tramp's advantage. The winter is already here, and promises to be a most severe one. Now, if you would like to rest and grow fat during the coldest months, come with me to Michigan. You can there enter jails without committing offence of any kind, and take ten, fifteen, twenty or thirty days, all at your own sweet discretion. No work to do, good food to be had, and tobacco daily supplied. There is nothing else but begging before you, for the coming winter,' said Brum, warming to his subject, 'but if you like to enter with me those blessed havens of rest, where one can play cards, smoke or read the time away, you will become strong and ready for work when the spring of the year arrives.'

This project did not seem to me to be very attractive. For one thing, it was a long journey to that part of the country, and the weather being cold, we were forced to travel at night and sleep in the day. I was certainly not a very pleasant companion at this time, being occupied so much with my own dreams, which ever took the one shape of a small comfortable room with a cosy fire; books, papers, tobacco, with reading and writing in turns. At any rate, we decided to follow Brum's suggestion, and, instead of going to New York, we got off, and took another road.

We had a rough time in beating our way to Michigan. We were marched out of one town by the marshal, where we were waiting to catch a train. This necessitated us either to walk three miles to catch a train as it was on a grade, or to walk ten miles to the next watering tank, where all freight trains stopped. We decided on doing the former. To do this required an activity of which I hardly thought Brum to be capable. The grade was long and before the train reached the top, its speed would be slackened to about ten miles an hour, or less, if it had heavy freight. It was necessary to lie low, and out of sight, until the train appeared, and then run beside it, so as to leap and catch the handle bar, the feet at the same time catching the iron step; after doing which we could step on to the bumpers, or climb the ladder to the top of the car. If either the hand or foot failed to do its duty, it meant a fall, and a very serious accident or death. I was the youngest and most active, and leapt the first part of the train. As soon as I was safe I looked around the car, and had the pleasure of seeing Australian Red succeed just three cars behind, and Brum succeeding on the next car to him. When we reached the next stopping place, we all got together on the same car, so as to be prepared for any trouble with the train's crew. A brakesman passed over the top, and shouted to us in a friendly manner; passed and repassed several times before the train reached its destination, but treated our presence with the utmost indifference, which is often the case in that part of America.

What a difference it made to our feelings, this changing of seasons! It seemed but a few days ago the birds were singing, the orchards were heavy and mellow with fruit, and we could sleep in the open air all night. It was now necessary to light great fires, when the front parts of our bodies burned whilst a cold chill crept up and down the spine; and the first fall of snow, which was likely to occur at any time, would soon make it difficult to enjoy even this small comfort.

At last we reached a small town in Michigan which, Brum informed us, was the county town; and which, said he, chuckling with delight, had an exceedingly pleasant jail.

CHAPTER VIII

A PRISONER
HIS OWN JUDGE

'Now,' said Brum, as the freight train steamed into the town and came to a standstill, 'we must see the marshal.' With this end in view we walked towards the passenger depot, which, Brum informed us, was visited by the marshal several times a day, so that he might the better accost such tramps as were going through that town. We arrived at that place and stamped up and down the platform, to circulate our blood, for it was now snowing heavily, and the wind blowing in small gusts that discovered us, shelter wherever we would.

How the snow falls in the north! Flake on flake falling incessantly, until the small dingles are almost on a level with the uplands. It throws itself on the leaves of Autumn, and holds them down in security from the strongest winds. It piles great banks against people's doors, and mothers and daughters are made prisoners to their own hearths, until fathers and sons set to and cut a path to the open thoroughfare. Special snow trains are at work clearing the track to make the way easier for passenger trains and freight trains that run on passenger lines, being loaded with cattle or other perishable goods; whilst other freight is often delayed for days, and sometimes weeks.

We had been here some fifteen minutes, when we saw the marshal coming down the road leading to the station, the bright star of his authority being seen distinctly on his breast. 'Now,' said Brum, 'let me be the spokesman, and I will arrange for a month's comfort.' By this time the marshal stood before us. 'Boys,' he began, 'cold weather for travelling, eh?' 'We don't feel the cold,' was Brum's reply. 'You will though,' said the marshal, 'this is but the beginning, and there is a long and severe winter before you, without a break. You would certainly be better off in jail. Sixty days in our jail, which is considered one of the best, if not the best, in Michigan, would do you no harm, I assure you.' 'As for that,' said Brum, 'we might take thirty days each, providing of course, that you made it worthwhile. What about tobacco and a drink or two of whiskey?' 'That'll be all right,' said the marshal, 'here's half a dollar for a drink, and the sheriff will supply your tobacco.' 'No, no,' objected Brum, 'give us a dollar and three cakes of tobacco, and we will take thirty days, and remember, not a day over.' The marshal produced the three cakes of tobacco, seeming to be well prepared for these demands, and giving us a paper dollar, requested us to go to Donovan's saloon, which we would find in the main street, where he would see us later in the day; 'when of course,' he added, winking, 'you will be supposed to be just a bit merry.'

'What is the meaning of all this?' I asked Brum, as we went ourway to Mr. Donovan's saloon. 'It simply means

57

this,' he said, 'that the marshal gets a dollar each for every arrest he makes—in our case three dollars; the judge receives three or four dollars for every conviction, and the sheriff of the jail is paid a dollar a day for boarding each prisoner under his charge; we benefit by a good rest, warmth, good food and plenty of sleep, and the innocent citizens have to pay for it all.'

We had not much difficulty in finding Donovan's saloon, which we entered, and called for whiskey. It so happened that two strangers were there, who had made a considerable stake in the backwoods, and had come to this town to squander their earnings. We therefore came into many a free drink, through the liberality of these men. About an hour and a half had elapsed when we discovered ourselves to be alone in the bar, and without means of procuring more liquor. 'We had better be going,' said Brum, and we passed into the street. Brum saw the marshal coming up the road and began singing in a lusty voice, to the astonishment of some of the storekeepers. Australian Red, being the worse for drink, and forgetting that we had only to feign this part, began to roar like a bull, merry in earnest. On this the marshal quickly crossed the street and in the hearing of several citizens, shouted in an authoritative voice—'I arrest you for being drunk and disorderly,' and we followed him like lambs. We were then led to the sheriff's house, adjoining the jail. That gentleman, being in, received us with open arms saying—'Welcome, boys, you want thirty days, and thirty you shall have, no more or less; and you will be none the worse for it, I promise you, at the end of the month.' He then made a few casual items in a large book, roughly descriptive of our weight, height, and personal appearance, and then led the way through two or three corridors, until we were confronted by a large iron door. This he opened with an iron key, and we were ushered into a large room, where were assembled between thirty or forty prisoners. Some were reading, some were pacing to and fro, and several batches of them were playing cards. What a reception we had, bringing in a fresh supply of information from the outside. 'Have you seen Detroit Fatty?' asked one. 'Or the Saginaw Kid?' asked another. 'Or Chicago Slim?' asked another. Brum, who seemed to know these wonderful persons, answered according to his knowledge.

In this large room, for the common use of the prisoners, were twenty or more cells, to which they retired for sleep, but were never locked in—except maybe, an occasional prisoner, who might be waiting trial under a charge of grand larceny, manslaughter, or murder. Supper was soon brought in, and it was a good substantial meal. Its quantity seemed to be more than idle men needed, if they had three such meals every day, and its quality would satisfy me in any position in life. What a pleasure it was that night to be in warmth, and with our minds eased of a month's anxiety. 'What time are you going to do?' asked one. 'Thirty days,' answered Brum. 'Plenty,' said the other. 'There is more jails than this, and not much difference in them, and to go out in the cold for a day or two makes us better appreciate the warmth and comfort within.'

Next morning we were taken by the sheriff to the courthouse, where a number of town people were assembled, owing to the more interesting trial of a local man. I have often thought with amusement of this scene. Despite the judge's severe expression, and his solemn deliberate

59

utterance, we knew what to expect—thirty days, no more or less. The sheriff whispered to the judge, and the judge nodded sagely, at the same time casting his eyes in our direction. We were charged with being drunk and disorderly, and with disturbing the public peace. 'He did not see,' he said, 'why peaceable citizens should be disturbed in this way by drunken strangers,' and would fine us seven dollars and costs, in default of which we would be lodged in the county jail for thirty days. We were then led back by the sheriff, and when we were again among the prisoners, they seemed to express very little curiosity as to our sentences, knowing it was our wish that we should receive thirty days, and that the judge was at our pleasure—we being in fact our own judges.

Every morning the sheriff required half a dozen prisoners to sweep and clean the courthouse, which was situated about half a mile from the jail. Australian Red and myself went with him several mornings, for a little fresh air, but prisoners could please themselves, and Brum, I know, never left the jail during the whole thirty days. It was an understood thing that any prisoner could discharge himself on these occasions, if inclined, without any fear of capture. The marshal and the judge had had their dollars for arrest and conviction, and I suppose, the sheriff charged for board and lodgings, without mention of a prisoner's escape. Perhaps they were afraid of bringing back an escaped prisoner, for fear he might make some awkward disclosures. At any rate, liberty could be had by a very deliberate walk and there was certainly no need to make a desperate dash for it. Of course, there was no reason why any prisoner should seek to escape these conditions, which were of his own seeking, and which, during this unpleasant time of the year, could not in any way be bettered by homeless men.

After serving our sentence, and the sheriff exacting a promise from us to return again that winter, if not the following, we sought another jail some twenty miles from the last, which prisoners had spoken highly of. We were told that there was no necessity at this place of going through the form of an arrest, but that we could go straight in out of the cold. The sheriff would at once receive us at his house, learn our wants, while the judge would attend to us on the following morning.

We arrived at this place, and everything turned out as described. This jail was no different from the other. We were catered for as customers that would, if treated with courtesy and good living, return winter after winter, and patronise this place in preference to visiting the more congenial climate of the south. At this place we sentenced ourselves to another thirty days. Our room, like the other, was a large iron cage, in which were twenty-four cells in a double row, main floor and gallery, like little cages within it. As we entered this large cage, the sheriff opening the iron door, a number of jailbirds were singing merrily, not for liberty, but enjoying such captivity. There was only one real prisoner here, who was waiting trial under a charge of manslaughter, and he was the one prisoner to be locked in his cell at night; and, in that cell, had waited trial a most cold blooded murderer. Here we had the usual amusements of card playing, singing and relating experiences.

The real prisoner—for none of the others had been guilty of any offence, having entered of their own free will—was very unfortunate in having a pair of wags quartered in the cell above him. These two practical jokers made a figure of their bed clothes, and letting it down, dangled it in front of this prisoner's cell. The poor wretch, happening to be awake, and thinking this was Bill Henderson, murderer and late occupant of the cell, come to haunt him, leaped from his bed, crying with a horror-stricken voice—'Bill Henderson, by God!' Before he could recover from his fear and make a more calm investigation, the figure was withdrawn. All this happened as expected, and the prisoners were delighted, for they had been hinting all day about Bill Henderson's ghost, so that it might take hold of this poor wretch's nerves. Once only during the night was this accomplished, so that their victim might have no suspicion as to its being a genuine ghost. Every time the sheriff appeared the prisoner complained to him of this ghost murderer, pleading for a removal, or an early trial. That gentleman invariably listened with a sarcastic smile, seeming to have some notion of the truth, by glancing at the faces of the other prisoners. How these sheriffs, marshals and constables despise cowardice, and how they respect the intrepidity of dangerous men. Many a sheriff, I believe has surrendered his prison keys to the lynchers and the lawless mobs, forgetting his duty in disgust at the exhibition of fear in one for whom he is responsible. And many a sheriff would lay down his life to protect a criminal who with cool nerve faces his cell, callous and indifferent.

We visited, and were entertained, in several jails during this winter, and emerged from the last in the middle of April.

I have heard since that this system of boodle, as it was called, was in the following winter entirely squashed. A sheriff, it seemed, being of an avaricious disposition, had interfered with the quality and quantity of the prisoners' rations. Therefore, when respectable citizens visited the jail to speak a few sympathetic words to the prisoners, which they usually did on Sunday, those discontented jailbirds complained of insufficient picking; and informed the citizens that they had been guilty of no offence; that they had entered the jail through being promised enjoyment, and that those expectations had not been realised. On hearing this, the citizens formed a committee, and soon discovered the whole system to be rotten. Seeing how they had been robbed, they deposed several officers and the upshot of it was that travellers never again visited that part of America in quest of comfortable jails.

For a day or two the least exertion tired us, owing to our winter's inactivity, but take it all in all, we were certainly in good bodily condition. It was now that Australian Red made his first proposal. He knew a fruit farm, where he had been previously employed: 'In this very State,' said he, 'on the shores of Lake Michigan.' 'How long does the work last?' I asked him. 'All the summer,' he answered, 'and good pay for an active man.' 'All right,' I said, 'if I can make a pretty fair stake, I shall then return to England and home.' Brum agreeing to this, we lit a fire that evening near a water tank, intending to take the first freight train that came our way. When the train arrived, we still dallied at the fire, which was a considerable distance from the track, It whistled before we expected and began its journey. 'Break away,' cried Australian Red, making a rush for the departing train. The speed of the train was increasing and when I reached its side I was almost afraid to attempt to board it. Australian

Red succeeded, but when we reached the next stopping place, we were greatly disappointed to find that Brum had been left behind. We got off and waited the arrival of other trains, thinking that he would soon follow us, but as Brum did not appear on any of them, we continued our journey, thinking to see him later. I never saw him again. He had complained of the year not being sufficiently aired for freedom, and had proposed another short term in jail. No doubt, after losing us he had done this.

CHAPTER IX

BERRY PICKING

We reached the fruit country a week or two before picking commenced, but although we were in advance of time, and without a cent, the generosity of the farmers supplied all our wants. The authorities did not in the least interfere with us, though we lit large campfires on the outskirts of the towns, took possession of hayricks and empty outhouses, and loafed for hours in their principal streets. They knew well that the assistance of every man would be needed to strip the vines of their berries, which promised a supply exceeding that of former years. Friday morning, it being generally known that picking was to commence on the following Tuesday, Australian Red remarked that it was now time to interview the farmer, for whom he had previously worked. With this object in view, we left the pretty inland port of St. Joseph, and strolling leisurely, we reached that farm in two hours, it being only five miles from the town. The farmer and his wife, who employed several servants of both sexes, but were without children of their own, at once recognised Australian Red, and gave him a kindly welcome, which spoke well for Red's gentlemanly behaviour in the past. The old man told him, in his bad English, that there would always be plenty of work for Red, and for others whom he might bring with him.

I was about twenty-three years of age at this time, appeared much younger and not in any way looking like a dangerous youth, was soon on the best of terms with the old people. So much so, that at the end of the summer, when the pickers were leaving, the result being as satisfactory to themselves as to the farmer, the kind old couple inveigled me into a private place and proposed to adopt me as their own son, and that they would teach me how to run the farm, which they said would become mine at their death. The only way to answer these kind people was to say that I already had a good home, and parents living in England, and that I intended to return there with the profits of this summer's work.

The earliest fruit was the strawberry, whose vines grew from six inches to a foot above the ground. We knelt in the hot blazing sun which beat so powerfully on our bended necks that the flesh became in a day or two the dark colour of walnut stain. The soil, being dry and sandy, burned through the clothing until our knees were covered with a red rash. The effect of this extreme heat often affected people's reason, and sometimes killed them outright. Berry picking in the South has other dangers of a worse kind. I shall never forget seeing a man leap screaming to his feet, at the same time wringing his right hand in agony. He had parted the thick vines, in quest of the berries that were concealed under the leaves, and in doing so, had disturbed a deadly snake, which had bitten his offending hand. The snake was very small, but far more deadly than many others of twenty times its length and weight. Several deaths occurred this way in my berry picking experience in the South. There was not much fear of this happening in the State of Michigan, but we often wished we could crawl under the low green leaves of the vine to escape for a time the rays of the sun. The farm extended to the shores of the lake, and when our day's work was at an end, we hastened there, and plunged into the cold and unsalted water which never grew warm, and could be swallowed with impunity. After which we would return, cook supper in the open air, and wrapping ourselves in blankets lie all night under the thick foliage of a tree. The berries were sent every night to Chicago for the morrow's market; but, there being no market on Sunday our day of rest was Saturday, and we picked on Sunday for Monday's market. Early every Saturday morning Australian Red would go to town in the farmer's buggy, and return to us later in the day with papers, tobacco, matches, and such provisions as were needed; for eggs, butter, milk, potatoes and fruit could be had of the farmer, the latter delicacy being free for the trouble of picking.

Red seemed to me to be a man above the average intelligence, and, as far as my knowledge went, seldom made an error in grammar or the pronunciation of words. But that he should think words required a different pronunciation in reading from what they did in speaking, was a great shock to me, and made some of his most illiterate hearers look from one to another with stupefaction. Now, I was always greatly interested in fights and glove contests, and Red, claiming to have personal acquaintance with the best of Australia, and himself claiming to be an amateur middle weight, whose prowess many a professional had envied, often entertained me with little anecdotes of them, which had escaped the notice of sporting papers. So, on the first Saturday of our picking, Red had returned from town with a paper which gave a full and graphic account, round by round, of a contest for the light weight championship of the world, the principals hailing respectively from Australia and America. Red's sympathies, of course, were with the former, who, to his elation, had defeated his opponent. Being a very modest man, Australian Red had always quietly perused his paper, making a few comments, so as to avoid all argument; but on this occasion, he opened his paper and began to read with a boldness that astonished me. But what surprised me most was the way in which he made use of an expletive syllable, which sounded so quaint as to make laughter irresistible. For instance, this passage occurred in describing the fifth round: 'After he was knocked down, he picked himself up painfully, and the blood flowed from his nostrils in copious streams.' I could not help laughing out at his strange delivery, and Red, thinking my sympathies were with the bruiser from the Antipodes, chuckled with a real, but more quiet delight. We had enough food for conversation that day, in commenting on this contest. I like to see a good scientific bout by men who know the use of their hands, but would rather walk twenty miles than see animals in strife. Although of a quiet disposition, my fondness for animals is likely at any time to lead me into danger. After reading cases of vivisection I have often had dreams of boldly entering such places, routing the doctors with a bar of iron, cutting

68

the cords and freeing the animals, despite of any hurt I might receive from bites and scratches. Perhaps I should cut a ridiculous figure, walking through the crowded streets with a poor meek creature under each arm, but that would not bother me much in the performance of a humane action.

After a good month's work at the strawberries, we had three weeks at picking raspberries, followed by four weeks' blackberry picking. There was good money to be made at the strawberries, but much less at the raspberries. The blackberry picking was as lucrative as the strawberry, and, being cultivated on low bushes that seldom required us to stoop, was not such a tedious occupation as the latter, whose vines were often half buried in the soil. After paying all expenses, I had, at the end of the season, cleared over a hundred dollars.

It was now the last of the picking, and the farmer paid us off. He was a German, and nearly all the farmers in that part of the country were the same, or of that descent, and they used the German language at every opportunity, and never used English except when it was necessary to do so. 'You vos come again, next summer,' said he to Australian Red and myself as we were leaving—'for I know you two plenty.' This remark made me blush, for it seemed as much as to say that his knowledge of us was more than he desired—but we understood his meaning. He offered to drive us to St. Joseph, but we preferred to walk, as we had all day and half the night to wait before the boat started from that place to Chicago.

'Now,' I said to Australian Red, as we jogged along, 'I am going to hoard the bulk of my dollars, and shall just keep two or three handy for food and incidental expenses, for I

69

am now about to beat my way from Chicago to New York. From the latter place I shall pay my passage to Liverpool, clothe myself better, and then take train for South Wales, and still have a pound or two left when I arrive home.' 'Come and have a drink,' said Red, 'and I will then inform you how any man without former experience on sea or ship, neither being a sailor, fireman or cook, can not only work his passage to England, but he paid for doing so.'

We had had no intoxicating liquor for several months, and, though we had passed one or two of these places on our way to St. Joseph, on which he had gazed in a rather too friendly manner, his courage, up to this moment, had not been equal to an invitation. 'Well,' I said, pleased with the prospect of not only saving my passage money, but also of earning my train fare in England—'it will certainly be cold, taking this deck voyage across the lake in the early hours of morning, and a glass of whiskey will keep some warmth in us.' Alas! the usual thing happened—we got full; and what with the dead effects of the drink, and a rough passage across, we arrived in Chicago feeling cold, stiff, and in many other ways uncomfortable.

I have often heard salt water mariners sneer at these fresh water sailors, but, after crossing the Atlantic some eighteen times, and making several passages across the lakes, my opinion is that these vast inland lakes are more dangerous to navigate, and far less safe than the open seas.

Of course we had to have more whiskey, after the voyage, and, having had no sleep, its effect was almost instantaneous. Not altogether losing my senses, I suggested to Red that we should go to some hotel, have breakfast, and then go to bed for an hour or two, say till dinner time, which would refresh us. It was now eight o'clock in the morning, and Red had unfortunately got into conversation with a gentleman who knew something of Australia. 'Yes,' he said, gravely, after listening to my proposal—'you are young, and you certainly look drunk and sleepy, and had better follow your own advice. The hotel is next door but one to this, and you will find me here when you return.' Not liking to take him by the shoulder, and to gently try to force him away from this stranger in whose conversation he evidently seemed to take a great delight, not to mention doing such an action before the landlord's face, I left him, made arrangements at the hotel for two, and then went to bed. Having had a good sleep, and a substantial meal, and feeling thoroughly refreshed, I now returned to Red, whom I found in the centre of half a dozen loafers, besides the gentleman to whom I have already referred. On my appearance, he staggered to his feet and came to meet me, and then, taking me on one side, began in this way: 'You have just come in the nick of time, for the glasses, as you see, are empty. Pay for all drinks called for, and I will make it all right with you in the morning.' 'What is the matter?' I asked. 'What have you done with over eighty dollars?' Winking artfully, and with a smile meant to be cunning, he said—'I have hidden my money, as I usually do in these cases. Most likely it is in the lining of my coat; but wherever it is, you may depend on it as being quite safe.' If he had had the assistance of a score of the most inveterate drunkards, I know he could not in this short time have squandered between eighty and ninety dollars. Red had earned ninety-five dollars and a half, and, up to the time of my leaving him, had spent but very little. I came to the conclusion that he had been robbed, and that this befell him in all his sprees. After calling for a round of drinks, I left the house, knowing that Red would soon follow, which he did, and at once. I persuaded him to bed, and the next morning saw the same peculiarities as before—his going into corners, up side streets, to feel the lining of his clothes. He was not satisfied at seeing no tear in the lining of his cap, but must hold it in his hand and feel every inch of it. 'Somewhere on my person,' he reiterated, 'I have secreted three twenty dollar bills. I have a distinct recollection of doing so, but for the life of me I cannot remember what part.' 'You have been robbed,' I answered, with a little disgust. Not willing to leave him in his present circumstances, and only too sorry that I had not done so when he was almost as well off as myself, I shared my dollars with him, saying in an offended manner—'The sooner we squander this stuff the better it will please us.' We spent it in one week in Chicago, and were again without a cent. 'Again,' I said with some exaggeration, 'winter is here, and we are in the same position as at the end of last summer. What now?' 'We are without money,' said Red, 'but there is still nothing to prevent us from our first intention of visiting England. We will beat our way to Baltimore without delay. I am known in that port by the cattle foremen and owners, and we are almost sure of a ship as soon as we arrive.' After all, I thought, eager for a new experience, one trip will not come amiss.

CHAPTER X

THE CATTLEMAN'S OFFICE

We found the Baltimore and Ohio Railroad easy to beat, and were at the end of our journey in a very few days. When we entered the cattleman's office, from which place owners and foremen were supplied with men, it was evident to me that Red was well known in this place, hearing him make many enquiries of Washington Shorty, New York Fatty, Philadelphia Slim, and others. At this place I made the acquaintance of Oklahoma Sam, an extremely quiet man, very much respected in that he had a cold-blooded fashion of whittling wood and paring his nails with a steel blade nearly a foot long. Another queer character was Baldy, of whom Australian Red related this anecdote. When stranded in Liverpool and hungry, he once took up a position in front of a confectioner's shop, and, being an extremely lazy man, placed his shoulder against the lamp-post, and settled himself for a long reverie. He might have been there an hour or more, when the baker came out and complained of

Baldy's person, being ragged and dirty, as the reason why people hurried past his establishment; telling Baldy straight that his presence was detrimental to the trade of any shop that catered to the inner man. Baldy, too lazy to speak, much less show any sign of anger, took a firmer bearing on the post and settled to a more prolonged reverie. Two or three hours elapsed when the baker, who had come several times to stare at him through the window, rushed out and shouted with much irritation—'For Heaven's sake go away: Here, take this sixpence, and let me see the last of you.' Baldy who had not wished the baker good morning, wished him good afternoon, and strolled quietly away, with the price of a good meal in his hand. Nobody, who thoroughly understood Baldy's disposition, would wonder at this; for this success, after all, was only the result of laziness, but most of his companions gave him credit for using unique strategy in obtaining money.

Shelter only was supplied at this office, and that of the barest kind, being no other than the hard floor and blanketless. Owing to this the men, who, after making a trip often had to wait sometimes two or three weeks for another chance, were all good beggars. Some of them had begged Baltimore off and on for ten years, and knew every good house in the city. One would say—'I shall go to the dressmaker for my breakfast'; another intended to go to the dairy, the fat woman or the dentist; the latter being always good for money in the shape of a ten cent piece.

We had been at this office three days, when the shipper sent Australian Red and myself, with four others, to rope cattle at the yards. Seven hundred and fifty head of cattle had to be shipped that night, and the ropes had to be placed on their necks or horns, with which they had to be fastened to their places aboard ship. After Red had taken a rope, and given me a practical illustration of what was to be done, the cattle began to arrive. They were very wild, having just come from the plains of the west. There was a long narrow shoot in the yards, with one end blocked, and when a number of cattle had been driven into this, and had wedged themselves too close and fast to be capable of any wild movement, it was our business to slip a noose around their horns, or necks, draw this rope as tight as possible, and fasten it with a knot, so as to prevent it from slipping. When this was accomplished, the end of the shoot was opened, and they were rushed out with their ropes dangling, and a fresh batch were then driven in and served likewise. After which they were put in cars and sent to the ship. Now the foreman, knowing Red, asked him if he would like to go with him, to which Red answered yes, at the same time putting in a good word for me, which at once met with the foreman's approval. We were not therefore surprised, on our return, when the shipper called us into his private office to sign articles—Red to receive two pounds for the trip, and myself thirty shillings, an amount seldom paid to a raw hand, except on the recommendation of owner or foreman.

I shall never forget the first night's experience, when the cattle were brought to the ship in a train of cars. A large sloping gangway was erected to span the distance between ship and shore, and up this incline the poor beasts were unmercifully prodded with long poles, sharpened at the end, and used by the shore cattlemen. The terror-stricken animals were so new to the conditions, that they had no notion of what was expected of them, and almost overleaped one another in their anxiety to get away. What with the shout of savage triumph, and the curse of disappointment, and the slipping and falling of the over-goaded steers, I was strongly tempted to escape the scene. As the cattle were being driven aboard, we cattlemen, who had signed for their future charge, caught their ropes, which we were required to fasten to a strong stanchion board. Sometimes one would run up behind, and prevent himself from turning. On one of these occasions, I crossed the backs of others, that had been firmly secured, so as to force this animal to a proper position. The animal, whose back I was using for this purpose, began to heave and toss, and at last succeeding in throwing me across the back of the other, this one tossing and rearing until I was in danger of my life, only the pressure of the other beasts preventing him from crushing my limbs. Taking possession of his rope, I held it to a cattleman, who was standing waiting and ready in the alley, and he quickly fastened this refractory animal to the crossboards. Now the foreman had been watching this, and coming to the conclusion that I was a good man with cattle, said he would like me to be the night watchman. This undoubtedly does require a good man, as I soon discovered, on the first night out. There were two lots of cattle aboard, and for these two foremen, two lots of cattlemen, and two watchmen. As all hands are available in the day, any difficulty with the cattle can soon be attended to; if necessary, all hands taking part. But when there is any trouble at night, one watchman only has the assistance of the other, who, of course, expects the same aid from him, in cases of emergency. Now if a number of cattle have broken loose, and worked themselves into intricate positions, the watchman is supposed to awake the foreman and his men to assist him, but one would rather struggle all night with his difficulties than to take these men at their word, knowing their peevishness and dislike for a man who has disturbed them from a sound sleep. A watchman is therefore told to call up all hands, if he cannot cope with the cattle under his charge, but he is never expected to do so.

What soon breaks the spirit of these wild animals is the continual motion of the vessel. There is always plenty of trouble at first, when they slip forward and backward, but in a few days they get their sea-legs, and sway their bodies easily to the ship's motion. The wild terror leaves their eyes, and, when they can no more smell their native land, they cease bellowing, and settle calmly down. This restlessness breaks out afresh when nearing shore on the other side, and again they bellow loud and often, long before the mariner on the lookout has sighted land.

We also had on this trip two thousand head of sheep, quartered on the hurricane deck. When we were six days out there came a heavy storm, and the starboard side was made clean, as far as pens and sheep were concerned, one wave bearing them all away. This happened at night, and on the following morning the sheep-men were elated at having less work to do during the remainder of the voyage. The cattle, being protected on the main deck, and between decks, and their breath filling the air with warmth, make the cattleman's lot far more comfortable than that of the sheep-men. The condition of the cattle can be seen without difficulty, but ten or fifteen sheep lying or standing in the front of a crowded pen, may be concealing the dead or dying that are lying in the background. For this reason it is every morning necessary to crawl through the pens, far back, in quest of the sick and the dead, and it is nothing unusual to find half a dozen dead ones. The voyage would not be considered bad if thirty sheep only died out of two thousand.

What a strange assortment of men were these cattlemen and sheepmen. One man, called Blackey, a bully without being a coward, fell in love with a small white cat, which we had found in the forecastle. His ruffianism at once disappeared, and every time he was at liberty, instead of looking for trouble with his fellow men he could be seen peacefully nursing this cat, at the same time addressing it endearingly as 'Little White Dolly', and such simple language as a child might use.

It was our duty to keep the cattle standing, and not to allow them to rest too long on their knees; and not let them, on any account, stretch full length in the pens. One reason for this was that a kneeling steer would be overstepped by his nearest neighbour, and if the latter happened to rise, their ropes, which were so fastened as to give them very little freedom, would be tightened and crossed, bringing their heads together in such close proximity that they would make frantic efforts to escape each other's presence. And another reason for not allowing them to lie down for any length of time was that their joints would become so stiff as to make them almost incapable of rising, though goaded by the most heartless cruelty. I used the most humane methods to attain this end, and sought to inspire terror in them by the use of a most ferocious war-cry, which often succeeded. If that failed to raise them, I struck them with a flat stick on the haunches, which they could scarcely feel, at the same time not forgetting to use my voice. Not succeeding in this,

I resorted to the old remedy, which rarely fails, standing at their backs and twisting their tails. A bullock can kick in any direction. There is terrible power in his side kick, also his front kick, throwing his hind leg forward with a speed that is remarkable for such an unwieldly animal but his back kick, when you stand back to back with him, has not the least power to cause hurt. The other watchman and myself had about an equal number of cattle under our charge, and when I was in difficulty he kindly came to my assistance, and I did likewise for him, although he seldom seemed to need other help than his own. We made our rounds about every half hour. Sometimes I found a steer in the alley; by some means or other he had cleared the headboard and, still being a prisoner, stood fastened outside the pen instead of inside. Another time we would find one standing with his tail to the headboard, instead of his head, owing to the rope getting loose, or being broken; after which he had turned himself around to see if there was any way of escape behind him. It required great care, in cases of this kind, to place them again in their original positions.

Up till the fourth night we had experienced no bad weather, and the cattle had been quiet and requiring little care. On this particular night my attention had been drawn several times to a big black steer, which, time after time, had persisted in lying down. At last, in pity for the poor beast, I let him rest, thinking to get him into a standing position at the last moment, when I went off duty, after calling the foreman and his men. But when that last moment came I failed in all my efforts to raise this animal, whose joints, I suppose, had become stiff after a prolonged rest. I was not therefore greatly surprised when the foreman came, after I had gone off duty, to the forecastle, with the complaint of having found a number of cattle lying down, and one, he said, in particular, which must have been lying down half of the night. 'When I left the cattle,' I said, 'nothing seemed to be wrong.' 'Come up and see this one,' he answered. I followed him on deck, and there I saw several cattlemen standing in front of a pen, in which I recognised the big black steer. He was now lying full length in the pen, the others having had to be removed for his convenience. 'See this,' said the foreman, 'this creature should be standing. Twist his tail,' he continued, to a cattleman, who at once obeyed. During this operation another cattleman fiercely prodded the poor creature's side with a pitchfork, which must have gone an inch into the body. At the same time another beat the animal about the head with a wooden stake, dangerously near the eyes. The animal groaned, and its great body heaved, but it made no attempt to move its legs. 'Wait,' said the foreman then, 'we will see what this will do.' He then took out of his mouth a large chew of tobacco, and deliberately placed it on one of the animal's eyes. My heart sickened within me, on seeing this, and I knew that I would have to be less gentle with these poor creatures to save them the worst of cruelty. In a second or two the poor beast, maddened by pain, made frantic efforts to rise, tried again and again, and after seeing its great sides panting, and hearing a number of pitiful groans, it succeeded in the attempt.

These cattlemen are, as a rule, great thieves, and well the sailors and firemen know it, and especially the steward and cook. One evening, when the men had finished their day's work, and I was preparing to go on duty for the night, I

80

heard Blackey propose a night's raid on the captain's chickens, which were kept in a small coop under the bridge, and rather difficult to rob, considering the bridge was always occupied by the captain or one of his first officers. But, next morning, on coming to the forecastle, I was not greatly surprised to smell a peculiar and a not unpleasant odour, coming from that place. Blackey and another had made their raid during the previous night, leisurely killing the chickens on the spot, which was certainly the best plan. When I descended the forecastle steps, I saw that the stove was red hot, on which was a large tin can full of potatoes, onions and chicken. I am not ashamed to say that I did not scruple to partake of this rogue's mess, knowing from experience how this company ran their boats, allowing their stewards such miserly small amounts for provisions, that the common sailors and firemen did not get sufficient food to eat, bad as its quality was.

When we arrived at Liverpool, we were not long clearing our decks of cattle. After one is forced to lead, which is often difficult to do, they all follow, and it is the same with the sheep. It is more often necessary to control their mad rush than to goad them on. We received payment aboard— Red two pounds, myself thirty shillings, one other a pound, and the rest ten shillings each, which was to board and lodge us ashore for six days, when we would have passenger tickets back to the port from which we had sailed. If the ship, from any cause, was delayed over this number of days, we were to receive an extra half a crown for every day over. Red, having been in Liverpool several times previously, led the way to a cheap house, at which place I persuaded them to pay down six nights' lodging, so as to make sure of some shelter, not forgetting to caution them against drink, as they would need every penny of the remainder for food, which would be more difficult to obtain in this country than their own.

These cattlemen are recognised as the scum of America, a wild, lawless class of people, on whom the scum of Europe unscrupulously impose. They are an idle lot, but, coming from a land of plenty, they never allow themselves to feel the pangs of hunger until they land on the shores of England, when their courage for begging is cooled by the sight of a greater poverty. Having kind hearts, they are soon rendered penniless by the importunities of beggars. Men waylay them in the public streets for tobacco, and they are marked men in the public houses—marked by their own voices. First one enters and makes a successful appeal, who quickly informs another, and others as quickly follow. These wild, but kind-hearted men, grown exceedingly proud by a comparison of the comfortable homes of America with these scenes of extreme poverty in Liverpool and other large sea-ports, give and give of their few shillings, until they are themselves reduced to the utmost want. And so it was on this occasion. The next day after landing, I made my way to the public library, for I had not enjoyed books for a considerable time. When I returned from this place, Australian Red at once approached me to borrow money, with his old hint of having some concealed. On questioning the others, six in number, I found that these men had not the price of a loaf of bread among them. As for myself, I had not been drinking, and had only spent seven shillings, and a part of that had been given away in charity. For even in the coffee-house ragged lads set their hungry eyes on one's meal, and sidle up with the plaintive remark that they will be thankful for anything that is left. In such cases, who could help but attend to them at once, before attempting to enjoy his own meal? As far as my money went I maintained Red and the others, but the day previous to sailing, there was not one penny left. We were to sail the following night, but would not be supplied with food until breakfast time the next morning. When that hour arrived we were all weak from hunger, not having had food for over forty hours. When the food did arrive in the forecastle, these hungry men strove for it like wild beasts, without any system of equal shares.

What a monotonous life we now had for thirteen days. No work; nothing to do but to eat and sleep. And how I had intended to enjoy this part of the trip! The few hours I had spent in the library, had brought back my old passion for reading and, had it not been for the distress of others, I had now been the happy possessor of some good books. This was not to be; for I was to lie in my bunk with but one consolation—that I had sufficient tobacco under seal with the steward to last me until the end of the voyage. This new experience was a disappointment, and it was my firm resolve, on returning to Baltimore, to seek some more remunerative employment, to save, and then to work my passage back to England in this same way, and go home with my earnings.

We had a rough passage back, the ship being light, with little more than ballast. One night the vessel made a fearful roll, and the lights went dark, and we thought every moment that she would turn over. A coal bunker was smashed by the waves, and large pieces of coal bounded across the deck with a force that would have broken every bone in a man's body. Pieces of heavy wood, that would have cut off a man's feet as clean as a knife, slid across the deck from side to side. We thought the end had come, especially when we saw an old sailor rush on deck in his bare feet, his shirt being his only apparel. Sleep was out of the question for some hours, for we were forced to cling to our bunks with all our strength, to save ourselves from being thrown out, when we would be rolled here and there, and soon battered into an unconscious state.

We reached Baltimore on the thirteenth day, and at once made our way to the cattlemen's office, intending on the morrow to make better arrangements for the future.

CHAPTER XI

A STRANGE CATTLEMAN

It was now the beginning of October, and the mornings and the evenings were getting colder. Although Baltimore is a southern town, and was therefore free from the severe cold of towns further north, it was not so far south as to make plenty of clothes dispensable. We two, Australian Red and myself, tramped this city day after day for work, but without success. There were only two courses left open to us: to make three or four more trips on cattle boats, until the coming of spring, when there would probably be work in abundance, or to go oyster dredging down the Chesapeake Bay, a winter employment that was open to any able-bodied man in Baltimore, experience not being necessary. Red soon placed the latter beyond consideration by relating his own hard experience of the same. First of all the work was very hard, and of a most dangerous kind; the food was of the worst; and, worse than all, the pay was of the smallest. A man would often cut his hands with the shells, which would poison and swell, and render him helpless for some time to come. 'Again,' said Red, 'a man is not sure of his money, small as it is. A few years ago,' he continued, 'it was a common occurrence for a boat to return and have to report the loss of a man. These dredgers were never lost on the outward trip, but when homeward bound, and the most hazardous part of their work was done. The captain on coming to shore, would report a man lost, drowned, and his body unrecovered. This drowned man, being an unknown, no relative came forward to claim wages from the captain. How the man met his death was no secret among the dredgers, and they had to keep a wary eye on their own lives; for a captain would often move the tiller so suddenly as to knock a man overboard, accidentally, of course. A board of enquiry looked into these things, and a captain was tried for murder, and escaped with a sentence of seven years imprisonment. There were not so many accidents after this, but they have not altogether ceased.' After hearing this account, I was not very eager for more practical knowledge of this profession, called dredging, so I agreed with Red to make three or four more trips as cattlemen, until the spring of the year made other work easy to be obtained.

We returned to the office, where between thirty and forty men were waiting an opportunity to ship. As I have said before, some of these men were notorious beggars, and the kind-hearted people of Baltimore never seemed to tire of giving them charity. One man, called Wee Scotty, who had been a cattleman for a number of years, begged the town so much in some of the rather long intervals when he was waiting a ship, that he could take a stranger with him three time a day for a month, to be fed by the different good people that were known to him. He could take up a position on a street corner, and say—'Go to that house for breakfast; come back to this house for dinner, and yonder house with the red gate will provide you a good supper.' In this way he kept me going for two weeks when, at last, I was asked to sign articles to go with cattle to Glasgow.

Some days before this, a man came to the office, whose peculiar behaviour often drew my attention to him. He asked to be allowed to work his passage to England, and the shipper promised him the first opportunity, and a sum of ten shillings on landing there. This was the reason why some of us had to wait so long, because, having made trips before, more or less, we required payment for our experience. The man referred to above, had a white clean complexion, and his face seemed never to have had use for a razor. Although small of body, and not seeming capable of much manual labour, his vitality of spirits seemed overflowing every minute of the day. He swaggered more than any man present, and was continually smoking cigarettes—which he deftly rolled with his own delicate fingers. In the intervals between smoking he chewed, squirting the juice in defiance of all laws of cleanliness. It was not unusual for him to sing a song, and his voice was of surprising sweetness; not of great power, but the softest voice I have ever heard from a man, although his aim seemed to make it appear rough and loud, as though ashamed of its sweetness. It often occurred to me that this man was playing a part, and that all this cigarette smoking, chewing tobacco and swaggering, was a mere sham; an affectation for a purpose, I could not, after much watching, comprehend. He was free of speech, was always ridiculing others, and swore like a trooper, yet no man seemed inclined to take advantage of him. Blackey took him under his protection, laughing and inciting him to mischief. He was certainly not backward in insulting and threatening Blackey, which made the latter laugh until the tears came into his eyes. The men were spellbound at his volubility. He shook that red rag of his, and a continuous flow of speech ensued, and the surrounding creatures were mute, but not at all infuriated. His audacity may have slightly irritated one or two, but no man had the least idea of inflicting on him corporal punishment. I and Red were called to the office to sign articles for Glasgow, and, when doing so, Blackey and this strange new companion of his were signing for England, the two ships leaving for their destination on the same tide. We were sorry to lose this man's company, knowing that his tongue would have gone far to amuse our leisure hours aboard.

We had a very pleasant voyage, and this line of boats gave us very little cause to complain, either of sleeping accommodation or diet, the officers and ship's crew also being sociable in their dealings with us. The same thing happened at the end of this voyage, and we would have suffered the same privation—had it not been for an accident. On the fourth morning ashore there was not a penny among us, and the boat would not sail for another two days. Australian Red was rummaging his pockets and piling before him a large assortment of miscellaneous articles. 'It wouldn't care much', said he, 'if I had the paltry price I paid for this,' at the same time throwing on the table a thick, heavy, white chain. Picking this up, for an indifferent examination, I became interested, and enquired as to how it came into possession. It seemed that a poor fellow had offered to sell

Red the chain for a penny. Red, seeing the man's condition of extreme want, had given him sixpence, at the same time refusing to accept the chain. The poor fellow had then persisted that Red should accept it as a gift. Red, being now filled with his own troubles, wished that he could dispose of the chain to the same advantage. The chain was, without doubt, silver, being stamped on every link. 'What!' cried Red, suddenly roused, while the cattlemen in their deep interest moved forward, making our circle several feet smaller —'What!' he cried, 'silver did you say? Let me see it!' He snatched the chain and, without looking at it, or putting it in his pocket, rushed out of the room without another word. In five minutes he returned, and throwing towards me eight shillings, the value of the chain in pawn, said: 'None of this for drink; keep a tight hand on it for our food supply until the boat sails.' He knew his own weakness. On first coming to shore I had taken the precaution to buy several books, to make sure of them, indifferent whether we suffered hunger or no. For this reason I thoroughly enjoyed the voyage back, and we arrived safely at Baltimore, having been away a little over five weeks.

The first man we met, on entering the cattlemen's office, was Blackey, who, having made a shorter trip, had returned some days previous. 'What became of your strange friend, Blackey?' I asked. 'Did he remain in England, or return to America?' 'Why, haven't you heard about it all?' asked Blackey, 'the English papers were full of the case.' 'We have heard nothing,' I said, thinking the poor fellow had either been kicked to death by one of the wild steers, or that he had either leaped at the waves in a mad fit of suicide, or that the waves had leaped at him and taken him off. 'He worked side by side with me for eleven days,' said Blackey, 'and by his singing, laughing and talking, he made a play of labour. Down in the forecastle at night he sang songs and, in spite of our limited space, and the rolling of the ship, he gave many a dance, and ended by falling into his low bunk exhausted, and laughing still. In all my experience this was the first time that I was not eager to sight land, and fill myself with English ale. On the eleventh day out, we were hoisting bales of hay for the cattle, and he was assisting me in the hold of the vessel. I know not whether we failed to fasten properly the bales, or whether the cattlemen on deck blundered when receiving them, but all at once I heard a shout of—"Look out, below!" and down came a heavy bale, striking my companion on the shoulder. He spun around once or twice, and then fell unconscious into my arms. The ship's doctor was at once called, and the poor fellow was taken aft. Several times a day I made enquiries about him, and heard that he was out of danger, but needed rest. I never saw him again. When we landed in England he was not to be seen, and I thought, perhaps, that he was too ill to be removed without the assistance of a vehicle. Next day I happened to pick up a paper, in which was a full and lengthy account of how a woman had worked her way as a cattleman from the port of Baltimore, making mention of the ship's name. My companion was that woman, and I never had the least suspicion,' continued Blackey, 'although, I will say, that I always thought him a queer man.'

I had scarcely been in the office a week, when I was offered a boat for London. Only one two pound man was required, all the others, with the exception of one, who was to receive fifteen shillings, were ten shilling men. Red had no chance on this boat, and I was not sorry, knowing how his extravagant habits would spoil the trip's enjoyment. This was a voyage of some delight, both aboard and ashore. Having been in London before, I knew what enjoyment could be had with but little expense—of museums, parks, gardens, picture galleries, etc. I made friends with a decent fellow, who had been a schoolmaster, and, persuading him out of Deptford, we procured lodgings in Southwark, and from that place we paid our visits to the different scenes. We saw none of the other cattlemen until the hour of sailing. Many of the poor fellows had lost their money on the first night ashore, and now had strange experiences to relate of workhouses, shelters, soup-kitchens, and unsuccessful begging. When we arrived at Baltimore it wanted one week to Christmas Day, and there was not much chance to ship again for two or three weeks, owing to the number of men waiting.

As I have said before, the people of Baltimore are extremely kind-hearted, and no man need starve if he has the courage to express his wants. The women seem to be as beautiful as they are good, for I have never seen finer women than those of Baltimore, and a man would not he making the worst of life if he idled all day in a principal street, reading the face of beauty, and studying the grace of forms that pass him by. But it is of their kindness and generosity that I would now speak. For Christmas Eve had come, and Australian Red, accompanied by Blackey, had taken me on one side, the former beginning in this way: 'Will you join this night's expedition? What we want you to do is to carry a small bag, no more, and all the begging will be done by us.' I had visions of the police stopping me and enquiring the contents of such a strange burden, but being an unsuccessful beggar, and feeling too independent to have others perform this office for me, without making some little effort to deserve their maintenance, I agreed to their proposal, and that evening at six p.m., we sallied forth together. They both started on a long street, Red taking one side and Blackey the other, whilst I waited the result some yards in advance - a safe distance away. They could scarcely have been refused in one house, for in less than ten minutes they were both at my side, dropping paper parcels into the empty bag, the mouth of which I held open. All at once Blackey disappeared, having been called in to supper. The same thing happened to Red, two or three minutes after. When they approached me again with other parcels, they both agreed to accept no more invitations to supper, but that they would excuse themselves as having families at home. They continued this for half an hour, hardly more, when the bag was full to the mouth. 'Now,' said Blackey, 'take this to the office, and we will remain to fill our pockets, after which we will follow as soon as possible. Or do you prefer to wait for us?' I preferred to go, and, avoiding the main streets and lighted places, succeeded in getting back without rousing the curiosity of the police. They soon followed, with another supply stored in their capacious pockets. What delighted them most—but of which I took very little account, knowing to what use it would be put—was that they had received several small amounts in money, the total being one dollar and seventy five cents. I shall never forget this begging expedition. When the different parcels were unrolled, we beheld everything that the most fastidious taste could desire, for not one parcel, I believe, consisted of simple bread and butter, much less the former by its own common self. There were fried oysters, turkey, chicken, beef, mutton, ham and sausages; Irish potatoes, sweet potatoes and yams; brown bread, white bread; pancakes, tarts, pie and cake of every description; bananas, apples, grapes and oranges; winding up with a quantity of mixed nuts and a bag of sweets. Such were the contents of over sixty parcels, got with such ease. Blackey had been refused at three doors; and Red had failed at five, but had been requested to call back at two of them, and had not troubled to do so, not having properly located the houses.

CHAPTER XII

THIEVES

Cockney More was a cattleman, hailing from the port of Baltimore. He was a born thief and, strange to say, nearly blind; but, without doubt, he was a feeler of the first magnitude. If he borrowed a needle, and the said article was honestly returned, it behoved the lender, knowing the borrower's thievish propensities, to carefully examine it to see that the eye had not been abstracted; for, as Donovan remarked—'Cockney More could steal the milk out of one's tea.'

When I have looked at Cockney's long thin fingers, I have often wondered whether he had power to disjoint them at will, letting them down the legs of his trousers to rummage the locality, while he stood innocently talking to us with his hands in his pockets. That honour which is supposed to exist among thieves was not known to Cockney More, for he would rob his best friend, and do it in such a way that no man could take umbrage. For instance, six of us had landed in Liverpool, having been paid off that morning. Cockney, knowing the ins and outs of that city, and its numerous pitfalls for strangers, escorted us at once to a cheap lodging-house, where we paid in advance for a week's bed, thus being assured of shelter until the ship was ready to return. The next morning we sat six disconsolate men in the lodging-house kitchen, not one of us having the price of his breakfast. Cockney, being the last to rise, entered at last, and noting our despondent looks enquired as to the cause. On being told he went out and returned in a few moments with tea, sugar, bread and sausages. In fact, he continued these kind deeds during our week ashore. The others, being mostly strangers, blessed him for a good fellow, but it occurred to me that he was simply returning us our own, for he spent three times more money during those few days than he had received for the trip.

I remembered a mean little trick that he had performed on one of the cattlemen that very first morning ashore. True, we were all getting drunk fast, but I never thought Cockney would be daring enough to attempt such a deed in our first stage of intoxication. He had asked this cattleman for a chew of tobacco and the man had generously offered him the whole plug to help himself Cockney took this plug and, biting off a piece, returned the bitten part to the owner, and himself pocketed the plug. I was speechless with astonishment at seeing this: and more so when the strange cattleman innocently received the bitten part, and put it in his pocket without having perceived anything wrong.

Cockney and myself were on the best of terms, and yet, sometime previous to the above episode, he had served me a trick which ought to have severed our friendship forever.

95

I was at the shipping office and had that morning signed for a trip to London. 'Have you sufficient tobacco, and a spoon, knife, fork and plate?' enquired Cockney. 'Yes,' I replied, 'and I have also a new pack of cards, so that we may enjoy our leisure hours aboard.' Cockney was pleased to hear this, although he was not to accompany me on this trip. 'Let me see them,' said he. This I did and being, as I have said, nearly blind, he took them to the window for examination, but returned them almost immediately. Then came a shout for all men who had signed for the London trip, and, hastily wishing Cockney and others goodbye, I left the office. On the second day out we were all at leisure for an hour or more, and enquiries went round as to who had a pack of cards. My cards were at once produced and, taking, partners, we were about to settle to a little enjoyment. Alas, when my cards were taken out of the new case, they were found to be a dirty, greasy old pack with several missing, and, of course, card playing, was out of the question. I at once knew what had happened: Cockney had substituted these old ones for the new, what time he pretended to be interested at the window. That little trick, meant twelve days' misery for eight men, for we could not get another pack until we landed in London.

On another trip, when I had the pleasure of Cockney's company, we had with us Donovan who, as a thief, certainly ran Cockney a good second. The truth of the matter is that all cattlemen are thieves, and the one who complains of going ashore without his razor, often has in his possession another's knife, comb or soap. On the second day out I missed my pocket-knife and, without loss of time, boldly accused Cockney More to his face, telling him that however much I admired his dexterity in other people's pockets I had not the least suspicion that he would be guilty of such a trick on an old pal. 'No more have I,' said he. 'What kind of knife was it?' On being told, he advised me to say no more about it, and that he would endeavour to find it. He succeeded in doing so, and the next day Donovan was shouting indignantly—'Who has been to my bunk and stolen a knife?' After this I lost my soap, but did not think it worthwhile mentioning such a petty loss. On approaching Cockney More for the loan of his, he—giving me strict injunctions to return it at once, and not leave it exposed to the eyes of thieves—lent me my own soap.

This trip was a memorable one, and no doubt Cockney made the best haul of his life. We were together in Liverpool, Cockney, Donovan and myself, and as usual drinking. A stranger, hearing by our conversation that we hailed from America, invited us to drink; and in the course of conversation expressed a regret that he was out of work, and had no means of visiting America—'Nothing is easier,' said Cockney, 'if you place yourself unreservedly in our hands. We are to sail on Thursday, and I can stow you away, as I have successfully done with others.' 'Many thanks,' replied the other, and so it was agreed.

On the following Thursday we went aboard, the Cockney carrying a large bag which contained the stowaway's clothes, etc. When the ship's officers entered our forecastle the stowaway was, of course, not present, but when they were searching other places, the stowaway was then sitting comfortably among us, these things being well managed by Cockney More. After this search they would pay us no more visits, and the stowaway was safe, and could go on deck at night for fresh air. The only danger now was to land him in America. This, the Cockney affirmed, was a danger of little account.

Now, as I have said, this stowaway had a bag, and Cockney More and Donovan were great thieves. Therefore, it was not at all surprising to hear that the poor fellow was soon without a second shirt to his back. He had lent me a book, the value of which I did not think him capable of appreciating, and I had made up my mind that it should not be returned until asked for. But when I heard him complain of losing so many things, through pity I became honest and returned it. But where was his watch and chain, his brushes, and where were his clothes, his tools, razor, strop, and many other useful articles? All these things were in possession of Donovan, and Cockney knew it and appeared to be grieving over lost chances; for he was supposed to have that honour which is among thieves, and as Donovan had been too fast for him, he had no other option than to sit quiet under the circumstances.

On the day before our arrival at Baltimore, I happened to enter the forecastle and found Donovan, his face pale, feverously rummaging Cockney More's bunk. 'What do you think?' said he. 'That blasted Cockney has robbed me of everything.' And so he had. He had allowed Donovan to do all the dirty work, of abstracting the goods one by one, as the chance occurred; he had allowed him the pleasure of their care and possession for many days, and then he had robbed him. But the artful part of the business was this: he had not left Donovan any chance to recover the goods, for he had made friends with one of the sailors—the latter having a forecastle to themselves—and had prevailed on that person to take charge of a parcel for him until all the cattlemen landed; 'for,' said he, 'these cattlemen are born thieves.' Yes, he had done the business neatly, for the desperate and much aggrieved Donovan who intended on landing to recover the goods by force, saw Cockney More walk ashore as empty-handed as himself, and he was almost shaken in his belief that the said Cockney was, after all, the thief triumphant.

CHAPTER XIII

THE CANAL

I now left Baltimore, travelling alone, making my way as fast as possible towards Chicago, where a canal was being built to facilitate commerce between that large inland city, and deep water, at which place I soon arrived.

On the banks of that canal were assembled the riff-raff of America and the scum of Europe; men who wanted no steady employment, but to make easy and quick stakes—for the pay was good—so as to indulge in periodical sprees, or in rare instances, for the more laudable purpose of placing themselves in a better position to apply for more respectable employment. They came and went in gangs, for the work was so hard that there were few men that did not require a week's rest after a month's labour. So much for the rough but honest working element. But unfortunately these canal banks were infested by other gangs, who did not seek work, and yet were often to be seen loafing about the various camps. Then how did these men live? For they could not successfully beg, seeing that work was to be had for the asking. Perhaps the explanation is that seldom a day passed but what a dead body was dragged out of the water, and more than two-thirds of these bodies bore the marks of murder. The bodies were not those of men coming from the city in search of employment, but of such men as had been known to have quit work a few days previous, having then had a month's or more pay on their persons, and who had been on the way to the city for enjoyment. Yes, these loafers were undoubtedly the thugs and murderers, and if a man was inclined to hazard his life, all he had to do was to make it known that he on the following day was to draw his earnings, with the intention of walking the canal banks to one of the distant towns. It was hardly likely that he would reach his destination, but would be taken out of the canal some days later—a murdered man. To defeat the purpose of these unscrupulous life-takers, the more timid workmen waited for one another until they were sufficiently strong in number to discharge themselves and travel without fear. But alas! there was many a man who prided himself on his own heart and muscles for protection and dared the journey alone. At the time of which I write there had been no houses built on those banks, therefore no women walked to and fro, and no children played there. No doubt such are to be seen there at the present day, innocent of the violence and the blood that was shed there in the past.

I had applied for work at one of these camps and being sickened of the same in a little more than three weeks demanded my earnings at the same time Cockney Tom and Pat Sheeny drew theirs, with the intention of accompanying them to Chicago. Being somewhat delayed in business, owing

101

to the absence of the timekeeper, and being then compelled to remain for dinner, we soon saw the impossibility of reaching the city before midnight. Therefore it was arranged between us that we should settle for the night at some place half way between the camp and the city, and rise early so as to enter the latter before noon on the following day. With this intention we started, after receiving dinner and pay, and after several hours' walk settled down.

There would be six hours' darkness and it was proposed that I should keep awake for the first two hours' watch, after which Cockney Tom would relieve me, and Pat would then keep watch until daybreak.

Now, in my two hours' watch I had on several occasions heard a stir in the adjoining bush, but not being able to see whether it was a man or a beast, I had not thought it necessary to alarm my companions. At last I considered my duty to be at an end, and, after rousing Cockney Tom, settled for sleep. Before I closed my eyes I noticed that the second watch was still lying recumbent, although he seemed to be wide awake; but I was too intent on my own sleep to care whether he would be faithful to his trust or not. I don't think I could have been asleep more than fifteen minutes when I was startled by a loud shout and, springing to my feet was just in time to see Cockney Tom in pursuit of one who was then entering the bush. The Irishman was also up, and we both followed the chase. We soon reached our companion, finding him standing dazed and confused as to which way the quarry had gone. He explained to us that when on watch he was lying down with his eyes closed, but with his ears wide open, and his mental faculties at work. Suddenly, he heard a step near and opening his eyes saw a stranger standing within three feet of him. It was at that moment that he gave the alarm, but the stranger was too fleet to be overtaken. 'No doubt,' said Cockney, 'there is a gang of them at no short distance from here and if we are wise, we will continue our journey at once. I have seen the man's face before, at the camp, and know I shall recognise him if we meet again.' His advice of continuing our journey was hardly necessary, for sleep was now out of the question.

In less than a week after the above incident we three, having squandered our earnings in Chicago, were back at the old camp seeking re-employment. There happened to be only one vacancy, which the Irishman persuaded Cockney to accept, whilst we two would travel on to the next camp, a distance of two miles. We were about to do this when the boss ganger asked me if I would like a position in the boarding shanty as assistant cook. Knowing that an assistant cook meant no more than carrying water, peeling potatoes, washing dishes, keeping a good fire and opening cans of condensed meat and preserves—I felt quite confident in undertaking such a position. So the Cockney and I started to work at once, but before doing so, arranged for the keep of Pat until a vacancy occurred, his meals to be entered to our account. The next morning his chance came and he was set to work.

We had been working four days, and on the evening of that fourth day we three and a number of others were resting ourselves in a quiet place near the camp. Whilst seated there, smoking and talking, there came along four strangers, who seated themselves some distance from us, but within earshot of our conversation. No one paid much heed to them, for it was not unusual to be visited by strangers in quest of work. But there was one man who could not keep his eyes from them, and that was Cockney Tom. 'Yes,' he said to me after several long puffs at his pipe, 'that stranger, showing us his side face, is the very man who attempted to rob us.' Saying this the Cockney took off his cap and laying it carefully on the ground with its inside uppermost, placed therein his dirty clay pipe, as gently as a woman putting a sleeping babe in its cradle—and to the no small surprise of his companions began to address them in this oratorical fashion: 'Gentlemen, some time ago a man attempted to rob me and two others, and ever since then I have been longing to meet him face to face. At last we meet, and I would like to know what is to be done with him.' 'Why, give him a good hiding, of course,' cried several angry voices. On hearing this the Cockney at once turned towards the strangers—whom he had hitherto pretended not to notice— and in three bounds was standing over them. Placing his hands on the shoulders of one he said in a calm voice, 'This is my man.' The man referred to rose deliberately to his feet, as though he had expected this, and his companions did likewise. 'Well,' said he, 'what is the trouble?' 'You know quite well,' replied the Cockney, 'so you may as well strip without further question.' Whatever the stranger was, he certainly was no coward, for his coat and waistcoat were soon in the hands of his companion. The Cockney lost no time, and the next minute they stood squaring before each other in such a scientific way as promised the onlookers a most interesting exhibition. Although the stranger was the taller of the two, the Cockney seemed to possess the longer reach. Round after round they fought, and in spite of their heavy and muddy boots the footwork was neat, and the

dodging of their heads and the feinting of their arms made
the more gentle onlookers overlook the drawing of blood.
There was no wrestling, or mauling on the ground, and
there was no attempt at foul blows, for each of the principals
seemed to value the favour of that most appreciative
assembly. It looked more like a friendly exhibition than two
men attempting to take life. The spectators laughed approval
and buzzed with admiration until even the bleeding men,
hearing this, chaffed one another, and smiled at each other
grimly with their battered faces. Yes, it seemed friendly
enough until the tenth round when the Cockney, who the
round previous seemed to show signs of weariness called to
his assistance some latent force which set his arms to work
like a pair of axes on a tree, and down his opponent fell,
and the battle was lost and won. The stranger was borne
away by his companions, and Cockney Tom returned to the
camp to dress his injuries, which did not prevent him from
work on the following day. The Cockney was well pleased
with this exploit, and if his opponent was one of those thugs
and murderers, who had taken an active part in perhaps
fifty or sixty murders, he would certainly be lucky if he
never met with severer punishment.

CHAPTER XIV

THE HOUSE-BOAT

I worked long enough on this canal to save fifty dollars, and then quit, feeling the old restlessness return, which had unsettled me for some time. With this comfortable sum in my possession I kept beating my way west until I arrived at St. Louis, a large city on the Mississippi, having up till now lived frugally, and spent nothing on travelling. This kind of life was often irksome to me, when I have camped all night alone in the woods, beside a fire, when one good sociable companion might have turned the life into an ideal one. Often have I waked in the night, or early morning, to find spaces opposite occupied by one or two strangers, who had seen the fire in the distance, and had been guided to me by its light. One night, in Indiana, when it had rained heavily throughout the day, I had made my fire and camped under a thick leaved tree, where the ground was dryer than in the open. Sometime about midnight, I felt myself roughly shaken, at the same time a sudden shower fell that pinned me breathless to the earth. I looked here and there, but could see no one. Then I left the shelter of the tree and saw to my surprise that the night was fine, and that the stars were thick and shining. As I replenished the fire with wood, of which I always gathered in an abundance before darkness came, it puzzled me much to account for this. Although I thought the shaking must have been a dream, my wet clothes were a sufficient proof of the rain's reality. Every man I met on the following day enquired where I had lodged during the earthquake shock on the previous night, and that question explained everything. The earth had shaken me, and the leaves of the tree, which had been gathering all day the rain drops, had in one moment relinquished them all upon my sleeping form.

On reaching St. Louis I still had something like forty dollars, and being tired of my own thoughts, which continually upbraided me for wasted time, resolved to seek some congenial fellowship, so that in listening to other men's thoughts I might be rendered deaf to my own. I had bought a daily paper, and had gone to the levee, so that I might spend a few hours out of the sun, reading, and watching the traffic on the river. Seeing before me a large pile of lumber, I hastened towards it, that I might enjoy its shady side. When I arrived I saw that the place was already occupied by two strangers, one being a man of middle age, and the other a youth of gentlemanly appearance. Seating myself, I began to read, but soon had my attention drawn to their conversation. The young fellow, wanting to go home, and being in no great hurry, proposed buying a house-boat and floating leisurely down the Mississippi to New Orleans, from which place he would then take train to southern Texas, where his home was. 'We will go ashore,' he said, 'and see the different towns, and take in fresh provisions as they are needed.' The elder of the two, who had a strong Scotch accent, allowed a little enthusiasm to ooze out of his dry temperament, and agreed without much comment. 'Excuse me, gentlemen,' I said, 'I could not help but hear your conversation and, if you have no objection, would like to share expenses and enjoy your company on such a trip.' The Texan, being young and impetuous, without the least suspicion of strangers, jumped to his feet, exulting at the social project. Scotty, more calm, but with a shrewd eye to the financial side of the question, said that he thought the trip would certainly be enjoyed better by three, and that the expense would not be near so great per head. We had no difficulty in purchasing a house-boat. Hundreds of these are moored to the banks, lived in by fishermen and their wives, and others in various ways employed on the river. But, of course, the one we required was to be much smaller than these. We found one, at last, rather battered, and ill-conditioned, for which we were asked eleven dollars. Scotty, to our unfeigned disgust, acted the Jew in this matter of trade, and had succeeded in beating the price down to nine dollars and a half when we to his annoyance offered to pay that sum without more ado. But Scotty, although mean in these business matters, was strictly honest and just in paying an equal share; for, after I had paid the odd half a dollar, he did not forget that amount when we came to stocking the boat with provisions. We lost no time in getting these, and then went ashore for the evening's enjoyment and the night's sleep, intending to start early the next morning. And with these prospects before us, a very pleasant evening we had.

At nine o'clock the following morning, we weighed anchor —our anchor being a large stone—and drifted into the current, the young Texan using an oar as a tiller. And what a strange voyage we had, fraught with more danger than many would dream. This Mississippi river often had only a few yards for navigation purposes, even when the distance from bank to bank was between two and three miles. Sometimes we were in the middle of this broad river, and yet were in extreme danger of foundering, for we could touch the bottom with a short stick. Yes, we were in danger of foundering, and yet our ship drew less than six inches of water! Trees, whose branches were firmly embedded in the mud, had their roots bobbing up and down, bobbing up unawares, and we were often in danger of being impaled on one of these ere we could steer clear of it. Sometimes we would see villages and small towns that in the remote past had been built flush on the banks of this river: now they were lying quiet and neglected a mile or more away, owing to this river's determination to take his own course. Hundreds of lives had been sacrificed, dying of swamp fever, in building levees and high banks to prevent this, and millions of dollars utilised for the same purpose—but the Father of Waters has hitherto had his own will, and can be expected to be seen at any place, and at any time.

Towards evening we would put ashore on a sand bar, making a fire of driftwood, of which there was an abundance. Here we cooked supper, slept and enjoyed breakfast the next morning. There was no other water to be had than that of the river, which the natives of the south claim to be healthy. We had no objection to using it for cooking and washing, but it was certainly too thick for drinking cold—or rather lukewarm, for it was never cold in the summer months. We would fill a large can and let the water settle for twenty or thirty minutes, and, after taking great care in drinking, a sediment of mud would be left at the bottom a quarter or three-eighths of an inch deep.

We put ashore at one place where a number of negroes and white men had assembled in expectation of work, when man again proposed putting forth his puny strength against the Mississippi, where we decided to wait a day or two and take our chance of being employed. Unfortunately the ill feeling which invariably exists between these two colours, came to a climax on the first day of our arrival. The negroes, insulting and arrogant, through their superiority of numbers, became at last unbearable. On which the white men, having that truer courage that scorned to count their own strength, assembled together, and after a few moments' consultation, resolved to take advantage of the first provocation. This came sooner than was expected. A negro, affecting to be intoxicated, staggered against a white man, and was promptly knocked down for his trouble. The negroes, whose favourite weapon is the razor, produced these useful blades from different parts of concealment, stood irresolute, waiting for a leader, and then came forward in a body, led by a big swaggerer in bare feet, whose apparel consisted of a red shirt and a pair of patched trousers held up by a single brace. These white men, who were so far outnumbered, said little, but the negroes were loud in their abuse. This soon led to blows and in the ensuing fight, knives, razors and fists were freely used. Only one shot was fired, and that one told. When the negroes, whose courage had faded at such a determined resistance, were in full flight, the tall swaggerer was left behind with a bullet in his heart. Several men were wounded, with gashes on necks, arms, and different parts of the body. Small fights continued throughout the day, but it was left for the night to produce a deed of foul murder. A white man was found next morning with his body covered with blood from thirty-nine wounds. Half a dozen razors must have set to work on him in the dark. The razor is a sly, ugly-looking weapon, but is far less dangerous than a knife, a poker, or even a short heavy piece of wood; and as it cannot pierce to the heart or brain, that is why this man took so long in the killing. This deed roused the sheriff and his marshal, and they followed the black murderers to the adjoining state, but returned next day without them.

We embarked again, but owing to the young Texan being taken sick with malarial fever, resolved to put ashore for medicine at the first large town. This malarial fever is very prevalent in these parts, especially this state of Arkansas, which is three parts a swamp. He suffered so much that we decided to call on the first house-boat seen, and ask assistance of the fishermen, and soon we had an opportunity of doing so. Seeing a large house-boat moored at the mouth of a small creek we put the tiller—which as I have said, was an oar—to its proper work, and sculled towards the shore. We ran to land within ten yards of the other boat, and the fisherman, who had seen us coming, stood waiting on the sands to know our wants. He was a typical swamp man, with a dark sickly complexion, thin-faced and dry-skinned and, though he was nearly six feet in height, his weight, I believe, could not have exceeded one hundred and twenty pounds. His left cheek was considerably swollen, which I thought must be due to neuralgia until the swelling began to disappear from that side; and, after witnessing for a few seconds a frightful, even painful contortion of the face, I saw the right cheek come into possession of the same beautiful round curve, leaving the left cheek as its fellow had been. It was now apparent that the one object of this man's life was to chew tobacco. To him we related our troubles, asking his advice, and for a little temporary assistance, for which he would be paid. Up to the present time he had not opened his lips, except a right or left corner to squirt tobacco juice, sending an equal share to the north and south. 'I guess there's some quinine in the shanty boat,' he said, after a long silence, 'which I reckon will relieve him considerably, but he ought ter go home ter th' women folk, that's straight.' He led the way to his boat, and we followed. We soon had the young Texan in comfort, and Scotty and myself returned to transfer some provisions to the fisherman's house-boat, for the evening's use. While doing so, we decided to sell our own boat, at any price, when we would walk to the nearest railroad, and send the young fellow home; after which we would seek some employment and settle down. We cooked supper, and then slept in the open air, beside a large fire, leaving our sick friend comfortable in the boat.

The next morning we offered our house-boat for sale for six dollars, with all its belongings. The fisherman explained to us that he not only had no money, but rarely had use for it. Everything he needed he paid for in fish, and often went months at a time without a glimpse of money of any description. To my surprise the one thing that did seem to claim his attention, for which he could not help but display some greed, was the large stone which we had brought with us from St. Louis, and which we had used for an anchor. This stone certainly had no vein of gold or silver in it, it was not granite or marble, and could boast of no beauty, being a very ordinary looking stone indeed, but it seemed to have a strange fascination for this man. The fisherman had no money, and had nothing to barter which might be of use to us, so we made him a present of the whole lot, and left him sitting on the stone, watching our departure. 'He seemed very eager to possess that stone,' I remarked to Scotty, as we followed a trail through a thicket, so that we might reach the high-road. 'Yes,' said Scotty, 'for in this part of the country, where there is little but sand, wood and mud, a stone, a piece of iron, or any small thing of weight, can be put to many uses.'

After reaching the road we had twenty miles to walk to reach the nearest railway station, at which place we arrived late that night, the young Texan being then weak and exhausted. A train was leaving at midnight for New Orleans, and, after seeing him safely aboard we sat in the station till day-break. Early the next morning we were examining the town, waiting for business to start, so that we might enquire as to its prospects for work. This seemed to be good, there being a large stave factory which employed a number of men. We succeeded in our quest, starting to work that morning, and at dinner time received a note of introduction to an hotel. That evening we associated with our fellow-workmen, and, in the course of conversation, we discovered that there was no particular time to receive wages, there being no regular pay day. Sometimes wages ran on for a month, six weeks, two months, etc. 'Of course,' he explained to us, 'anything you require you can easily get an order for on the stores.' We worked two weeks at this factory, when I was taken ill myself with malaria, and not being able to eat, soon became too weak for work. In this condition I went to the office for my money, but could not get it, and saw that nothing else could be done than to get an order on the stores, and take my wages out in clothes, shoes, etc. Scotty was scared at this, and quitted work at once to demand his wages in cash, and there I left him, waiting for a settlement. I intended going to Memphis, the nearest large town, and placing myself in its hospital, whilst Scotty was going to New Orleans, where I promised to meet him in a month, providing I was sufficiently recovered to do so.

I don't know what possessed me to walk out of this town, instead of taking a train, but this I did, to my regret. For I became too weak to move, and, coming to a large swamp, I left the railroad and crawled into it, and for three days and the same number of nights, lay there without energy to continue my journey. Wild hungry hogs were there, who approached dangerously near, but ran snorting away when my body moved. A score or more of buzzards had perched waiting on the branches above me, and I knew that the place was teeming with snakes. I suffered from a terrible thirst, and drank of the swamp-pools, stagnant water that was full of germs, and had the colours of the rainbow, one dose of which would have poisoned some men to death. When the chill was upon me, I crawled into the hot sun, and lay there shivering with the cold; and when the hot fever possessed me, I crawled back into the shade. Not a morsel to eat for four days, and very little for several days previous. I could see the trains pass this way and that, but had not the strength to call. Most of the trains whistled, and I knew that they stopped either for water or coal within a mile of where I lay. Knowing this to be the case, and certain that it would be death to remain longer in this deadly swamp, I managed to reach the railroad track, and succeeded in reaching the next station, where most of these trains stopped. The distance had been less than a mile, but it had taken me two hours to accomplish. I then paid my way from this station, being in a hurry to reach Memphis, thinking my life was at its close. When I reached that town I took a conveyance from the station to the hospital. At that place my condition was considered to be very serious, but the doctor always bore me in mind, for we were both of the same nationality, and to that, I believe, I owe my speedy recovery.

CHAPTER XV

A LYNCHING

Upon leaving the hospital, I remained several days in Memphis, spending most of my hours enjoying the shade and sunshine of a small park, which is pleasantly situated in the main portion of that town. One morning, while doing this, I was accosted by one whom I soon recognised as a fellow-worker of mine in the stave factory. From him I learnt that the firm had smashed, no pay day had come, and the stores had all absolutely refused to honour the firm's orders; while some men had left the town disgusted, and others were patiently waiting a settlement that would never come. This man was going north, so I left him at Memphis, intending to beat my way to New Orleans, and from that town to the state of Texas.

These states of Tennessee, Arkansas, Mississippi and Louisiana, are the homes of the negroes of old. It is a strange contrast to see the old negroes, who in their young days were slaves, reverently raising their hats to any seedy looking white man whom they meet, calling him such titles as captain, major, colonel and even general—and the half defiant gloom of the free, young generations, who are still in some respects slaves to the white men. These negroes lived in small wooden shanties, and rarely received money for their labour. They worked for the planter at so much a day. This gentleman kept on the plantation a large general store, and supplied their wants at such an exorbitant price that the negroes were seldom out of debt, when the busy season commenced. In the cities, silk would be far cheaper than the common flimsy muslin which poor black Dinah so much coveted from her master's store. I have heard many an old negro say that he was far worse off as a freeman than as a slave.

The prisons in the north were like hotels, but here in the south went to the extreme of cruelty. In some places a man would be tried and perhaps fined ten dollars and costs. A citizen, having need of a cheap labourer, would pay this fine, take possession of the prisoner, and make him work out his fine on the farm. This citizen would buy the prisoner cheap overalls, dungarees, shirts, shoes, etc., for a few dollars, and charge the prisoner four times their amount. The prisoner was not free to refuse these, and being forced to work out their price, was kept in this way twice the number of his days. I was very much afraid of all this, although a wandering white man was not in nearly so much danger as a negro.

Some days after leaving Memphis, I arrived at a small town, where I was surprised to see an unusual amount of bustle, the surrounding country for miles having sent in all its able bodied men. Every man was armed with a gun, and they stood in small groups talking outside the various stores. It seemed as though there had been rumours of an invasion, and that these men were organising to defend their homes and country, but I had not the least idea of what had really happened. The small groups now began to join together into larger ones, and the larger groups joined until they became one large body of men. This one body then shouldered guns and moved quickly along the main street, the men's faces being drawn and pale. I followed on, perhaps the one unarmed man among them, curious to know the meaning of it all. They came at last to a halt, and, to see the reason for this, I stepped across the way, and saw that they had halted before a large building, which, by its barred windows, I had no difficulty in recognising as the jail. One man had curled around his shoulders a long rope, and this man with two others knocked loudly with the butt ends of their guns on the prison door. Almost in an instant the door was flung wide open, and the sheriff stood in the open way to know their wants. The men must have demanded the prison keys, for I saw the sheriff at once produce them, which he handed to these men without the least show of resistance. This man with the rope and several others then entered the jail, and the silent crowd without cast their eyes in that direction. Up to the present time I had not heard a distinct voice, nothing but the buzz of low whispering. But suddenly from the jail's interior there came a loud shriek and a voice crying for mercy. Men now appeared in the open doorway, dragging after them a negro at the end of a rope. This unfortunate wretch was possessed of a terror that is seldom seen in a human being. He fell on his knees to pray, but was jerked to his feet ere he could murmur the first words, O Lord. He staggered to and fro and sideways, at the same time howling and jabbering, foaming at the mouth, and showing the horrible white of his eyes. I can well understand a man screaming, trembling and crying for mercy, when actually enduring bodily pain, but that one should show such a terror at the thought of it, filled me more with disgust than pity. That this prisoner should have been so brutal and unfeeling in inflicting pain on another, and should now show so much cowardice in anticipation of receiving punishment inadequate to his offence, dried in me the milk of human kindness, and banished my first thoughts, which had been to escape this horrible scene without witnessing its end. For it was now I remembered reading of this man's offence, and it was of the most brutal kind, being much like the work of a wild beast. They now marched him from the jail, their strong arms supporting his terror stricken limbs, but no man reviled him with his tongue, and I saw no cowardly hand strike him. Soon they came to a group of trees on the outskirts of the town, and, choosing the largest of these, they threw the rope's end over its strongest branch, the prisoner at the same time crying for mercy, and trying to throw his body full on the ground. When this was done a dozen hands caught the rope's end, made one quick jerk, and the prisoner's body was struggling in the air. Then all these men shouldered their guns, fired one volley, and in a second the body was hanging lifeless with a hundred shots. In five minutes after this, nothing but the corpse remained to tell of what had occurred, the men having quietly scattered towards their homes.

A few days after this, I was in New Orleans, intending to spend a week or two in that city, before I started on my journey to Texas. It was in this city, three days after my arrival, that I became the victim of an outrage which was as unsatisfactory to others as to myself. Having been to the theatre, and being on my way back home late at night, half a dozen men, whom I scarcely had time to recognise as negroes, sprang from a dark corner, and, without saying a word, or giving the least chance of escape or defence, biffed and banged at my face and head until I fell unconscious at their feet. Their motive, without a doubt, was robbery, but having my money concealed in a belt next to my body, they had to be satisfied with a five cent piece, which was all my pockets contained. Such brutal outrages as these are seldom committed by white men, who, having the more cool courage, demand a man's money at the commencement, and do not resort to violence, except it be their victim's wish. But this not very intelligent race half murder a man without being sure of anything for their pains. White men will search a man as he stands, and if he possesses nothing, he may go his way uninjured, followed perhaps, by a curse or two of disappointment; but these negroes prefer to murder a man first, and then to search the dead body. They are certainly born thieves. On the river boats, that ply the Mississippi from St. Louis to New Orleans, which are all manned by negroes, with the exception of those holding the higher offices, a negro chief will often spoil a six dollar pair of trousers in robbing his victim of a twenty-five cent piece. When a man is asleep the negro will bend over him, feeling the outside of his trousers where the pockets are. If he feels the shape of a coin, instead of working his fingers carefully into the mouth of the pocket, he takes out his razor and, holding the coin with the fingers of his left hand, cuts it out, bringing away coin, part of the lining, pocket and trousers. When the victim wakes he, or some one else, sees the hole, and they at once know the meaning of it. I remember a trip on one of these boats when a white man feigned a sleep, lying on his back on a bale of cotton, with his hands in his coat pockets. In his right pocket was a revolver, which his right hand held ready cocked for use. These negroes are always on the look out for sleepers, and one of these thieves was soon bending over his expected victim. He had felt a coin and, taking out his razor, was in the act of cutting it out, when there was a sharp report, and the negro fell back shot through the brain. The supposed sleeper quietly rose to his feet, and when the captain and some officers came, he simply pointed to the negro and the fallen razor, and no other explanation was needed. At the next stopping place the captain had a few words with the authorities, and the dead body was taken ashore, but the white passenger continued his journey without being bothered about a trial or examination. There was no more thieving during that trip.

I soon left New Orleans, being possessed with a restless spirit, and, after visiting Galveston, Euston, and many more towns of less importance, I made my way through the heart of Texas to the town of Paris, which lies on the borders of the Indian territory. It was in a saloon in the main street of this town that I had my attention drawn to a glass case, wherein was seen hanging a cord, at the end of which was something that looked very much like a walnut. On looking closer, I saw a small heap of dust at the bottom. Seeing that this case contained no stuffed animal, nor any model of ingenious mechanism I began to read the printed matter, curious for an explanation. This small thing dangling at the end of the cord purported to be the heart of a negro, whom the people had sometime previously burned at the stake. He had suffered a terrible death: so had his little victim, a mere child of a few years, who had been found in the woods torn limb from limb. This negro had been arrested by the sheriff, and sentenced to a short term adequate to his offence. After he had been released, he had taken his revenge on the sheriff's child, bearing her off when on her way to school. The sheriff's wife, being the child's mother, had with her own hand applied the torch to this monster, and if her hand had failed, any woman in this land of many millions would have willingly done her this service.

I left Paris that night, catching a fast cattle train, and arrived the following morning at Fort Smith, Arkansas. Bill Cook, the train and bank robber, and his gang, were being tried this morning, and a special train was now waiting to convey them to the penitentiary. I saw this notorious freebooter, when he was brought to the station—a young man between twenty and thirty years, receiving a sentence of forty years' imprisonment. One of his gang, Cherokee Bill a desperado of nineteen years, was indicted for murder, and remained in Fort Smith to be hanged. The train steamed out with its many deputies to guard a few prisoners—few, but proved to be very dangerous.

CHAPTER XVI

THE CAMP

Who would have dreamt that so many well-known beggars would have met together at one camp, without any pre-arranged plans? The time was morning and the scene was on the outskirts of Pittsburg, and the characters were Philadelphia Slim and Wee Shorty, who had all night ridden the freight car and had now dismounted near the camp, which they knew of old. They both had cold victuals in plenty, with dry coffee and sugar, and they were not long in making a blaze and fetching water from the spring before they were seated comfortably to their breakfast, after which they intended to sleep, for they were more weary than working men.

They were not without money; for Wee Shorty and Slim had, the day previous, been encamped with others about a hundred miles from the present spot, at which place there had come to the camp an unfortunate blacksmith who possessed society papers but lacked courage to beg with them. On which Wee Shorty had conceived a most daring plan, which was to borrow the aforesaid papers, with the blacksmith's consent, and to make his way to the nearest blacksmith's shop. With this idea in his mind the Wee Man had bound his hand in white linen, so that he could plead disablement in case the blacksmith doubted him to be the legitimate owner of the papers, and to prove his veracity, would test him with a little job. After binding his hand in this way, Wee Shorty, who was no more than five feet in height, and who had small white hands and a pale face, and whose weight never exceeded seven stone and a half, and who looked more like a sickly tailor than a blacksmith— after taking this precaution, Wee Shorty made his way to the blacksmith's shop. In less than twenty minutes he had returned with a dollar in small change, and had returned the poor blacksmith his papers, and generously given him one fourth of his makings. Yes, it would indeed be a hard town if this wee fellow failed to make money.

As I have already said, Slim and the artful one were tired after their night's ride, and they were well pleased to find the camp unoccupied by strangers. But they had scarcely made their coffee and swallowed the first mouthful, when the dried twigs were heard to crack beneath a heavy tread and, the next moment, there walked into the camp the Indian Kid, whom the present proprietors had not seen for over twelve months.

What a meeting was there, and what confidences were exchanged. There was good reason for the Kid not having been seen, for he had been incarcerated in a jail. He had committed his first and last burglary, which had not been done with an eye to profit, but out of a mean spirit of revenge. He had been refused charity at a house and, on leaving the place, had spied a small outhouse in which he saw many things easy to carry, and easily to be converted into money. Bearing this in mind he had returned after dark, scaled the back wall, and was soon in possession of a large bundle consisting of shirts, frocks, shoes and various carpenter's tools. All this had been done through a spirit of revenge, for the Kid swore that he could have begged the worth of the bundle in half an hour. Being in possession of that bundle at that strange hour of the night, he was afraid to carry it into the town for fear that the police would enquire his business, so he hid it in the bushes, which in the night looked so dark and thick; after which he had artfully walked some distance away, and laid himself down to sleep until morning. it must have been daylight for several hours when the Kid rose hastily and went in quest of his bundle. But the bundle had disappeared, and the Kid had been cruelly robbed, by early workmen he at first thought, who had spied the bundle in the bushes, which appeared so much less heavy by day than by night. However it was not the early workman who had done this, but a plain clothes policeman who still hid behind the bushes and, seeing the Kid searching for his bundle, sprang from concealment, saying—'You are looking for a bundle, and I am looking for you.' Such was the Kid's story, recited at great pains, for he often rambled in his discourse to laud himself as a successful beggar who would, on no account, commit burglary for profit; all of which accounted for his twelve months' disappearance.

His story was scarcely at an end when who should walk into the camp but Windy, the talkative Windy, whose tongue had entertained many a camp with strange and unique experiences. Of course, at his heels was Pennsylvania Dutch, a faithful friend enough but a poor beggar, who was no more than a pensioner on Windy's bounty, and acted the part of a man-servant.

But there was another surprise to follow; for English Harry, who had been in Pittsburg for some time past, having now walked out of the city to take a glance at the camp, walked into it at this very time, and to his astonishment and joy found the place in possession of good beggars instead of common work seekers, as he had at first feared.

Only imagine all these notorious men meeting together haphazard in this manner. They could scarcely recover their astonishment. There was nothing else to be done but to make a muster of what money was in the camp, and to send Pennsylvania Dutch for its worth in whisky, so as to celebrate such an event by a carousal. This was at once done, and Windy's pensioner shook off his laziness from head to foot, which made Wee Shorty sarcastically remark—'Dutchy would rather buy than beg.' To which Windy, in a voice of despair, answered—'He will never make a beggar and, if I did not keep a sharp eye on him, or anything occurred to part us, he would live in orchards and turnip fields until he saw a chance to become a working man. He confessed, when I first met him, that he had lived for ten days on green corn and apples, so I took him in hand and kept him, thinking my example would rouse him to action, but it was of no use, for the poor fellow has not the heart. However, I never forget poor Dutchy when I am foraging,' said Windy, rather tenderly.

It was not long before the object of these remarks returned and placed before his companions two bottles of whisky.

'Now, boys,' said Windy, after he had become affected by several lots of spirits—'Now, boys, I propose that we hold this camp down for a whole week, and we will all rag up'— meaning that they would beg clothes and put on the appearance of gentlemen. His proposal was unanimously seconded, and was quickly followed by a suggestion from the Indian Kid that they should finish the whisky, which also met with no objection. 'We will hold the camp,' cried Windy, 'against all comers.' They would certainly find no necessity for defending their privacy, for one glance at these six men, especially in their present condition, would have been sufficient to deter any decent-minded person from entering. This camp was now far more private than Mrs. Brown's house in town, who had a neighbour that never entered other people's doors without first knocking; but which neighbour never gave Mrs. Brown, or anyone else, the chance to remove sundry things that were better concealed, nor waited to hear the cry 'come in'; for she entered as she knocked, saying— 'Don't be alarmed, Mrs.Brown, it is only Mrs. White.'

Alas, the whisky soon gave out, and there was no more money, and what was to be done? 'I propose,' said English Harry, 'that we leave Pennsylvania Dutch in charge of the camp while we go out foraging for an hour.' To this they all agreed, and made their way towards the town. On reaching the suburbs they divided and went in different directions, with the understanding that each man should be returned to the camp in less than two hours, and that each one should have no less than half a dollar.

How it was done was a mystery, but Wee Shorty was back in less than an hour, not only with half a dollar but with twenty cents' worth of whisky in a bottle. He was soon followed by Windy, who had begged fifty-five cents. After which came in English Harry and the Indian Kid together, each with half a dollar. But where was Philadelphia Slim, Wee Shorty's boon companion? For these were good beggars all, who could have almost persuaded the birds to feed them in the wilderness, and Slim was by no means the worst, even though the Wee Man was by a small degree the best. Until they knew the fate of poor Slim they felt very little inclination to continue their carousal.

It might have been three quarters of an hour after the return of English Harry and the Kid, when they heard a step coming through the bush and, turning their eyes that way, were soon confronted by their late companion Slim. He had a large bundle under his arm, but to the surprise and anxiety of his companions, was holding to his nose a blood-stained pocket handkerchief. 'Who has done that, Slim?' cried Wee Shorty, who had surreptitiously fortified himself with whisky, and who, being the smallest man, was naturally the most ferocious—'Who has done that?' he cried, springing to his feet and, with his hands dangerously clenched, standing to his full height. Slim did not answer this question at once, but threw down his bundle; after which he produced a dollar bill and placed it thereon. Pointing then to the twain with his right hand—his left hand still being occupied with his bleeding nose—he said, 'Here is a suit of clothes and a dollar bill, and I have well earned them.' Such words were mysterious to his associates, for they knew that Slim would never at any price perform labour, and they came to the conclusion in their own minds that he had forcibly taken these things in a very high handed fashion, and had suffered in the act. What a disgrace to the profession!

After enquiring if there was any whisky to be had and being supplied with the same by his particular friend Wee Shorty, Slim proposed that Pennsylvania Dutch should be again despatched with all speed for a fresh supply. Seeing this done he then seated himself and proceeded to give his experience.

It seems that Slim had had more difficulty than was expected. A full half hour had elapsed, and Slim had not received one cent, although he had told his pitiful story to a number of people. He almost began to despair of success, but firmly resolved not to return without something to show for his trouble. Seeing a very large house he went to the front door and rang the bell, but the door remained unanswered. Not to be baffled by this, and beginning to feel desperate, he made his way to the back of the house, and was just about to knock at the back door when a voice hailed him from an adjoining shed. Turning his eyes in that direction he saw a man in his white shirt sleeves, who seemed to be the master of the house. Now, as Slim looked across, he saw into the shed, and behold there was a punching ball hanging from the ceiling, which was still moving as though this gentleman had only that moment finished practising. On Slim explaining his wants, which had been increasing in number through his ill-success, the gentleman quietly went to a shelf and taking there from a pair of boxing gloves told Slim that if he would oblige him with ten minutes' practice with the same, he would reward him with a dollar. Now it happened that these things were not entirely unknown to Slim, and once or twice in his life he had actually had them in his hands—but not on—and he had come to the conclusion that they could do but very little hurt. Therefore he donned the gloves, being as eager to earn an easy dollar as the master of the house was eager to practise. Alas! it was this difference in their motives which gave the gentleman an overwhelming victory and poor Slim a bloody nose and such aching bones. 'For,' said Slim to us, 'suppose I had knocked him out, who was to pay me my dollar? He attacked me like a mad bull, and all I dare do was to act on the defence. Several times he left an opening which, had I taken advantage of, would have ended in his collapse; and if he had died, there had been no witness to hear what bargain had been made between us. Being at such a disadvantage as I was,' Slim continued, 'he would, no doubt, have made matters worse if my nose had not bled, which I began to wipe with the gloves. Seeing this he was afraid my blood would be conveyed by means of the gloves to his own person, so he asked me if I had had enough. I thanked him that I had and, as we made our way towards the house, told him I would be thankful for any old clothes to replace my own, which were now stained with blood. He seemed to be so pleased at having drawn my blood that I believe he would have given me anything I asked for. Here are the clothes, but I don't know what they are like.'

Such was Slim's experience. On an inspection of the bundle it was found to contain a clean shirt, a pair of socks, two handkerchiefs, and an almost brand new suit of clothes. Just as Philadelphia Slim ended his story, Pennsylvania Dutch returned with the whisky, and we all caroused until sleep overpowered us.

CHAPTER XVII

HOME

I had now been in the United States of America something like five years, working here and there as the inclination seized me, which, I must confess, was not often. I was certainly getting some enjoyment out of life, but now and then the waste of time appalled me, for I still had a conviction that I was born to a different life. The knowledge that I had the advantage over the majority of strangers in that country, often consoled me when feeling depressed. For my old grandmother had left me one third profit of a small estate, my share at that time amounting to ten shillings per week, and during these five years I had not drawn one penny, therefore having over a hundred pounds entered to my account. So, when one would say how much he desired to return to his native land, but had no means of doing so, I would then explain how it could easily be done on the cattle boats. And if he protested, saying that he had not the courage to return penniless after so many years abroad, although I had no answer to console him, his objection was a pleasant reminder of my own expectations. It was this knowledge that made me so idle and so indifferent to saving; and it was this small income that has been, and is in a commercial sense, the ruin of my life.

It was now the end of October, and I was in Chicago squandering a summer's earnings, having during the previous months worked on a fruit farm in Illinois. I had been idling for three weeks, visiting the various theatres at night, and reading during the day. One Sunday, I had bought a weekly paper, wherein I read an appreciation of the poet Burns, with numerous quotations from his work. My thoughts wandered back to the past, the ambition of my early days, and the encouraging work of my elders.

'Ah!' I said, with a sigh, 'if during these five years I had had the daily companionship of good books, instead of all this restless wandering to and fro in a strange land, my mind, at the present hour, might be capable of some little achievement of its own.'

These thoughts haunted me all day, and that night a great joy came over me; for after my thoughts had tugged and pulled at my heart, all pointing in the one direction, which I saw was towards England, I settled with myself to follow them to that place. So, that night I resolved to leave Chicago early the following day, beat my way to Baltimore, work a cattle boat to either Liverpool or London, and from one of these places make my way back to where I belonged. With this object, I was up early the next morning, had breakfast, and in as happy a mood as when I first landed in America, left Chicago for the last time.

The Baltimore and Ohio Railroad was an easy road to beat. I had taken with me a good lunch, with a small flask of whisky, so that I might attend to travelling for twenty or thirty hours without suffering thirst or hunger. At the end of thirty-six hours I got off a train, now being hungry and thirsty, at a small town, having by then traversed half the distance between Chicago and Baltimore. Without staying any length of time in Pittsburg, I caught a train for Connesville, and, arriving there in a few hours, had to dismount and wait the next train for Cumberland, in the state of Maryland. A train was now being made up consisting of flat cars loaded with iron rails, and coal cars, also loaded. There was not much necessity on this road of concealing oneself, so I boldly mounted a coal car and there I sat, exposed to the elements, and to the curious gaze of people at various small towns through which we passed. What surprised me not a little was that I seemed to be the only man that was beating his way on this train, whereas, this being such an easy road, most trains had a number of tramps, some of them having two score or more. It did not take me long to notice that these people at the different stations and villages stared at me with something like awe, had pale faces, pointed at me in an unusual manner and whispered to each other. Now, between Connesville and Cumberland, the Baltimore and Ohio Railroad crosses the Alleghenny mountains, and often the train, if heavy, can scarcely crawl up, after which it runs down at a terrific speed. We had just mounted a steep elevation, had reached the top, and the train men were making fast their brakes for the steep incline on the other side of the mountain, when my attention was drawn to a large number people assembled

133

in the valley below, some distance ahead. I then saw that the mountain side was covered with coal, and between forty and fifty trucks lay in a heap at the foot of the mountain. This train had apparently through some cause or another, jumped the rails, and the cars had rolled over and over from top to bottom. When I reached Cumberland, still being stared at, and pointed out at various stations and villages on the way, it was not long before an explanation was forthcoming. I, it seemed, had followed a train that had killed forty-four men—two brakesmen, the engineer, conductor and forty tramps who were beating their way. On coming down the mountain side, the brakes had refused to work, the fireman had jumped off in time to save his own life, and the others had all been precipitated with the train into the valley and killed. It had run with such a reckless speed that it could not possibly maintain its hold of the rails. And this accounted for the one traveller on this train, and how horror-stricken the people had seemed at my temerity, which, of course, was no more than ignorance of the mishap. After this ride I never again felt comfortable on a train, much preferring to take my chance on the water, however stormy it might be. It made me pause when this same night an unknown man was struck down by a fast express train, mangled and cut into pieces. Two or three trains left this town of Cumberland before I could summon sufficient courage to ride. I was standing, still wondering whether I should ride or walk from this town to Baltimore, when a switchman, who had just helped finish making ready a train, said—'Hallo, lad; which way are you going, to Baltimore?' On answering in the affirmative, he said, pointing to this train, 'Jump on: you will be there early in the morning!' Which I did, at the same time saying to myself, 'This is my last train ride in America, whether I live or die.' No sleep that night, and I was not sorry to reach Baltimore.

I had something like fifty dollars at this time, and intended to go at once to the cattleman's office, and to ship at the first opportunity, so that I might still have a few pounds left when I landed in England. So, when I reached Baltimore, I soon made my way to that place, and on entering, recognised several of the old cattlemen, among whom was no less a person than Australian Red, who it seemed had lost all ambition for a more respectable life. I invited him out, with two others, and we had several drinks, and at night visited the theatre. 'Now,' I said, after leaving the theatre, well knowing that these men would unscrupulously bleed me to the last cent, and would take a cunning delight in robbing me and bearing all expenses themselves—'now,' I said, 'one drink more, and we have reached the end of my resources.'

Shipping, Red explained to me on the following day, was rather slow for experienced hands. He had been begging Baltimore for more than six weeks, and was still without prospect of making a trip. He explained that he could go at any time for a pound, and had had a chance or two to go for thirty shillings, but very few two-pound men had been called for during the last three months. 'Are you going out for breakfast?' he asked. 'If you have any more money left, don't be foolish enough to spend it on food, for I can get you more than you want of that, and the money can be used for pleasure.' 'You already know that I have no more money,' I said to him, feeling myself change colour with guilt, which he did not notice. 'Wait here till I return,' he said. 'If you don't feel inclined to beg, for a day or two, you need have no fear of starving.' He then left me, and, after he had gone, I followed, and feeling guilty and ashamed, turned into a restaurant for breakfast. Later on, when I returned to the office, Red was waiting for me with an abundance of food, for he had made extra exertion on this particular morning. 'Come,' he said, 'you must be hungry by this time.' Knowing that I had this part to keep up, I sat down, but after slowly eating a morsel or two, which had been difficult to swallow, I found it necessary to plead a full stomach. Red was persistent, and so dissatisfied at this that I could not help but feel grateful for such kindness, and, feeling more shame than ever at playing such a part, I arose, telling him I would wait for him outside the office. He soon followed, and, leading the way to another part of the city, I commenced with him a spree that ended in a week's debauchery. Both of us then being penniless, we returned to the cattleman's office, to find that a good chance had been lost in our absence, when the skipper had enquired for us.

'What,' cried Red, 'go home for good next trip, eh? Why, you are cursed, like myself, by restlessness, and, mark me, you will not remain six months in your native town.' 'Perhaps not,' I said, 'but I assure you, that neither this town, nor this country, shall again feel my tread!'

Some days after this I was sent with several others to rope cattle at the yards, and there met a foreman under whom I had made a former trip. 'Hallo,' said he, 'I have not seen you for some time; are you going with this lot of cattle?' 'I don't know,' was my answer, 'but I should certainly like to, if there is need of a two-pound man.' 'Well,' he said, 'I'll put in a good word for you at the office.' That night the shipping master approached me on the subject. 'Look here he said, 'I can only give you thirty shillings for this trip. If you like to wait, you can have two pounds, but I warn you, the chance may be a long time coming. What do you say?' 'I'll sign for thirty shillings,' I said, with difficulty trying to conceal my eagerness; which was at once done. I was alone on this trip, among strangers. Had Australian Red accompanied me, no doubt I should have spent my train-fare, and been forced to return to America on the same boat.

What an enjoyable trip this was from beginning to end! What music heard in the weighing of the anchor, and what a delightful sensation when the good ship moved slowly from her dock! I performed my duty with a new pleasure, leaping here and there at any sign of danger, giving one steer longer or shorter rope, as the case required, knowing what pleasant dreams would be mine at night, when the day's work was done. And when this pleasant time came, I would lie in my bunk and take an inventory of all the old familiar things which had been stored in my memory, unthought of for over five years, and nothing would now escape me. I had written home only three times during this long absence, three short letters in my first year abroad. Probably they had given me up for dead, and I would appear at their door as a visitant from another world. One thought often troubled me, and that was to be going home without money, after such along stay in a new country. For every man thinks that fortunes are more easily made in other lands than his own, and I knew that people would expect me to be in possession of ranches, flourishing towns and gold mines; and I felt much shame in having to admit that I had returned poorer than ever. Had it not been for the money saved during my absence, which had not been convenient for use, this thought had been likely to prevent my return for some years longer, perhaps for my whole life. On the tenth day we were passing Ireland, on which I gazed with deep feeling, taking her to my heart as a sister isle, knowing at the same time that her heart was her distressful own. When I reached Liverpool, and the cattle had gone ashore, I received my pay, and, slipping away from the other cattlemen, went alone up town, made a few purchases in the way of clothes, and arrived at the railway station with three shillings and a few coppers over my fare. With this insignificant amount, the result of five years in a rich country, and something like one hundred and twenty pounds standing to my account, I arrived that evening at my native town.

Here I wandered lost for several hours, making enquiries for my people, who, during my stay abroad, had moved from the place I knew. I had just made up my mind to seek a favourite aunt of mine, who, previous to my leaving England, had been a number of years in one house, and did not then seem likely to leave, when a strange woman in the street where I was making enquiries, recognised me by my likeness to mother, and at once directed me to her place. I knocked at the door and mother, who always was and is full of premonitions, and is very superstitious in the way of signs and dreams, opened the door at once, knew who I was in the dark, though we could not see much of each other's form or face, and, to my surprise, called me by name. 'That's me, mother,' I said. 'Yes,' she answered, 'I thought it was your knock,' just as though I had only been out for an evening's stroll. She said in the course of the evening, that they had all given me up for dead, except herself, and that

138

she had also, three years before, given up all hopes of seeing me again, having had a dream wherein she saw me beat about the head and lying bloody at the feet of strangers. She mentioned the year, and even the month of this year, and a little consideration on my part placed its date with that of the outrage at New Orleans, but I did not then trouble her with an account of this.

When I was very small an aunt took me to live with her for a couple or more months in a small town in Gloucestershire, a county in which mother had never been. But she had a dream in which she saw me leaving the house with my uncle's dinner, and that I had to follow the canal bank to his works. She saw me returning that same way, and, beginning to play near the water, fall in head first, she, in her dream, just reaching the spot in time to save me. Early the following morning, after this dream, mother came by train to this village, walked the canal bank to my aunt's house, without enquiring its whereabouts, and demanded her son before he was drowned. There was certainly a possibility of this happening, for I was very small at that time, and the canal was deep. She had never before been in this place, but the locality seemed to be well-known to her as it was seen in her sleep.

.

CHAPTER XVIII

OFF AGAIN

Of course at this homecoming I vowed that I would never again leave my native town. True, I found great difficulty in sleeping on a soft bed, and lay awake several hours through the night, tossing and turning from one side to another. The food itself did not seem so palatable coming out of clean pots and shining ovens, as that which was cooked in close contact with the embers, and in the smoke and blaze of a camp fire. The unplucked chicken, covered with a thick crust of mud and baked under a pile of hot ashes, after which the hard crust could be broken to show the chicken inside as clean as a new born babe, with all its feathers and down stuck hard in the mud—this meat to me was far more tasty than that one at home, that was plucked and gutted with care, and roasted or baked to a supposed nicety. This food of civilisation certainly seemed to suffer from a lack of good wholesome dirt, and I should like to have had my own wood fire at the end of the backyard, were it not for shame.

For several weeks I walked the streets, renewing old acquaintance, accosted here and there by my old schoolmates. Most of them were married, but married or single, they all seemed to be poor and unsuccessful. I began to drink immoderately at this time, meeting one and the other, and very soon began to realise that my hundred and twenty pounds were going at the rate of a sovereign a day. Scarcely had I been home one month; when, to escape from so much drink, I made a trip to Bordeaux, on one of the local steamers. But it was of no use: for I saw the time coming when I would again be without prospects. I had not worked at my trade since leaving Bristol, six years before, and had no intention of doing so again. The fever of restlessness that had governed me in the past, broke out afresh, and after two months of this idle life, I suddenly made a pretence of being filled with a desire for business, saying it was my intention to open a bookshop in London, and as soon as possible, which I have often had thoughts of doing. With this end in view, I drew the remainder of my money, which in two months had dwindled by a half, divided a few pounds among the family, and took train for London. 'Yes,' I repeated to myself, several times on this journey. 'I will open a bookshop and settle down to a quiet life of study, for which there will be ample time during the intervals of business.' In London I saw a number of vacant shops that would have answered the purpose, but unfortunately, I had not the least notion of how or where to obtain books, the greater part of which were to be second-hand. If when on this quest, I could have bought a bookshop ready fitted and filled, no doubt I would have closed with the offer at once, and settled quietly down. Not seeing any way out of

141

this difficulty, I continued my rambles through the city, day after day, invariably visiting the theatre at night. This happened for over a week, and the money was still going out and none coming in, and poverty never appeared worse to me than at that time.

One afternoon, when passing through Trafalgar Square, I bought an early edition of an evening paper, and the first paragraph that met my eye had this very attractive heading —'A Land of Gold'. It was a description of the Klondyke, and a glowing account of the many good fortunes that daily fell to the lot of hardy adventurers. It would cost me sixty pounds, or more, to travel to that remote part of the world, and forty-four pounds were all I now possessed. This thought did not for long discourage me from making the attempt. I knew that I could beat my way across the Canadian continent, without using a cent for travelling, and I could save these few pounds for food, and cases in which payment would be absolutely necessary, when forced to travel on foot, at the other end of Canada.

That night I exchanged thirty pounds for their equivalent in paper dollars, placing the latter in a belt which I wore next to my skin, determined that this money should not see the light until my journey was nearly done.

It was now the month of March, and the navigation of the St. Lawrence had not yet opened, so that I would be compelled to beat my way from Halifax, or St. John's, to Montreal, which would not be necessary later in the Spring, when the latter port would be the destination of all emigrant ships. I was very happy at this time, with these prospects in view, which were really too bright to decoy any man who had an average amount of common sense. My conception of that wonderful land, for all my travels, was childish in the extreme. I thought the rocks were of solid gold, which so dazzled the sun that he could not concentrate his glance on any particular part, and that his eye went swimming all day in a haze. I pictured men in possession of caves sitting helpless in the midst of accumulated nuggets, puzzled as to how to convey all this wealth to the marts of civilisation. What I wanted with all these riches I cannot say, for it was never a desire of mine to possess jewellery, fine raiment, yachts, castles or horses: all I desired was a small house of my own, and leisure for study. In fact I made up my mind not to waste time in hoarding more wealth than would be necessary to these small comforts, but to return home satisfied with a sum not exceeding two thousand pounds, the interest from which would, I thought, be ample for any student who remained true to his aims, and was sincere in his love for literature.

In this month of March, the first day in the second week, I left Euston Station at midnight, and arrived cold and shaking in Liverpool, early the next morning. On making enquiries, I learnt that a ship was leaving for St. John's on the following Wednesday, from which place emigrants must needs go by train to Quebec or Montreal, owing to the ice-bound condition of the river. I decided on making St. John's my destination, from which port I would beat my way towards the west, going easy at first, and faster as the spring of the year advanced.

The accommodation for steerage passengers on this ship was abominable, and their comfort seemed to be not in the least considered. This was owing to the small number of English speaking people that were travelling as steerage

143

passengers, and the disgusting, filthy habits of the great majority, who were a low class of Jews and peasantry from the interior of Russia. None of the ship's crews could be expected to treat these people as one of themselves, seeing them sit to eat in the filth of their skin and fur clothes, without the least thought of washing; and again, hiding food in their bed clothes, making the cabin too foul to sleep in. After seeing the first meal fought for, and scrambled for on the steerage floor, where it had fallen, we Englishmen, five in number, took possession of a small table to ourselves, only allowing one other, a Frenchman, to sit with us. This did not succeed without some protest. On the second day out, when we went below for our mid-day meal, we found the table to be already occupied by these people, who maintained our seats, looking defiantly at us to show that they had taken no accidental possession of the same. It was owing to these defiant looks that we determined to repossess this table. 'Stick close together,' said a young Englishman, who was a blacksmith, with the accredited brawny arms. Saying which he caught one of the usurpers in his arms, and, with great force, threw him in the midst of his people, knocking several of them down. There was great commotion at this. Two hundred of these haters of soap and water began to jabber and wildly gesticulate, and no doubt every foul word in that unknown tongue was used against us. Instead of seating ourselves at once at the table, which was now unoccupied, we stood in our small body waiting with a quiet determination which did not seem at all to their relish. This attitude conquered them; and, as none of us were quarrelsome, and did not again in any way interfere with them, either on deck or below, the trip was ended without any further trouble.

So many of these aliens were landing in Canada at this time, that when I approached the Custom House officers, one of them, judging by my features and complexion, which were not much unlike those of a native of the south, addressed me in an unknown tongue. I looked at him in surprise, which made him repeat his question, probably in another tongue, equally unknown. Being rather incensed at this, and flushing indignantly at this tone to a dog, I lost no time in answering him according to Billingsgate. 'Ho, ho!' he laughed, 'so you are a blooming cockney, and so am I. Why didn't you say so at once!'

The blacksmith had booked through to Quebec, and would take train to that place before morning. Three other Englishmen had booked through to Winnipeg, and would travel with him by the same train. The other Englishman, a carpenter by trade, had relatives in Montreal, and, having only a couple of dollars in his possession, was willing to take instructions from me how to get there. I promised to get this man to Montreal in three or four days, providing he did not at any time question my actions. He kept his promise, and I kept mine, for on the fourth day after landing, I wished him good-bye outside his sister's house, which he had had some difficulty in finding. I was now alone, and seeking a companion for my journey west.

Now, once upon a time, there lived a man known by the name of Joe Beef, who kept a saloon in Montreal, supplying his customers with a good free lunch all day, and a hot beef stew being the mid-day dish. There was not a tramp throughout the length and breadth of the North American Continent, who had not heard of this and a goodly number had at one time or another patronised his establishment.

Often had I heard of this famous hostelry for the poor and needy, and the flavour of its stew discussed by old travellers in the far states of the South. When I thought of this, I knew that a companion for any part of America could most certainly he found on this man's premises, and I would there hear much valuable information as to the road I was about to travel. So I went strolling along quietly, intending to wait until I met some needy looking individual before I made enquiries. Now, whenever Joe Beef's name had been mentioned it had invariably led to the mention of French Marie, and the name of the latter as invariably introduced the name of Joe Beef, for these two establishments seemed to be patronised by the same class. These names were well-known to me, for, as I have said, their fame was abroad throughout America.

I was strolling along with these thoughts, when I met the man of my desire, leaning lazily against a post. Not wishing to accost him outright, and yet eager for his conversation, I stood beside him lighting my pipe, striking several matches for this purpose and failing owing to the wind blowing in small gusts. Seeing my dilemma, the man quickly produced matches of his own, and striking one, held it lighted between the palms of his hands, leaving just enough space for the bowl of my pipe to enter. For this I thanked him, and secondly, invited him to a drink, asking him where we should go, being in hopes he would mention Joe Beef. 'Well' he answered, pointing to the opposite corner, 'the nearest place is French Marie's.' We entered that place and, in the course of conversation, I told him how I had beat my way from state to state, but that this was my first experience in Canada. 'The United States,' said this man sagely, 'are nearly played out, and of late years there are far too many travellers there. You will find the Canadian roads better to beat, and the people's hearts easier to impress, for they are not overrun. When did you get here?' Knowing that this man was under the impression that I had just beat my way into Canada from the States, and not willing to undeceive him, I answered quickly 'This morning,' and for a time changed the conversation into a praise of the beer. 'Where are you going to sleep?' he asked. 'Meet me here in half an hour, after I have begged the price of my bed, and a drink or two—and we will both go to Joe Beef's, where I have been for this last week.' Not wishing to lose sight of this man, I told him that my pocket could maintain the two of us until the next day. 'All right,' said he, appearing much relieved, 'we will go at once and settle for our beds, and come out for an hour or so this evening.' Leaving French Marie's we walked beside the river for some distance, when my companion halted before a building, which I knew must be Joe Beef's, having just seen two seedy looking travellers entering. We followed, and to my surprise, I saw it was a rather clean looking restaurant with several long tables, with seats and a long bar on which the food was served. But what surprised me most was to see a number of Salvation Army men and officers in charge of this place. Without saying a word to my companion, I took a seat at one of the tables, to order a beef stew, asking him what he would have, and, for his sake, the order was doubled. 'When Joe Beef kept this place,' whispered my companion, 'he was a true friend to travellers, but you don't get much out of these people except you pay for it!' Although I winked at him, as though the same thoughts were mine, I noticed that the meals were well worth what was charged for them, and, in after days, I often compared this place favourably with similar institutions in London, that were under the same management, and where men did not get the worth of their money.

CHAPTER XIX

A VOICE IN THE DARK

At this place I remained several weeks, watching the smiling Spring, which had already taken possession of the air and made the skies blue—unloosing the icy fingers of Winter, which still held the earth down under a thick cover of snow. What a glorious time of the year is this! With the warm sun travelling through serene skies, the air clear and fresh above you, which instils new blood in the body, making one defiantly tramp the earth, kicking the snows aside in the scorn of action. The cheeks glow with health, the lips smile, and there is no careworn face seen, save they come out of the house of sickness or death. And that lean spectre, called Hunger, has never been known to appear in these parts. If it was for one moment supposed that such a spectre possessed a house in this country, kind hearts would at once storm the place with such an abundance of good things that the spectre's victim would need to exert great care and power of will, if he would not succumb to an overloaded stomach. This spectre is often seen in the overcrowded cities of Europe, and one of its favourite haunts is the Thames Embankment, in front of the fine hotels where ambassadors and millionaires dine sumptuously. Where they sit or stand at their windows watching the many lights of the city, and to see the moon dipping her silver pitcher in the dark river, and they swear, by Jove! it is worth seeing. But they cannot see this spectre of Hunger, moving slowly, and sometimes painfully, from shadow to shadow, shivering and anxious for the sun, for they have no other fire to sit before, to make their dreams of the past pleasant.

I remained three weeks in this inexpensive hotel, and decided to travel on the following Monday, although the snow was still deep in Montreal, and would be yet deeper in the country. I had a small room for sleeping purposes, at a cost of fifteen cents per night. There were several others of the same kind, each divided one from the other by a thin wooden partition, which was high enough for privacy, but did not prevent curious lodgers from standing tip toe on their beds, and peering into another's room. Going to bed early on Sunday night, previous to continuing my journey on the following day, I was somewhat startled on entering my room, to hear a gentle rap on the partition which divided my room from the next. 'Hallo!' I cried, 'what do you want?' The man's wants, it seemed, were private, for he seemed frightened into silence at this loud tone of demand, which would most certainly draw the attention of others. At last he cleared his throat by a forced fit of coughing, and then whispered, in a low distinct voice—'I want a match, if you can oblige me with one.' Of course, smoking was not allowed in the bedrooms, but in this respect we were nearly all breakers of the law. Taking a few matches from my pocket, I threw them over the partition, and heard him feeling in the semi-darkness, after hearing the sound of them falling. Then he gently struck one, and, by its light, gathered in the others. In a moment or two he addressed me in his natural voice, and, to my surprise, it sounded familiar, and filled me with curiosity to see this man's face. I encouraged him to talk—which he seemed determined to do—thinking a word might reveal him to me, and the circumstances under which we had met.

His voice in the dark puzzled me, and I could not for my life locate it. A hundred scenes passed through my memory, some of them containing a number of characters. In my fancy I made them all speak to me, before dismissing them again to the dim regions from which they had been summoned, but not one of their voices corresponded with this voice heard in the dark. Above this voice I placed thin and thick moustaches, black, grey, brown, red, and white; under this voice I put heavy and light beards of various hues, and still, out of all my material, failed to make a familiar face. Still sending Memory forth in quest of the owner of this voice, and she, poor thing! bringing forward smiling men and stern men, thin men and fat men, short men and tall men, tame men and wild men, hairy men and bald men, dark men and fair men—until she become so confused as to bring back the same people the second time; still sending her forth on this vain quest, I fell asleep.

It was a dreamless sleep; no sound broke its stillness, and no face looked into its depths; and, when I awoke the next morning, this voice seemed to be already in possession of my thoughts. I lay awake for about ten minutes, and was just on the point of rising, thinking the man had left his chamber, when I heard a stir coming from that direction. He was now dressing. Following his example, but with more haste, so as to be the first ready, I waited the unbolting of his door, so that I might meet this man face to face. I unbolted my own door, and opened it when I was but half dressed, but there was no necessity for doing this, for my arms were in the sleeves of my coat when his bolt was slipped back and we simultaneously appeared, at the same time wishing each other good morning. I recognised this man without difficulty, but apparently had the advantage of him. To make no mistake, I looked at his right hand, and saw the two fingers missing, knowing him for a certainty to be Three Fingered Jack, who had been a cattleman from Montreal, whom I had met in Glasgow when I had gone there from Baltimore, three years previous to this. On that occasion I had been in this man's company for only half an hour, and since that time had heard thousands of voices, but was still positive that I had heard this voice before.

We stood side by side washing, and preparing for breakfast, and, although I remained a stranger to him, as far as former acquaintance was concerned, I mentioned to him in confidence that I was going west that very morning, after breakfast. 'So was I,' he said, 'as far as Winnipeg, but thought to wait until some of this snow cleared. Anyhow, as a day or two makes little difference, we will, if you are agreeable, start together this morning. I know the country well,' he continued, 'between Montreal and Winnipeg, having travelled it a number of times, and, I promise you, nothing shall be wanting on the way.'

This man had lost his two fingers at work in the cotton mills, some ten years before, and ever since then had been living in idleness, with the exception of two or three trips he had made as a cattleman. Certainly he lived well on the kindness of these people, as any able bodied man might do in this country, without being in any way afflicted. Though he was going to Winnipeg, he was in no hurry, had no object in view, and had not the least idea of where that town would lead him, and he soon tired of one place.

Three Fingered Jack was a slow traveller for, as he with some emotion said—'It broke his heart to hurry and pass through good towns whose inhabitants were all the happier for being called on by needy men.' This slow travelling suited me for the time being, for we were having another fall of snow, and I half regretted having left Montreal, although, day after day I was certainly getting a little nearer to the gold of Klondyke. But I determined to shake off this slow companion on the first approach of fine weather.

We loafed all day in the different railway stations, in each of which was kept a warm comfortable room for the convenience of passengers. Although we were passengers of another sort, and stole rides on the trains without a fraction of payment to the company, we boldly made ourselves at home in these places, being mistaken for respectable travellers, who were enjoying the comforts for which we paid. Sometimes a station master would look hard on us, suspecting us for what we were, but he was very diffident about risking a question, however much he was displeased at seeing us in comfortable possession of the seats nearest to the stoves. Towards evening we made application for lodgings at the local jail, at which place we would be accommodated until the following morning. I was now without money, with the exception of that which was concealed and reserved for the most hazardous part of the journey, which would be its western end. Now, in all these jails we were searched and examined before being admitted for a night's shelter, but often in a very indifferent manner. One night we arrived at a small town where a double hanging was to take place in the yard of the jail early the next morning. A woman, it seems, had called on her lover to assist in the murder of her husband, which had been brutally done with an axe, for which crime both had been pronounced guilty and condemned to die. Thousands of people had flocked in from the neighbouring country, which in this province of Ontario was thickly settled, and a large number of plain clothes detectives had been despatched from the cities, there being supposed some attempt might be made at rescue, owing to one of the condemned being a woman. We arrived at this town early in the afternoon, and were surprised at the unusual bustle and the many groups of people assembled in the main thoroughfares. Thinking the town contained, or expected, some attraction in the way of a circus or menagerie, we expressed little curiosity, but returned at once to the railway station, intending to possess its most comfortable seats against all corners, until the approach of darkness, when we would then make application at the jail for our night's accommodation. When this time came, we marched straight to the jail, and boldly hammered its door for admittance. It was at once answered by a police officer, to whom we explained our wants, and he, without much ado, invited us indoors. Expecting the usual questions, and being prepared with the usual answers—expecting the usual indifferent search, and having pipe, tobacco and matches artfully concealed in our stockings—we were somewhat taken by surprise to find a large number of officers, who all seemed to show an uncommon interest in our appearance. The Officer, who was examining us previous to making us comfortable for the night, had finished this part of the business to his own satisfaction, when one of these detectives stepped forward, and said—'We cannot admit strangers to the jail on the present occasion, so that you had better make them out an order for the hotel.' This order was then given to us, and we immediately left the jail; and it was then, curious to know the reason for this action, that we soon made ourselves acquainted with the true facts of the case. When we arrived at the hotel, we were informed that every bed had been taken since morning, and that, as it was, a number of men would be compelled to sit all night dozing in their chairs, and it was with this information that we returned to the jail. For the second time we were admitted, and were advised to walk to the next town. This, Three Fingered Jack absolutely refused to do, saying that his feet were too blistered and sore to carry him another hundred yards. All these detectives then got together, and, after a rather lengthy consultation, one of them came forward and, after plying us with a number of questions, proceeded to examine our clothes, and that so thoroughly that I feared for the result. At the beginning of the search, I gave him my razor, a small penknife, my pocket-handkerchief and a comb, but he was not satisfied until his hands were down in my stockings, and bringing up first my pipe, then my tobacco, and lastly the matches. What worried me most was the belt next to my body, which contained my money. I had not much fear of Three Fingered Jack, when confronting each other openly, though he was a tall active man, but had he known of these dollars, I had not dared in his presence to have closed my eyes, believing that he would have battered out my brains with a stone, wooden stake or iron bar, so that he might possess himself of this amount. This detective certainly discovered the belt, and felt it carefully, but the money being in paper, and no coin or hard substance being therein, he apparently was none the wiser for its contents. At last this severe examination was at an end, and we were both led through an iron corridor and placed in a cell, the door of which was carefully locked. I don't believe we slept one moment during that night but what we were overlooked by a pair, or several pairs, of shrewd eyes. They could not believe but that we were other to what we pretended and had come there with designs to thwart the ends of justice. Next morning our things were returned to us, and we were turned adrift at a cold hour that was far earlier than on ordinary occasions.

The snow was still deep and the mornings and evenings cold when, a week after this, we reached Ottawa. This slow travelling was not at all to my liking, and I often persuaded my companion to make more haste towards Winnipeg. This he agreed to do; so the next morning we jumped a freight train, determined to hold it for the whole day. Unfortunately it was simply a local train, and being very slow, having to stop on the way at every insignificant little station, we left it, at a town called Renfrew, intending that night to beat a fast overland passenger train which would convey us four or five hundred miles before daybreak.

With this object we sat in the station's waiting room until evening, and then, some twenty minutes before the train became due, we slipped out unobserved and took possession of an empty car, stationary some distance away, from which place we would see the train coming, and yet be unseen from the station's platform. This train would soon arrive, for passengers were already pacing the platform, the luggage was placed in readiness, and a number of curious people, having nothing else to do, had assembled here to see the coming and going of the train. At last we heard its whistle, and, looking out, we saw the headlight in the distance, drawing nearer and nearer. It steamed into the station without making much noise, for the rails were slippery, there still being much ice and snow on the track. 'Come,' I said to Jack, 'there is no time to lose,' and we quickly jumped out of the empty car.

This fast passenger train carried a blind baggage car, which means that the end nearest to the engine was blind in having no door. Our object was to suddenly appear from a hiding place, darkness being favourable, and leap on the step of this car, and from that place to the platform; this being done when the train was in motion, knowing that the conductor, who was always on the watch for such doings, rarely stopped the train to put men off, even when sure of their presence. If he saw us before the train started, he would certainly take means to prevent us from riding. When we had once taken possession of this car, no man could approach us until we reached the next stopping place, which would probably be fifty miles, or much more. At that place we would dismount, conceal ourselves, and, when it was again in motion, make another leap for our former place. Of course, the engineer and fireman could reach us, but these men were always indifferent, and never interfered, their business being ahead instead of behind the engine.

The train whistled almost before we were ready, and pulled slowly out of the station. I allowed my companion the advantage of being the first to jump, owing to his maimed hand. The train was now going faster and faster, and we were forced to keep pace with it. Making a leap he caught the handle bar and sprang lightly on the step, after which my hand quickly took possession of this bar, and I ran with the train, prepared to follow his example. To my surprise, instead of at once taking his place on the platform, my companion stood thoughtlessly irresolute on the step, leaving me no room to make the attempt. But I still held to the bar, though the train was now going so fast that I found great difficulty in keeping step with it. I shouted to him to clear the step. This he proceeded to do, very deliberately, I thought. Taking a firmer grip on the bar, I jumped, but it was too late, for the train was now going at a rapid rate. My foot came short of the step, and I fell, and, still clinging to the handle bar, was dragged several yards before I relinquished my hold. And there I lay for several minutes, feeling a little shaken, whist the train passed swiftly on into the darkness.

Even then I did not know what had happened, for I attempted to stand, but found that something had happened to prevent me from doing this. Sitting down in an upright position, I then began to examine myself, and now found that the right foot was severed from the ankle. This discovery did not shock me so much as the thoughts which quickly followed. For, as I could feel no pain, I did not know but what my body was in several parts and I was not satisfied until I had examined every portion of it. Seeing a man crossing the track, I shouted to him for assistance. He looked in one direction and another, not seeing me in the darkness, and was going his way when I shouted again. This time he looked full my way, but instead of coming nearer, he made one bound in the air, nearly fell, scrambled to his feet, and was off like the shot from a gun. This man was sought after for several weeks, by people curious to know who he was, but was never found, and no man came forward to say—'I am he.' Having failed to find this man, people at last began to think I was under a ghostly impression. Probably that was the other man's impression, for who ever saw Pity make the same speed as Fear?

Another man, after this, approached, who was a workman on the line, and at the sound of my voice he seemed to understand at once what had occurred. Coming forward quickly, he looked me over, went away, and in a minute or two returned with the assistance of several others to convey me to the station. A number of people were still there; so that when I was placed in the waiting room to bide the arrival of a doctor, I could see no other way of keeping a calm face before such a number of eyes than by taking out my pipe and smoking, an action which, I am told, caused much sensation in the local press.

CHAPTER XX

HOSPITALITY

I bore this accident with an outward fortitude that was far from the true state of my feelings. The doctor, seeing the even development of my body, asked me if I was an athlete. Although I could scarcely claim to be one, I had been able, without any training, and at any time, to jump over a height of five feet; had also been a swimmer, and, when occasion offered, had donned the gloves. Thinking of my present helplessness caused me many a bitter moment, but I managed to impress all comers with a false indifference.

What a kind-hearted race of people are these Canadians! Here was I, an entire stranger among them, and yet every hour people were making enquiries, and interesting themselves on my behalf, bringing and sending books, grapes, bananas, and other delicacies for a sick man. When a second operation was deemed necessary, the leg to be amputated at the knee, the whole town was concerned, and the doctors had to give strict injunctions not to admit such a number of kind-hearted visitors. At this time I was so weak of body, that it was thought hopeless to expect recovery from this second operation. This was soon made apparent to me by the doctor's question, as to whether I had any message to send to my people, hinting that there was a slight possibility of dying under the chloroform. A minister of the gospel was also there, and his sympathetic face certainly made the dying seem probable. Now, I have heard a great deal of dying men having a foresight of things to be, but, I confess, that I was never more calm in all my life than at this moment when death seemed so certain. I did not for one instant believe or expect that these eyes would again open to the light, after I had been in this low vital condition, deadened and darkened for over two hours, whilst my body was being cut and sawn like so much wood or stone. And yet I felt no terror of death. I had been taken in a sleigh from the station to the hospital, over a mile or more of snow; and the one thought that worried me most, when I was supposed to be face to face with death, was whether the town lay north, south, east or west from the hospital, and this, I believe, was the last question I asked. After hearing an answer, I drew in the chloroform in long breaths, thinking to assist the doctors in their work. In spite of this, I have a faint recollection of struggling with all my might against its effects, previous to losing consciousness; but I was greatly surprised on being afterwards told that I had, when in that condition, used more foul language in ten minutes' delirium than had probably been used in twenty four hours by the whole population of Canada. It was explained to me that such language was not unusual in cases of this kind, which consoled me not a little, but I could not help wondering if the matron had been present, and if she had confided in her daughter. The latter was a young girl of sixteen years, or thereabouts, and was so womanly and considerate that her mother could very well leave her in charge of the patients for the whole day, although this had not been necessary during my stay.

For three days after this operation I hovered between life and death, any breath expected to be my last. But in seven or eight days my vitality, which must be considered wonderful, returned in a small way, and I was then considered to be well out of danger. It was at this time that the kindness of these people touched me to the heart. The hospital was situated at the end of a long road, and all people, after they had passed the last house, which was some distance away, were then known to be visitors to the matron or one of her patients. On the verandah outside sat the matron's dog, and, long before people were close at hand, he barked, and so prepared us for their coming. When it was known that I was convalescent, this dog was kept so busy barking that his sharp clear voice became hoarse with the exertion. They came single, they came in twos and threes; old people, young people and children; until it became necessary to give them a more formal reception, limiting each person or couple, as it might be, to a few minutes' conversation. On hearing that I was fond of reading, books were at once brought by their owners, or sent by others; some of which I had not the courage to read nor the heart to return; judging them wrongly perhaps by their titles of this character: *Freddie's Friend*, *Little Billie's Button*, and *Sally's Sacrifice*. With such good attendance within, and so much kindness from without, what wonder that I was now fit to return to England, five weeks after the accident, after having undergone two serious operations! My new friends in that distant land would persuade me to remain, assuring me of a comfortable living, but I decided to return to England as soon as possible, little knowing what my experience would be in the years following.

When the morning came for my departure, the matron, in a motherly way, put her two hands on my shoulders and kissed me, her eyes being full of tears. This, coming from a person whose business was to show no emotion, doing which would make her unfit for her position, made me forget the short laugh and the cold hand shake for which my mind had prepared itself, and I felt my voice gone, and my throat in the clutches of something new to my experience. I left without having the voice to say goodbye. On my way I had to wish goodbye to everyone I met, and when, at last, this ordeal was over, and I was in the train on my way back to Montreal, I felt that I was not yet strong enough to travel; my courage forsook me, and I sat pale and despondent, for I never expected to meet these people again, and they were true friends.

Soon I reached Montreal. Only two months had elapsed, and what a difference now! Two months ago, and it was winter, snow on the earth, and the air was cold; but I was then full limbed, full of vitality and good spirits, for summer like prospects golden and glorious possessed me night and day. It was summer now, the earth was dry and green, and the air warm, but winter was within me; for I felt crushed and staggered on crutches to the danger of myself and the people on my way. I soon got over this unpleasant feeling, roused by the merry-makers aboard ship, the loudest and

163

most persistent, strange to say, being a one legged man, who defied all Neptune's attempts to make him walk unsteady. Seeing this man so merry, I knew that my sensitiveness would soon wear off; and, seeing him so active was a great encouragement. I was soon home again, having been away less than four months; but all the wildness had been taken out of me, and my adventures after this were not of my own seeking, but the result of circumstances.

CHAPTER XXI

LONDON

Sitting at home, thinking of future employment, manual labour being now out of the question, it was then for the first time that I expressed gratitude for my old grandmother's legacy, which on my home coming from the States had been reduced from ten shillings to eight shillings per week. In the past it had been sniffed at and scorned, being called several ill-natured names, such as 'a week's tobacco', 'a day's grub,' or 'an evening's booze without cigars'. I had been very bitter, on the reading of her will, that the property had not come into my hands, to sell or retain, spend or save; but a little common sense now told me that if such had been the case I would, at the present time, have been without either property or income, and had been so less than twelve months after her death. The old lady, no doubt, had noted my wildness, and to save me the temptation to squander my brother's share, who was incapable of taking charge of his own affairs, and whose share I must have ill managed, after the passing of my own she had wisely left this property to remain in the hands of a trustee, which now turned out as lucky for myself as for my brother.

I was now more content with my lot, determined that as my body had failed, my brains should now have the chance they had longed for, when the spirit had been bullied into submission by the body's activity.

It was now the middle of Summer, and daily I sat dreaming, reading, and occasionally writing in a leafy bower in the garden. I could now dispense with crutches, having just received from London an artificial limb, and on this was practising, taking short walks at night, with a success that was gratifying. A far different Klondyke had opened up before my eyes, which corresponded with the dreams of my youth. I pictured myself returning home, not with gold nuggets from the far West, but with literary fame, wrested from no less a place than the mighty London. This secret was never divulged to my people, and, in the after years, this reticence saved them from many a pang of disappointment, and freed me from many an awkward question. Determined to lose no time in the conquest of that city, which I expected would be surrendered to me some time within twelve months, I began, without wasting more time in dreams, to make preparations for this journey. Alas! how many greater men failed in a lifetime at this attempt, although they now stand triumphant in death, holding in their spiritual hands the freedom and keys of the whole world's cities!

With a cotton shirt, a pair of stockings and a handkerchief in a brown paper parcel, and the sum of two pounds in my pocket, after the expense of train fare, I started for London, filled to the brim with the aforesaid designs. My failure in the States, and again in Canada, had made me a little more chary with my confidence, but I was not in the least the less optimistic. My first dreams were, and are, my best. I scorn clothes and jewellery; I would rather take a free country walk, leaving the roads for the less trodden paths of the hills and the lanes, than ride in a yacht or a coach; I would rather see the moon in the ruins than the gaslight of an assembly room; gluttony I despise, and drink is seldom taken except at the invitation of other eyes: then what, in the name of everything we know, would be to me the silver and gold of all Alaska!

I arrived in London early the following morning and at once made my way towards Lambeth. Early that night, being tired with the exertion of an unusually long day, I went seeking for lodgings in Blackfriars Road, and, seeing several signs that claimed to accommodate working men with good clean beds at sixpence per night, entered one of these establishments, paid the amount demanded, and was then ushered into a long kitchen, preferring to sit and smoke for an hour before retiring for the night. Some thirty or forty men were in this kitchen, but the British Workman had either not yet arrived, was out drinking his pint, or had gone early to bed. This was not by any means my first experience in England of lodging houses, for I had been forced to live in similar places on my visits in cattle ships from America; but I certainly did not like the look of this place, where no sign of authority was to be seen, and which seemed to be entirely left to the control of these noisy men. Some of these lodgers had been old soldiers, had just received their pensions—the accumulation of three months. A number of them were bringing in cans of beer, and the kitchen was in an uproar. Many of them were too drunk to perform this task, but were sufficiently sober to sit awake and give money and orders to others, and there was no lack of willing hands to bring them what they required. I left the kitchen at once, determined to seek another place, without troubling the landlady to refund my money. As I left the kitchen, two drunken men began to fight; others interfered, and this fight threatened to become an all round affair. When I had reached the top of the stairs, feeling my way in the dark, I found the landlady standing at the office door. Seeing me, as I was about to pass her, she said, in a voice which was the worse for drink—'So you want to go to bed? Here, Jim, show this gentleman to his bed.' Jim obeyed, a small, pale-faced child, whom I mechanically followed up two flights of stairs, which were better lighted than those leading to the kitchen, which was in the basement of the house. He then showed me into a room where there were a number of beds, and, pointing to one, said—'You are number forty-five,' and then he left the room. Many of the beds already contained sleepers. I sat down on the edge of mine, wondering if there would be any disturbance in the night, whether any of these men would take a fancy to my clothes, or in the dark were likely to rummage their contents. The man in the next bed coughed, and then, turning towards me, said gently—'The beds are good, I admit, but that is about all you can say of this house.' Second voice, not far away: 'You've come to a good house, you have, and yer don't know it.' First voice: 'If I hadn't been drunk last night and got chucked out of Rowton's, I wouldn't, on any account, be here.' A third voice, distant, but loud and angry: 'Give over, will yer: when are you coves going to sleep? I ain't done any labour for three weeks, and now as I've got a chance at four in the mornin', blow me if I ain't robbed of my slumber. Take care I don't set about yer at once, yer blooming lot of bleeders. If I come arter yer body, yer'll know it, and no mistake about it, either.' No more was said after this. I at once made up my mind to try Rowton House on the following day. That they had refused this man a bed owing to his being drunk, and, more than likely, quarrelsome in drink, was a strong recommendation to me after my experience here, where it would be impossible to either read, write or think, or to even partake of my meals in comfort.

The following morning, after having had breakfast at an eating house, I enquired for Rowton House, and when the first person I addressed asked which one I wanted, I answered him—'the nearest one.' This proved to be in Newington Butts and, after receiving instructions, I proceeded accordingly, and was soon standing outside that place, where I was to remain for two years, without in the least impressing London. To my surprise, I found this house to be a fine large block of red buildings, with an imposing front, and a fine entrance, polished and clean; and, facing its many front windows, was an old church tower and clock, set in an old leafy churchyard that had stones for the dead and a number of wooden seats for the living.

On making an application for a bed, I learnt that this could not be granted until nine o'clock in the evening, but was courteously allowed the privilege of remaining indoors until that time. This place surprised me by its accommodation of dining rooms, library, sitting rooms, baths, lavatories, etc., all being kept clean and in thorough good order by a large staff of men, its charge being sixpence per night.

On making my way into the library, and seeing two large cases of books, one containing fiction, and the other being enriched by the poets, historians, essayists, with biography and miscellaneous literature, and hearing how quiet this room was, in spite of the presence of over a hundred men, I at once made up my mind to pay a week's lodgings down, indifferent whether the sleeping accommodation was good or bad. This I did at nine o'clock, after which I sat sometimes reading the paper, and again watching the faces of this mixed assembly. Some of them were of refined appearance, with their silk hats, their frock coats, cuffs and collars, and spoke in voices subdued and gentle. Some of them were of such a prosperous appearance that no doubt I had already passed them in the street, thinking they were either merchants or managers of great concerns; and, more likely than not, the paper boys had followed on their heels, and the cabmen had persistently hailed them.

If I wanted to devote my time to study, living on eight shillings per week, this was apparently a suitable place for my purpose. Being my own barber, doing my own plain cooking, and living abstemiously, renouncing drink and the pleasures of theatres, and other indoor entertainments, and retaining tobacco as my sole luxury—I saw no reason why this could not be done, at the same time making up my mind that it had to be done.

I had been here little more than a week, when I set to work in earnest, and the result of two months' diligence was a tragedy, written in blank verse, and which I called *The Robber*. Never dreaming but what it would at once meet with success, owing to its being full of action—a very difficult thing to marry to verse, but which I thought was successfully accomplished—I was somewhat taken aback to have it returned to me on the third day, with the manager's regret. Now it seemed that the Rowton House had a bad name, owing to the great number of criminals that were continually in the Police Courts giving that address. Some of these lodgers, for that very reason, had their correspondence addressed to various small shops, where they were customers for tobacco, papers, and groceries.

On having this tragedy returned, I, thinking of this, came to the conclusion that no respectable person would be likely to consider or respect any work, or application for the same, that emanated from a house of this name. I spoke to a gentleman with whom I had become acquainted, on this difficult subject, and he agreed with me, saying that such were the true facts of the case. 'But,' said he, after a thoughtful pause, 'as your means are so limited, and the shopkeepers charge one penny for every letter they receive on a customer's behalf, would it not be as well to still have your correspondence addressed here, but in another way, of which you probably have not heard? Give your address as number one Churchyard Row, and, although people will not recognise this house under that name, yet the post office authorities will know it for its proper address.' This I did, without further question, and *The Robber* was despatched on a second journey. Fourteen days after my robber returned to number one Churchyard Row. Bothering my head to account for this, I came to the conclusion that my tragedy had not been read farther than the front page, and that a tragedy that was born and bred in such a place as

Churchyard Row—the address being so appropriate to the nature of the work—was enough to make any man, who had the least sense of humour, condemn it with a laugh. My conceit, at this time, was foolish in the extreme, and yet I was near my thirtieth year.

The next work was a very long poem, in which the beasts of the field, the birds of the air, and even the fishes of the sea, met in a forest glade to impeach man for his cruelty to them, and went on to describe their journey at midnight to the nearest town, and the vengeance they then took on the sleeping inhabitants. My confidence in this work being accepted could not have been altogether whole-hearted, for the following reason: I made two copies of this poem, and posted them simultaneously to different publishers. I felt quite satisfied that one of these would be accepted, but when a whole week had passed on, and I had received no communication from either publisher, I was then horrified to think that they both were giving the poem such a consideration that there was a probability that both of them would accept it, and that both publishers would call on me to make terms, perhaps at the very same hour. This thought so preyed on my mind that I did not feel at all easy until I had one of the copies returned; but it was a great disappointment to receive the second copy on the following day.

Thinking that short poems would stand a better prospect of being accepted, I set to work on a hundred sonnets, writing five, and sometimes six a day, but when this number had been accomplished and submitted, this work met with the same failure.

After this I wrote another tragedy, a comedy, a volume of humorous essays, and hundreds, I believe, of short poems. I was always writing at this time, either beginning or finishing a work, but, strange to say, none of this work was being sent out, but was safely treasured, under the impression that it would some day find its market.

After having had twelve months' practice, in the last months of which no attempt had been made at publication, I decided to make one more effort, this time with a small volume of short poems. This was immediately sent to a well known publisher, who in a few days returned answer, offering to publish at the author's expense, the sum needed being twenty five pounds. This success completely turned my head. With all my heart I believed that there would not be the least difficulty in procuring money for such a grand purpose, and at once wrote to several well known philanthropists, writing six letters. Two of them never murmured, and the other four set their secretaries to snap me up in a few words. Exasperated at this I wrote to several others, all my trouble being to no purpose.

Now, when I first entered this lodging house, I had something like thirty shillings to the good, being ahead of my income, and up to the present had no reason for spending this amount. Could I put this to some use?—My mind had several plans, and one in particular seemed good and feasible. I would write three or four short poems on a page, get them printed, and sell them from door to door. Two thousand of these sheets, sold at threepence per copy, would be twenty five pounds, and, no doubt, I could sell quite a hundred of these copies a day, providing I went from house to house, from street to street, from early morning till late at night. With this object I lost no time in seeing a job printer, and was told that thirty five shillings would be needed to defray expenses. This large amount disappointed me not a little, but I paid a deposit and went back to the house, where I lived and nearly starved in saving four shillings that were short, which was done in two weeks out of the sixteen shillings that were to maintain me in food and lodgings for fourteen days. At last, after great privation and sacrifice, it was done, and I received from the printer two thousand and some odd copies. Early the next morning I was to be seen in the suburbs of London, with my hands and pockets full of these copies, going from door to door. I mentioned to the inhabitants that I had had an offer from a publisher, and that he could not undertake to publish my work under twenty five pounds. All these people did was to stare, none of them seeming to understand, and no one seemed inclined to ask questions. I had, I believe, visited the doors of some thirty houses or more, and had not sold one copy. Most of these people were poor, and some had become sufficiently interested to enquire the price of my copies, seeming inclined and willing to trade with me in a small way, but none of them seemed to be anxious to give threepence for a sheet of paper which they did not understand. At last I chanced upon a house that was much larger than the others, at which place a servant answered the door. I lost no time in relating to her the true facts of the case, and she was standing there silent and puzzled as to my meaning, when her mistress called to her from the top of the stairs—'Mary, who's there?' On which the maiden gave answer in a halting voice—'Some man selling some paper.' At this there was a pause, and then the same voice said, from the direction of the stairs—'Give him this penny, and tell him to go away,' and, almost instantly, that copper coin fell at the bottom of the stairs, and came rolling rapidly towards us, as though aware of its mission. The girl handed me this penny, which I took mechanically, at the same time persisting in her taking a copy to her mistress. That lady, hearing our further conversation, and perhaps, guessing its import, cried again, this time in a warning voice—'Mary, mind you don't take anything from him.' This crushed the last hope, for I began to think that if this lady, who might be a woman of some cultivation and rich, could only see and read what had been done, she might have at once, in her deep interest, merged the whole twenty five pounds, at the same time befriending me for life. Alas! I have been unfortunate all my life in believing that there were a great number of rich people who were only too eager to come forward and help talent in distress.

I was so disgusted at receiving this single penny, and being so dismissed, that I at once put the sheets back in my pockets and returned to the city. How long would it take to get twenty five pounds, at this rate? What am I talking about! Money was lost, not even this single copper was a gain; for this penny-a-day experience had cost me three pennies in tram fare, without mention of a more expensive breakfast than I usually had.

When I got back to the house I started, with the fury of a mad man, to burn the copies, and did not rest until they were all destroyed, taking care not to save one copy that would at any time in the future remind me of my folly.

It was at this time that I came under the influence of Flanagan. That gentleman, seeing me often writing and apparently in deep thought, at once gave me credit for more wisdom than I possessed. He was a very illiterate man, having no knowledge of grammar, punctuation or spelling. The upshot of this acquaintance was that he informed me in confidence that he was the lawful heir to nearly half the county of Mayo, in Ireland; on which estate was a house like the King's palace. In exchange for this confidence I told him that I was the author of a book of verse, which could not be published except the author defrayed expenses. On which Flanagan expressed much sympathy—more especially when I read him aloud a few lines expressing my disapproval of landowners and rich tyrants—and promised sincerely to relieve me of all difficulty providing, of course, that he made good his claims to the estate. Flanagan then proposed that I should put some of his arguments in grammatical form, which he would immediately forward to the proper authorities. This I began to do at once, and some of Flanagan's arguments were so strong that I am surprised at the present day at being a free man. I told one eminent statesman that he should retire and give place to a more honest man, and another that though he was born in Ireland and bore the name of an Irishman, yet he was a traitor, for his heart had ever been in England. Despite these powerful letters, the County Mayo never to my knowledge changed hands, and I was disappointed in my expectations, and Flanagan grieved daily. At that time, I must confess, I thoroughly believed Flanagan, perhaps through being blinded by my own ambitions as an author.

Even at the present time, though I have cut down the estate considerably, from half a county to half an acre, and have taken out quite a number of windows from the estate's residence—after doing this, I still believe that poor Flanagan was robbed of a cottage and garden by an avaricious landlord.

This was at the time of the Boer War and Flanagan's long dark beard and slouched hat gave him the exact appearance of one of those despised people. Therefore we seldom took a walk together but what we were stoned by boys in the street, and even grown up people passed insulting remarks. In fact everywhere we went we were regarded with suspicion. Our clothes not being of the best, drew the attention of attendants at museums and art galleries, and we, being swarthy and alien in appearance, never paused near a palace but what sentry and police watched our every movement. One morning we were passing through Whitehall, what time a regiment of soldiers were being drilled and inspected by a gentleman in a silk hat. Now Flanagan was a man of great courage and never thought it necessary to whisper. Therefore a vein of savage satire broke in Flanagan's heart when he beheld a man in a silk hat inspecting a troop of soldiers. 'See!' he cried, 'there's a sight for the Boers.' A number of bystanders resented this remark, and there were loud murmurs of disapproval on which Flanagan asked the following question: 'Will the best man in the crowd step forward?' But no man seemed inclined to attempt Flanagan's chastisement, without being assisted. Although I did not entirely approve of him on this occasion, still, seeing that the words could not be recalled, I was quite prepared to be carried with him half dead on a stretcher to the nearest hospital; for I liked the man, and he certainly seemed to like me, since he always took his walks alone when I did not accompany him.

CHAPTER XXII

THE ARK

I had now been two years in London, at the same place, and though my literary efforts had not been very successful, I must confess that the conditions had not been the most unfavourable for study; and, no doubt, I had cultivated my mind not a little by the reading of standard works. The conditions of this place could not have been bettered by a person of such small means, and probably I would have continued living here until I met with some success, had I not known of one who would he thankful of a couple of shillings a week, and resolved to make a little sacrifice that would enable me to send them. To do this it was necessary to seek cheaper lodgings where, rent not being so high, this amount could be saved. I had heard something of such a place in Southwark which was under the control of the Salvation Army. A bed was to he had there for two shillings per week, therefore one and sixpence would be saved at the onset, as I was now paying three and sixpence. Following my first impulse, as usual, but with much regret at having to leave a place where I had not by any means been unhappy, I gathered up my few things and left, and that night settled in Southwark Street.

Speaking after six months' experience at the Salvation Army Lodging House, I am very sorry that I have nothing at all to say in its favour. Of course, it was well understood by the lodgers, whatever people on the outside thought, that no charity was dispensed on the premises. Certainly the food was cheap, but such food as was not fit for a human being, I do not know whether the place came under the control of the London County Council, being regarded as a charitable institution, or whether, in case of a surprise visit from its inspectors, beds were removed in the day: what I do know from experience is this, that it was with difficulty that a man could find room between the beds to undress. A row of fifteen or twenty beds would be so close together that they might as well be called one bed. Men were breathing and coughing in each other's faces and the stench of such a number of men in one room was abominable. I was fortunate in having, a bed next to the wall, to which I could turn my face and escape the breath of the man in the next bed.

The officers in charge were, according to my first opinion, hypocrites; which seemed to be verified some time after from Head Quarters, for both the Captain and his Lieutenant were dismissed from the Army. However, the Captain was well liked by the lodgers, and I have often seen him assist them out of his own private purse.

As for the Lieutenant, he was very gentle and fervent in prayer, more so than any man I have ever heard, but in conversation he had not a civil word for any one, except, of course, his superior officer. He sometimes made his deceit so apparent that I have been forced to laugh out. When the Captain arrived at night, or in the morning—he was a married man and did not live on the premises—he would stand with his back to the restaurant bar, looking down the long room at the faces of his many lodgers. It was at such a time that when I have looked up from my meal, I have been surprised, and not a little startled, to see this Lieutenant's pale thin face looking down through a glass window, eager to see what his superior officer was doing. So engrossed would he be that he would entirely forget that he exposed his deceit to the eyes of a number of men who had their faces turned towards him. Sometimes he would creep tiptoe to the kitchen door and peep in for an instant, and then creep back to the office. I have often wondered that the Captain never turned and surprised him in these doings, for there was not a lodger in the house that had not one time or another seen him perform them.

On Sunday afternoons, those two, the Captain and his Lieutenant, would conduct a meeting; the latter commencing it with a short prayer, after which the former would preach a sermon which was, I must confess, often interesting, and invariably eloquent. In all my life I have never heard a more pathetic address and prayer than that which was delivered by this Captain, on one of these Sunday afternoons. It so chanced that in this place there lived a poor half demented lodger, who was known by the name of Horace, whose profession was that of a flower seller. Every night this man would dress and garland himself with his unsold flowers, and return home drunk to the Ark. Now, this man suddenly disappeared, and, at the same time, a man committed suicide from London Bridge, which was well known to be the haunt of the man Horace. Whereat the following Sunday our Captain preached a funeral oration, giving for our interest the few facts he had gleaned from the past life of the deceased, who, the captain affirmed, had received a good education and had come of a respectable family. The Captain wept copiously, being overcome by his feelings, and the Lieutenant approved and encouraged him by an unusual number of sighs and broken sobs.The meeting then ended with an earnest prayer for the soul of the drowned Horace. About six days after this meeting had taken place, there came to the Ark a man drivelling and laughing idiotically, with wreaths and posies all over his person—no other than the lamented Horace. The Captain came out of his office, followed by his Lieutenant. The Captain looked at Horace with a melancholy annoyance; the Lieutenant looked first at his superior officer and, after receiving his expression into his own face, turned it slowly on Horace. The Captain then turned slowly on his heels, at the same time shaking his head, and, without saying a word, returned to the office, while his subordinate followed him in every particular. Never, after this, did this Captain treat Horace as a living man, and all chaff and familiar conversation was at an end between them. How the Captain came to the belief that the drowned suicide was Horace, the flower seller, was very strange, for this man was known to mysteriously disappear several times in the year, he, invariably, like the drowned man he was supposed to be, coming to the surface on the seventh day, seven days being the extreme penalty of his simple and eccentric behaviour.

There was no lack of strictness at this place; whether a man was ill or not, whether it rained, snowed or hailed, every lodger was compelled to quit the premises at ten o'clock in the morning, after which it would remain closed for cleaning purposes until one o'clock. And yet there was not a man in the house could keep himself clean. It was not thought necessary to close other establishments of this kind, that were not connected with the name of religion, which were kept cleaner without making the lodgers suffer any inconvenience. Why things should be carried on in this high handed fashion I cannot understand, seeing that there was not the least charity doled out. Whatever good the Salvation Army did for the homeless and penniless in their shelters, they certainly did not cater well for these poor, but independent, fellows whose wages ranged from a shilling to eighteenpence a day—being paper-men, sandwichmen, toy-sellers, etc., who received nothing but what they paid for.

I had been at this place something like four months, when I determined to make another attempt at publication. My plans at this time seemed to be very feasible, for I gave them a full half year for execution. I applied at the local police station for a pedlar's certificate, intending to stock myself with laces, pins, needles and buttons with which I would hawk the country from one end to the other. At the end of this time I would be some ten pounds in pocket, the result of not drawing my income, and would, no doubt, save between nine and ten shillings a week as a hawker. Being very impulsive, I proposed starting on this interesting business at once, but one idea—which could not for long be overlooked—brought me to a halt: my artificial leg would certainly not stand the strain of this enforced march from town to town on the country roads, that were so often rough and uneven. For even now it was creaking, and threatened at every step to break down. On mentioning these difficulties to a fellow lodger, he at once advised me to go to the Surgical Aid Society for a wooden leg, of the common peg sort; which, he was pleased to mention, would not only be more useful for such a knockabout life, but would not deceive people as to my true condition. This society was visited by me on the following day; at which place I was informed that fifteen subscription letters would be required for my purpose, and after paying sixpence for a subscription book, in which were the names and addresses of several thousand subscribers, I lost no time in buying stamps and stationery. Eighteen letters were without loss of time written and posted to their destination. These eighteen succeeded in bringing in two subscription letters, several letters of regret from people who had already given theirs away; several of my letters were returned marked 'not at home,' and a number of them elicited no response. Twelve more letters were quickly despatched, with the result of one subscription letter. To be able to do this I was forced to use the small weekly allowance that I had been making. In six weeks I had written nearly a hundred letters and was still several letters short of my allotted number. I again consulted my fellow lodger, who had at first referred me to the Surgical Aid Society, and his explanation was, undoubtedly reasonable and true. He explained that not only was the time of the year unfavourable, it being summer, and most of the subscribers were away from home on their holidays—but, unfortunately, the South African war was still in progress, and numbers of soldiers were daily returning from the front in need of artificial assistance, one way or another. Although I ruminated with some bitterness on the idea that I would almost pay in postage the value of that which I required, before it became mine, I still had enough common sense to see that no one was actually to blame. Several letters were received, offering to assist me on certain conditions. One lady would assist on a clergyman's recommendation, and another subscriber would have no other than a Roman priest. I offered to get these ladies a Salvation Army Officer's recommendation, which, apparently, would not do, for our correspondence came to an end. One lady, who did not recognise the house of Salvation under the address of 96 Southwark Street, regretted that she had already given her letters away, but advised me to go to the Salvation Army, who would most certainly attend to my wants. I explained to this person that I was already at one of their places, and had been here over five months; and that I had not been seen drunk in the place, and that my behaviour had not, at any time, raised objections, also that I was on the most friendly terms with the officer in charge; but that I could live here for many years to come, and no man would enquire my wants or offer to assist me.

One afternoon, when I returned to the Ark, after having been out all day, I was surprised to hear from a lodger that two gentlemen had been there that afternoon to see me. After which another lodger came forward with the same information, and still another, until I was filled with curiosity to know who these gentlemen could be. 'What did they look like?' I asked one. 'Like solicitors,' he answered. 'What kind of looking men were they?' I asked of another. 'Very much like lawyers,' he answered at once. 'Don't forget to remember yer old pals,' chimed in another, 'when yer come into the property.' First I examined my mother's side of the family, and then my father's, but could find no relative, near or distant, at home or abroad, whose death would be likely to befriend me. At last I went to the office, but found this place closed, the Lieutenant being out walking, and the Captain not yet having arrived. Never in my life did I have such an excitable half hour as this. When I saw the Captain coming forward, smiling, with an envelope in his hand, I went to meet him, and, taking the letter in my own hand, began to examine its outside. 'Of course,' said the Captain, 'you know who it is from?' 'Not the least idea,' I said, 'how should I?' and proceeded to open it. It was a short note, with a request that I should call on the Charity Organisation, between the hours of ten and eleven a.m. on the day following. The Captain went back to his office, and I sat down, thinking of what this would amount to. Again I decided to consult the Canadian, the lodger who had first mentioned to me the Surgical Aid Society. 'As to that,' said this man, 'it's a wonder to me that you have not run foul of these people before now. My friend, who sells papers in the city, was continually meddled and interfered with by these people, but they gave him no assistance, although they seemed curious to know all about him.' This information surprised me not a little, but I came to the conclusion that the Canadian's friend was addicted to drink and other bad habits, and was an undeserving case.

The next morning I arose, lighthearted in anticipation of hearing something to my good, and was leaving the house when I saw the Captain standing at the front door. Feeling some misgiving, I turned to this gentleman and asked him point blank—what was his opinion of the Charity Organisation. 'Well,' he replied slowly, 'to give you my candid opinion—although I may be mistaken—the object of the Charity Organisation is not so much to give alms, as to prevent alms being wasted.' How I remembered these words in the light of my after experience with these people!

At ten o'clock punctually, I was at their office in the Borough Road, and was at once shown into a side room, where I sat waiting patiently, for an hour. At last a gentleman in black came forward, saying, very politely—'Mr. Davies, will you please come this way.' I followed him up two or three flights of stairs and we entered a quiet room on the top floor. Seating himself at a table, and taking pencil and paper, he then asked me to be seated and began. 'Mr. Davies,' he said, 'I have received a letter from a lady who has become interested in your case, and wishes to better your conditions. So as to answer this lady, it is necessary to know something of yourself, for which reason I propose asking you a few questions, which, of course, you need not answer except you think proper.' This he proceeded to do, at the same time making notes of my answers. After answering a dozen or more questions truthfully, dealing with particulars of my family, and my past life—he brought the case up to that time. 'Surely,' he said, 'you do not live on eight shillings a week. I should have thought that to be impossible.' 'As for that,' I answered, 'not only has that sum been sufficient for myself, but I have been able to make another an allowance of two shillings a week, but have not been able to do so since I applied to the Surgical Aid Society.' 'Now tell me what is the matter with that leg?' asked this gentleman. 'I should have thought that it would last for another two years at least. Excuse me, did you get that through the Society?' 'No,' I said, 'it cost me twelve pounds, ten shillings, when I could ill afford the money, but, unfortunately, I knew nothing then of the Surgical Aid Society.' 'The Society, no doubt, does a large amount of good,' continued this gentleman, 'but I don't altogether agree with their methods. You have written quite a number of letters?' he asked; 'and I don't suppose any of the subscribers helped you with the postage, sending you a trifle to defray expenses?' At this point he made a long pause, and I began to tell him that all the help I had received was from a gentleman who, having no letters left to assist me with, had very considerately sent twelve stamps to help my correspondence. The Charity Organisation showed much interest at this point of the conversation, and said that he thought quite a number of subscribers would have done the same. 'As I have already said,' he continued, 'I don't altogether agree in the methods of the Surgical Aid Society; their cases are maintained too long without results, and allows too good an opportunity for writing begging letters.' Not even now could I see the drift of this man's questions— that he suspected me of being an impostor, of writing begging letters. Yes, I, who was bitter at having to bear all this expense, and was grieved at having to withhold two shillings a week from one who was very poor, so that I might be enabled to do so. 'How many letters do you now need?' he asked. 'Two,' I answered, 'but I don't intend to be at any further expense in postage; I will take in what letters I have already received, and explain to the Surgical Aid Society the difficulty I have had in trying to obtain the requisite number.' This ended our interview, and I went away satisfied that the

Charity Organisation would come to my rescue in the near future. But I did not again hear from them for over two years, which will be explained in another chapter. How they answered the kind lady who had become interested in me, I cannot say, but it could not have been other than to my discredit.

The day following this interview, three letters were at the office, all three coming by the first post. One of them contained a subscription letter, so that I now only lacked one of the required number. One of the other letters came from the Surgical Aid Society, saying that a subscriber had forwarded to them a letter to be entered to my account, and that if I would call at their office with the letters I then had, the Society would make up the number deficient. The required number was now made up, without having need to draw on the Society. I now took these letters to their office, and in a day or two received the article which had caused me so much bother in writing letter after letter, and such an expense in postage. By a sad irony, the worry and expense was by no means at an end, as I had expected. People were now returning from the continent, and other places where they had spent their summer holidays. Letters came to me daily from people returning home. Some of my own letters, which had been posted three, four, five and six weeks before, were now being considered. Several subscription letters came to hand—too late for use. Others wrote asking if I was still in need of assistance. I was now at as great an expense as ever, returning these subscription letters with thanks and writing to others to tell them that I had now succeeded in obtaining the required number. Letters were still coming when I left the Ark for the country; and, it was told me afterwards, that a goodly number had come, been kept for a number of days, and returned during my absence.

I was more determined than ever to tramp the country until I was worth thirty pounds, for an offer had again been made by a publisher, during my stay at the Ark, and this offer was much the same as the other. Seeing that there was no other way of getting this amount than by hawking the country, I determined to set out as soon as possible. So, when my business with the Surgical Aid Society was at an end, I spent three or four shillings on laces, needles, pins, buttons, etc., and started with a light heart and not too heavy a load. The Canadian, who had had some experience in this kind of life, prophesied good results from it, adding that a man situated the same way as I was, need carry no other stock in trade than that which I had received from the Surgical Aid Society, and that success was assured, on that very account.

CHAPTER XXIII

GRIDLING

It was a beautiful morning in September when I left the Ark with every prospect of fulfilling this mission. As I advanced towards the country, mile after mile, the sounds of commerce dying low, and the human race becoming more rare, I lost for the time being my vision of the future, being filled with the peace of present objects. I noted with joy the first green field after the park, the first bird that differed from the sparrow, the first stile in the hedge after the carved gate, and the first footpath across the wild common that was neither of gravel nor ash. I had something like nine shillings in my pocket, and I felt that business was out of the question as long as any of this remained. Reaching St. Albans on the first night, I walked through that town, and, making a pillow of my pack, lay down on the wild common. It seemed as though extra bodies of sun had been drafted that night into the heavens to guard and honour the coming of age of a beautiful moon. And this fine scene kept me awake for two or three hours, in spite of tired limbs. This seemed to me a glorious life, as long as summer lasted and one had money to buy food in the towns and villages through which he passed. For three or four days I walked and idled, standing on culverts and watching the water burst from darkness into light; listening to the birds; or looking at a distant spire that was high enough, and no more, to show that a quiet town was lying there under a thousand trees.

I reached Northampton, and it was in this town that I intended to start business on the following day, though I still had a few shillings left, having slept in the open air since leaving London. With this object I proceeded to examine my pack, with the intention of filling my pockets with the different wares, to draw them forth one or two at a time, as they would be needed. So, that night, previous to the great business that was to be transacted on the following day, I sought a quiet corner in the lodging house, and began to unroll my paper parcel. As I proceeded to do this, it seemed to me that the inner part of the parcel was damp, and then I remembered the two or three heavy showers that we had on the second day of my travels. On a further examination I discovered, to my horror, that the goods were entirely unfit for sale; that the parcel had been so bent and misshapen one way and the other, during my night's repose, that the needles had cut through their rotten packets, and were stuck in the pin papers, and that a great number of pins had concealed their whole bodies in the needle packets, showing plainly the guilty tops of their heads. The laces were twisted and turned, and their tags were already rusted. This was a great blow to me, as there seemed nothing else to do but send home for the few shillings that had now become due. But on second thoughts I made up my mind to travel without stock of any kind, not doubting but what I would rise to the emergency after the last penny had been expended, and I was under the force of necessity. Thinking Northampton too large a town in which to starve, I determined to remain here until my funds were exhausted, when desperation would urge me to action. With this idea I took life very easily for a couple more days, even inviting poverty by being unusually extravagant, going to the extreme of buying milk for my tea. But when I became reduced to the last sixpence, I decided to make all speed to Birmingham, as the resources of that city, it being so much larger, would be a better place to serve my wants.

Starting on this journey, without any more delay, I was soon going into the town of Rugby, tired, penniless, and hungry. What was I to do? Something had to be done, and that at once. I had to face the horrible truth that I was now on the verge of starvation. Whilst busy with these unpleasant thoughts, I heard a voice shout to me from the roadside, and, looking in that direction, saw a man sitting in the grass, eating from a paper parcel, which was half spread before him. On going over to see what this man wanted, I found an apparently tall man and large in proportion, who was dressed in seedy looking clothes, which were torn and patched in a good many places. In fact, something seemed to have been gnawing night after night at the bottom of his trousers taking advantage of him in his sleep, for these hung in tatters and rags just below the calves of his leg. The man had a freckled face, which was almost lost in an abundance of red hair, and his head was as thick with the same. What helped to make his appearance strange, and perhaps ridiculous, was a schoolboy's small cap to cover the crown of such a large head. 'Have a mouthful of this,' he said, inviting me to partake of some bread and meat. 'It is dry eating, I must say, but, as we go into Rugby, we can wash it down with a pint or two of beer.' I thanked him for his kindness, and, accepting his invitation, seated myself on the grass. 'What's in your bundle,' he asked, looking askance at a small brown paper parcel which contained a clean shirt, socks and a handkerchief, 'are you selling anything?' I explained to him that I was a licensed hawker, but had not yet been long enough at the business to make a success of it. 'What,' he cried with some surprise, 'a one legged man not to be successful? I get all I want by just opening of my mouth,' although he added with some scorn, 'I know that some people cannot beg unless they have something in their hands to sell. But if you travel with me, all you will have to do is to pick up the coppers.'

After I had finished eating, he proposed to set off immediately; and, as we walked leisurely along, I wondered how it was possible for a big healthy fellow like this to be able to exist in any other manner than by selling. On coming to the first public house he politely invited me to enter, which I did, when he called for two pints of beer. He then became communicative, telling me he was a gridler, and a good one too; which I understood to mean a grinder, although I had not seen tools of any description either in his hands or in his pockets. He paid for two or three pints of beer in quick succession, and, not having had much drink for a considerable time, I began to feel somewhat elated, and began to make a laughing joke of my circumstances. 'Now,' said this man, 'to business; for we must get the price of our beds and a little breakfast for the morning, not to mention the night's supper.

193

All you have to do,' he said again, 'is to pick up the coppers as they come.' Wondering what these words could mean. I followed him, on this pleasant afternoon, up several side streets, until we came to the end of one very long street, which had respectable looking houses on either side of the road. My strange companion walked several yards down this street, and then came to a sudden halt in the middle of the road. 'Now,' said he, for the third or fourth time, 'all you have to do is to pick up the coppers. I ask you to do no more; except,' he added, grinning rather unpleasantly, 'except to see that we are not picked up by the coppers.' His joke appeared simple enough, and I could not fail to understand it, but it was not at all to my relish. The last named coppers were police officers, who would be likely to take hold of us for illegally appropriating the copper coins of the realm. 'Are you going to pick up the coppers?' he asked a little impatiently, seeing me standing irresolute and undecided as to what to do. Scarcely knowing how to answer him, I said that if I saw any coppers he need have no fear but what I would pick them up. 'All right, that's good,' he said, at the same time moving several feet away from me. I stood still watching these mysterious movements, and thinking of the coppers, wondering from what source they would be supplied. He now turned his back, without more ado, and, setting his eyes on the front windows before him, began, to my amazement, to sing a well-known hymn, singing it in the most horrible and lifeless voice I have ever heard. In spite of the drink, which had now taken effect making my head swell with stupidity, I still felt an overwhelming shame at finding myself in this position. I stood irresolute, not knowing whether to wait the result of this, or to leave him at once with short ceremony. But, whilst ruminating in this frame of mind, I heard a window open with a loud creak, saw the shaking of a fair hand, and then heard a copper coin fall on the hard earth within a yard of where I stood. Being penniless I was nothing loth to take possession of this coin, and had scarcely done so, when a front door opened on the other side of the street, and a fat florid old gentleman appeared and beckoned me across to him. Going immediately to this gentleman, I received twopence and, after thanking him, joined my companion in the road. Now, as I belong to a race of people that are ever prone to song, whether it be in a public house or a prayer meeting, it will not surprise many to know that ere long I was making strong attempts to sing bass to this man's miserable treble, and only ceased to do so when it became necessary to stoop and pick up the coppers, which continued to come in at the rate of two to the minute. The effect of my voice on my companion was immediately apparent. His limbs shook, his knees bent and knocked together, and his voice quivered and quavered with a strong emotion. He was now singing another well-known hymn, better known perhaps than the last; and what with his tall form bent double to half its height, and the wringing of his hands in despair—a poor wretch who was apparently broken both in body and spirit—he was, at this particular stage, the most miserable looking mortal I have ever beheld. He was in this old man's broken attitude when, to my surprise, he suddenly straightened his great body, and gazed about one second down the street. After which he quickly turned on his heels, saying, in short peremptory tones—'Quick march,' at the same time suiting the action to the words, in sharp military steps. What the people in their different windows, and on their doors, thought of this change, I cannot say. I looked down the street, and then saw that a police officer had just turned its far corner, and was coming slowly in our direction. My companion waited for me at our end of the street, where I joined him as soon as possible. 'It is getting harder every day for a poor man to get a living,' he said, when I stood beside him. 'Suppose you count the earnings,' he said. 'We work together well.' On doing this, I found twenty pennies to be in my possession, and, at his suggestion, we there and then shared them alike. 'Friend,' he began, 'before we commence again, let me give you a word or two of advice. First of all, you sing in too lusty a voice, as though you were well fed, and in good health. Secondly, you are in too much of a hurry to move on, and would get out of people's hearing before they have time to be affected. Try to sing in a weaker voice: draw out the easy low notes to a greater length, and cut the difficult high notes short, as though you had spasms in the side. Your object is to save your voice as much as possible, indifferent to the demands of music, or the spirit of the song. When we start in another street,' he continued, —but at this admonitory point I cut him short, telling him that I had had enough of—eh—gridling. 'What, enough of chanting?' he cried in amaze. 'Why, my dear fellow, it is the best thing on the road, bar none. All right,' he said, seeing my determination not to make a fresh start, 'we will make our way to the lodging house: it is not far from here.'

We were soon comfortably settled in this place, and when, after having had a good tea, I was sitting smoking, and enjoying a newspaper, I felt more pleased than ashamed of what I had done; for I was going to bed with an easy stomach, and had coppers in my pocket for a good breakfast.

Therefore, when a fellow lodger, a hawker, who was now taking an inventory of his wares, and who had probably seen and heard us singing that day, when following his own calling - when this man enquired of me if the town was good for gridlers, I answered him very pleasantly indeed, that there was nothing to complain of.

After breakfast, the next morning, my companion of the preceding day proposed putting in a good eight hours' work, but I at once cut him short saying that such a business was not in my line. Now, several women were at this place; some of them were married, and some single, and most of them made and sold fancy work of embroidery. After I had spoken so decisively to my companion he had sat near to one of these women at the other end of the kitchen. This woman, who seemed to be the wife of a knife and scissors grinder, had a little girl of about seven years of age. 'Yes' said this woman, in answer to some question my companion had made, 'you can have the kid all day; it's not the first time, by a long way, for Mary Ann to be used by gridlers, and she knows as well as you what's wanted of her.' Not long after this remark my companion and the woman's child left the kitchen together. This I, subsequently, often saw done. Almost any woman, if she called herself a true traveller, would lend her child for this purpose; the woman or child, of course, deriving some part of the profit: so that when a man is seen with one or more children, it is not always to he granted that he is the father of them. These children are rarely subjected to ill usage—except that of enforced tramping—but are more often spoilt by indulgence, especially if they show early signs of that cunning which is needed for their future, and which is the boast of their parents.

What a merry lot of beggars were assembled here; and how busy they all seemed to be, making articles for sale, and washing and mending their clothes! two or three of them sitting shirtless during the process of drying.

It has become a common expression to say 'dirty tramp', or, 'as dirty as a tramp'; but this is not always true, except occasionally in the large cities; although such a term may be applied morally to them all. There is one species of tramp who wanders from workhouse to workhouse; and this man, having every night to conform strictly to the laws of cleanliness, is no less clean, and often cleaner, than a number of people whose houses contain bath rooms which they seldom use. Another species of tramp is proud of being a good beggar, who scorns the workhouse, but who knows well that a clean appearance is essential to his success. For this reason, anyone that enters a common lodging house can at once see what efforts are being made to this end. It seems strange to say, but the dirtiest looking tramp is often the most honest and respectable, for he has not the courage to beg either food or clothes, nor will he enter the doors of a workhouse. I have seen this so often the case that I would much prefer to believe a dirty ragged tramp who might tell me that he had a good home six months previous, than to believe his cleaner namesake, who seems so eager to impart this information unsolicited. It is certainly the man who has had a good home, and has been waited on by other hands, who soon succumbs to a filthy condition, when it becomes necessary to wait on himself by washing and patching his own clothes; and the higher his former position has been the lower he sinks in the social strata.

It is no difficult matter to get company when travelling. The pedlar, whom I have mentioned before, asked me if I was going towards Coventry, and if I intended to do business on the road.

To this question I answered that such might be the use, but I could not say for sure—at the same time knowing that it was very unlikely. 'Come along then,' he said, 'and do business, if you feel inclined; but, I warn you, it is a very poor road for a gridler.' We started at once, and, in the course of our journey I told him everything—from my first experience of gridling and my dislike to it, and how my wares had been spoilt by the rain, which had prevented me, through having no stock, nor money to buy it, from earning my living in a respectable manner as a pedlar. 'Of course,' he said, 'you have a pedlar's certificate?' I answered him in the affirmative, and added that I had not earned one penny with it up to that moment.

As we jogged along talking in this way, we came to a small village, when the pedlar, stopping short asked if I would like to help him to do a little trade. Knowing that something had to be done, as I had but twopence in my in my pocket, I assured him that I would. Hearing this he took two bundles of laces from his pack, leather and mohair, and placed them in my hands, at the same time saying—'You work on one side of the village and I'll attend to the other.' I passed several houses before I had the courage to knock at their doors, but seeing him go calmly from door to door, I nerved myself to follow his example, and was soon doing the same, and, as far as I could see, was meeting with more success. This so encouraged me that I was soon regretting that I had no more homes left on my side of the village. But, instead of waiting patiently until he had done, I took a desperate notion and went back to the houses which I had at first passed. After this we jogged on towards Coventry, which we reached that evening.

We worked Coventry together for four or five days, and the result was nine shillings and some odd pence in my pocket. This pedlar was going to spend a week or two with a brother in Birmingham, whom he had not seen for a number of years. But, before we left Coventry, he persuaded me to stock myself with three shillings' worth of stuff, and, said he, 'never let a day pass you without doing some business, however little; and never allow your stock to get low.' We reached Birmingham, and, after he had shown and recommended a lodging house, he wished me good-bye, with many hopes that we might meet again.

As usual, my first enquiry, after I had settled for my lodgings, was for the public library. This place I found so much to my liking, what with its variety of journals, its number of papers, and so much comfort and accommodation for its visitors—that business was entirely out of the question until the third day, when I woke to the awkward fact that my last three coppers were then being spent on a meal. At this I made up my mind to hawk on the outskirts of Birmingham for a month or more, so that my evenings might be enjoyed in its library. But, apparently, I was not cut out for this kind of business. Hawking required a perseverance which I certainly did not possess. For when a person declined to make a purchase, instead of crying up the cheapness of my wares, I walked away dumbfounded to the next house. Yes, the success or ill success of this buying and selling was all a simple matter of tongue. A big able-bodied fellow, with a persistent tongue, can talk charity out of the people who indifferently pass the silent blind man. Of course this business of hawking with a few cheap laces and a few packets of common pins or needles, was after all only another name for begging, and it was well for us that the people knew it, for they often paid for what they declined to receive. They knew that these things were to be had much cheaper at a store. In exoneration of this fraudulent selling, a man was expected to tell some tale of distress. This I found difficulty in doing, except on being asked direct questions; and the people would often stand after refusing to purchase with their hands in their pockets ready to assist on the first confession of distress. The number of times people have called me back, after I have left their doors, and assisted me, has often proved to me how they had waited to have their first feelings of pity strengthened by some recital of poverty. No doubt there was some sort of living to be made in this way, providing a man talked incessantly and went for hours from house to house, and from street to street; and when he failed in the line of business to plead for the sake of charity. It must have been over two hours and my takings had amounted to ninepence, nearly all profit I admit.

Looking at this paltry amount I now reversed my former opinion as to the resources of a large city, and came to the conclusion that the small country towns and villages were after all more willing, if not better able to support me. Therefore, instead of returning to the city I took the road towards Warwick, intending when I reached that town to use my tongue to some purpose. And how many houses have I visited with this same resolution, but, alas, many of the towns were passed through without anyone hearing the sound of my voice.

CHAPTER XXIV

ON THE DOWNRIGHT

On my way towards Warwick I joined company with a grinder, and we travelled socially together towards that ancient town. When we arrived, we lost no time in seeking a lodging house, which we soon found, but, to my surprise, the landlady, a big raw-boned, slatternly woman said, looking sternly at my companion: 'I will have no grinders in my house.' Of course, I did not know at that time what I have heard subsequently. Of all the men on the road, following various occupations, the grinder is, I believe, the most thoroughly detested. As a rule he is a drunken dissolute fellow, a swearer, and one who, if he picks up a quarrel, which is usually the case, is in no hurry to drop it. The more unpretentious lodgers hate his presence, seeing that he makes himself more at home than the landlord himself. I have often heard travellers tell of a small village in the north of England, which grinders dare not enter, pass through or lodge therein for the night, and it is the regret of many travellers that there are not more villages of its kind distributed throughout the country. It seems that some years ago, a great wind had visited that particular town, and floored the roofs of the houses, and grounded the church steeple, many of the inhabitants being injured, and not a few killed. Now, it happened that the day following this great disaster, two unfortunate grinders, who had arrived in town the night before, and slept at the village inn, appeared in the streets and made a great shout in soliciting orders. Some way or another the inhabitants connected these poor wretches with the great wind, and set upon them, and proceeded to beat them out of the town, coming near to killing them; and, since that day the town has been visited by neither grinders nor great winds. Even in larger towns these people often experience great difficulty in procuring lodgings. This state of affairs was not known to me at this time, or I should certainly not have been anxious for the company of one of these despised people.

We were admitted at the next lodging house, but even here the landlady seemed to have some compunction at so doing; for she followed us to the kitchen and without saying a word, placed her two hands on her broad hips, at the same time looking severely at my grinder, as much as to say —'If you are going to start any of your capers, let it be at once, my hearty grinder, now I am watching you, and we'll soon see who's who.' We sat down quietly, and the landlady, thinking that this attitude had had its desired effect, left the kitchen, not forgetting to throw a last glance at my grinder, who was trying his best to hide his nervousness by puffing hard at his pipe and nearly choking in the attempt.

Some ten or fifteen men were in this room, some of them busy preparing work for the next day. Two were busy making artificial flowers; one was working with copper wire, turning and twisting it into toasting forks, plate holders, and hangers to suspend flower pots. Two others were in the rag and bone trade, for I had seen them when I first entered, overlooking their stuff in the backyard. One man was a pedlar, for there was his pack, towards which he often turned his eyes, in distrust of his company. One was a musician, for there, sticking out of the top pocket of his coat, was a common tin whistle. 'There,' said I to myself, glancing at a man on my right hand—'here is the only respectable working man among them all.' This man had on a clean moleskin pair of trousers, a pilot cloth coat, and on his neck a large clean white muffler. 'Grinder?' asked this man, catching my eye before I could avoid it. 'No,' I answered, 'a pedlar.' 'Oh,' said he. 'I didn't notice you carrying a pack when you came in.' Alas! my little stock could easily be carried in my pockets. 'No,' I answered, 'as a rule I don't carry much stock.' 'I shouldn't think you would,' he said, glancing at my leg, 'a bible ought to be enough for you, and a good living too.' Now it happened when I left London, I had made room in my pockets for two books which, up till that time, I had very little opportunity of reading. One was the bible, and the other was a small printed and cheap paper cover edition of Wordsworth. So, hearing this man mention a bible, I became extremely curious to learn how a man could earn a living by carrying a book of this kind. Seeking this information I said to this man—'I shouldn't think that there was much money to be made by carrying a bible.' 'Why not?' he asked; 'if you carry in your hand a decent rake (a comb), a flashy pair of sniffs (scissors) and a card of good links and studs—that is certainly a good bible for a living; but there is not much profit in a pair of stretchers (laces) or a packet of common sharps (needles). As for me,' he continued, 'I am on the downright, and I go in for straight begging, without showing anything in my hand. That grinder, whom I thought you were with, and am glad you are not, works very hard at dragging that old rickety contrivance with him all over the country; and is he any better off than I am? I never fail to get the sixteen farthings for my feather (bed), I get all the scrand (food) I can eat; and I seldom lie down at night but what I am skimished (half drunk), for I assure you I never go short of my skimish.' Being curious to see this man at work, and to hear the tales with which he approached people, I told him I would accompany him the next day as far as Stratford, that was if he had no objection to my company, as I also intended to visit that town before I made my way towards London. To this proposal he seemed perfectly agreeable.

The next morning arrived and after having had breakfast, we set out. We had scarcely set foot outside the lodging house, when I saw this downrighter dodge in and out of shops with an astonishing alacrity, more like a customer than a beggar; but with what success I could not tell. He seemed to go in smiling, and to come out the same, until we were at last at the business end of the town. He did not confide in me as to his success or failure; but generously invited me to a smoke. We filled our pipes, but just as I was about to strike a match, my companion interrupted me with —'Wait until we are on the other side of the sky pilot.' Looking down the road I saw a clergyman approaching us at a fast rate, carrying something in his hand which proved on nearer view to be a book of prayers. When this black cloth was within three or four feet of us, my companion began to address him in a very serious voice, calling him in his ignorance, or perhaps excitement—'your reverend highness.' The gentleman in black cloth seemed to have been expecting something of this kind, for, without turning his head either to the right or left, he passed on, going if possible, at greater speed. On seeing which my companion shouted in a jeering voice—'Go it, old hearty, and remember me in yer prayers.' As we proceeded on our way he laughed immoderately. 'Yes,' he said, 'I have always found a bible or a prayer book in a person's hand to be the sign of an uncharitable disposition. Seldom do I get anything from them, but I like to pester them. Now, if this had been a man with a bottle, or a jug of beer in his hand, I would have had a civil answer at the very least.' The indifference of this reverend gentleman, and the experience my companion seemed to have had of this kind in general, surprised me not a little; for this man I was with certainly had the appearance of an honest working man of the better class; his clothes were good, and his flesh was clean, and he certainly had not forgotten the barber.

My companion allowed no person to pass us without making an appeal, and it was made apparent to me that he was successful in a number of cases. In times of failure people listened to this respectable looking fellow, and regretted that they had left home without having brought coppers with them. At one time we saw a man who had dismounted to examine his bicycle, probably having heard some part of it go click and fearing an accident, had paused for an investigation. We stood before this man, and my companion in straightforward, manly tones, asked him for assistance. The gentleman began to stammer, to hem and to haw, at the same time saying that he regretted that he was not at that moment exactly in the position to—'friend,'. broke in my bold downrighter, in a stern solemn voice, laying his heavy hand on the man's shoulder; 'friend, you see before you two men in extreme want, who must be relieved in this very hour.' We were standing in the man's way, and he could not possibly escape without knocking us over. Apparently the man was afraid, for he first looked at our faces, and after looking backward and then forward, he produced a silver sixpence, saying he trusted that that amount would be of some service to us. We made sure of this and then cleared ourselves from his path, allowing him space to mount and ride, an opportunity of which he quickly availed himself. This looked very much like highway robbery, but strangely, I was better satisfied at this open independent way of transacting business than by whining forth pitiful tales of want, however true they might be.

We were now entering the town of Stratford-on-Avon, and my companion was advising me as to my behaviour at the common lodging house. 'It is the only lodging house in the town,' he said, 'and the old lady is very particular and eccentric. Our very appearance may dissatisfy her, and then we will be compelled to walk some miles to the next town. She keeps a shop attached to the lodging house,' continued the downrighter, 'and if strangers, not knowing this to be the case, when applying for lodgings, have bread, tea, sugar, meat, etc. in their hands, that is bought elsewhere, this eccentric old landlady declines to receive them as lodgers, and they are forced, often late at night, to walk to the next town. Some time ago,' he continued, 'a lodger bought at her shop a half-pound of corn-beef, which he thought was underweight. Going to the public house opposite for a glass of beer, he requested the publican to weigh this meat, which being done, it was found to be two ounces short of the required weight. On returning to the house his lodger went quietly to bed, but the next morning he spoke his mind to her in a very straightforward manner, making mention of the publican as a witness. Ever since that time, any man who visits that public house is not allowed to sleep on her premises. If seen entering that place by day, they are objected to at night, and if seen visiting that house after their beds are already paid for, on their return their money is at once refunded without the least explanation.'

It certainly spoke highly for our respectable appearance when this particular landlady received our money, and admitted us without much scrutiny into the kitchen; although she lost no time in following us there, and stood for several minutes watching our movements. No doubt if one of us had thrown a match on the floor, or sat too near the fire; or complained that the kitchen only contained two tea pots, cracked and half spoutless, among the ten lodgers now patiently waiting a chance to make tea; and that there were only three cups, and one half rimmed plate like a vanishing moon—no doubt if we had uttered one complaint, our money would have been returned without advice or warning, and we would have found no other lodgings that would have answered our small means in the town. But we fortunately knew the old lady too well to implicate ourselves and we gave her no chance to complain.

After tea I wandered alone about the town, and as I went

here and there in this enchanted place, ambition again took possession of me, stronger than ever. It filled me with vexation to think that I was no nearer my object, for I was, comparatively speaking, penniless. Two months had I wandered, during which time I had not been able to concentrate my thoughts on any noble theme, taking all day to procure the price of a bed, and two or three coppers extra for food. True I had by now some three pounds saved, the income that I had not touched, but at this rate, I would never be able to attain my ends. November was here, and I was suddenly confronted with a long winter before me, and I pictured myself starved and snow bound in small out of the way villages, or mercilessly pelted by hailstones on a wild shelterless heath. Side by side with these scenes I placed my ideal, which was a small room with a cosy fire, in which I sat surrounded by books, and I sickened at the comparison.

The following morning I was up and on my way before the downrighter had put in an appearance. In two or three days I was again back on the outskirts of London, walking it round in a circle; sometimes ten miles from its mighty heart, or as far distant as twenty miles; but without the courage to approach nearer, or to break away from it altogether. Whatever luck I had good or bad, I always managed to escape the workhouse; and was determined to walk all night, if needs be, rather than seek refuge in one of those places. One desperate hour possessed me every day, sometimes in the morning, or in the afternoon, but more often in the evening, when I would waylay people on the high roads, go boldly to the front doors of houses, interview men in their gardens, stables or shops at the same time flourishing before their eyes a whip of a dozen laces. In this hour I seemed to be impelled by a fatality like that of the wandering Jew, cursed at having to perform something against my will. When this mad fit was at an end, during which I generally succeeded in getting a shilling or more, people might then come and go without fear of being molested, for I was satisfied that the workhouse was once more defeated for another night.

One morning at the beginning of December, I made up my mind to tramp home for Christmas. This was a new idea, and not much to my liking, for I had always written them hopeful letters, and although they knew that I had left London, they knew nothing of my present condition. As usual, under these active impulses I made astonishing progress, being on the borders of Wales in less than a week. The greater part of the journey accomplished, being now less than thirty miles from my native town, I regretted having started with such an intention, and tramped over the Welsh Hills day after day, ultimately finding my way to Swansea. I did not remain long in that town, but began other rambles, and the day before Christmas eve, was in a town twenty-seven miles from home; sleeping there that night I rose early the following morning and started for home. Keeping up a pace of three miles an hour, in spite of the one leg and the rough uneven roads of the hills, I accomplished the journey in nine hours, arriving home just after dark, without having once rested on the way.

I had now been tramping for over three months and thought myself entitled to a little rest, if such could be had. After all why had I done this, and to what end had I suffered? For I would now draw the few pounds that were due to me, would return to London in a week or two, and would again commence writing without any prospect of success, for I would once more be living on a small income. And such was the case: three weeks' comfort improved me wonderfully and vitality returned stronger than ever after the low state into which it had fallen. What cut me to the heart was not so much that I had not practised writing during these four months, but that I had been forced to neglect reading and had therefore been taking in no means to justify my hopes in the future of being capable of writing something of my own. The poor man, who has his daily duties to perform, has his quiet evenings at home, with friends to lend him books, and being known in the locality, a library from which to borrow them, but what privileges has the wanderer?

Feeling myself fit, I drew what money was due to me and returned to London.

CHAPTER XXV

THE FARMHOUSE

Yes, I returned to London, and to my surprise, began to look forward with pleasure to be again frequenting the old haunts for which, when leaving I had felt so much disgust. This feeling seems to be natural; that I felt inclined to see familiar faces, although they were red and blotchy with drink; to hear familiar voices, however foul their language might be. Therefore, on the first night of my return wonder not when I say that I was sitting comfortably in the Ark, as though I had not slept one night away. I looked in vain for my old friend the Canadian. Many recognised and spoke to me. One in particular, a toy seller, who was curious to know where I had been. Seeing that he suspected that I had been incarcerated in a jail, I told him something of my wanderings, and ended by making enquiries of him as to the whereabouts of the Canadian. Of this man he knew nothing, but gave information that 'Cronje', the fish porter, another of my acquaintants, was staying at the Farmhouse, and no doubt would be glad to see me, he having been at the Ark to enquire of me during my absence. Of course it was not my intention to stay long at the Ark, so I at once made my way to the Farmhouse, to see Cronje, where I found him.

The Farmhouse is very particular about taking in strangers, which certainly makes it a more desirable place than others of its kind; but, at Cronje's recommendation, I was without much ceremony accepted as a lodger. This man, nicknamed Cronje, who had been for a number of years in Australia, and had so many wonderful anecdotes to relate, was a sharp little man, the very image of a Jew in features, but fair, red, always happy and laughing, for a contradiction. He was clean in his habits, extremely generous to the poorer lodgers, and was well liked by all. It is true that many considered him to be a liar; but no man contradicted him, for no man was capable of talking him down. In his early days he had had a phenomenal voice, which he claimed to have lost through auctioneering. As a rower he had defeated all corners on the river Murrumbidgee, and had publicly disgraced the champion of Wagga Wagga at billiards. On seeing a man taking a hair out of his food, Cronje declaimed on the danger of swallowing this, relating how his friend Skinner of Australia—who had taken down all the best fencers of Europe —had swallowed a single hair which, taking root in his stomach, had grown to such a length that it had killed him before an operation could be performed. Again: hearing some one mention the names of two famous singers, one a tenor and the other a basso, Cronje, eager to create wonder, said that it was a most remarkable case that the tenor had at first become famous as a basso, and that the basso had at first received recognition as a tenor, and that each man's voice had changed after he had become famous.

What a strange house was this, so full of quaint characters. Some of these men had been here for fifteen, and twenty years. 'Haymaker' George was here, and had been here for some time; for he claimed to have gone haymaking from this very house, when he first came here; going and returning daily without the assistance of trains, buses or cars.

'Salvation' Jimmy was here; who had been so emotional that he had been desired as an acquisition to the Salvation Army, which he had joined, and donned the red jersey. At last the poor fellow had become so very emotional, probably influenced by such stirring music and the ready hallelujah of the members, that really, his frequent laughter, his fervent cries and his down-on-the-knees-and-up-in-a-trice, had provoked so many smiles and sarcastic remarks from his audience, that not only was he not promoted to rank from a private, but was discharged the service altogether. Even to this day, he knew no reason for his dismissal. He was mad enough now, in these latter days, laughing, dancing and singing up and down the Farmhouse kitchen, so that I can imagine the effect on his nerves when marching to the sound of loud music, under the spread of a blood red banner. Even now, in these days, he drew every one's attention to his eccentric behaviour, so that what must he have been then?

I soon knew them all by name, that is, by their nicknames, by which most of them preferred to be known. It was very interesting to hear, morning after morning, 'Fishy Fat' and John—the latter being in the last stages of consumption, and poor fellow peevish withal—sit down to breakfast and to abolish the House of Lords. It was often a surprise to me to see this noble edifice still standing, after hearing it abolished in such fierce language, and in terms of such scathing reproach. Strangely, these men had very little to say during the day; and did one get up earlier than the other in the morning, he would stand silent with his back to the fire, or pace quietly up and down the kitchen waiting the appearance of his friend. When one saw the other preparing breakfast, he would at once follow his example and when everything was ready, both would seat themselves opposite each other at the same table. Up till this time nothing would have been said, until each had tasted and sugared his tea to his own liking. After this being done, one would suddenly ejaculate a sentence of this kind 'Smother them lazy rotters in the 'upper 'ouse, the bleeding liars.' In accordance with that remark, the other would immediately answer—'Perish 'em all.' And then would follow oath after oath of the blackest character, and daring cold-blooded designs that would have gladdened the heart of Guy Fawkes.

Brown was also here, and always in a state of wonder. He had very little faith in print, and every hour things happened which made him—to use his own words—'know not what or what not to believe.' He presumed that the laity was a certain kind of religious sect, but to him they all seemed without difference. The only difference he could see between a vicar and a curate was that one had a larger corporation and a redder nose than the other. Brown, who was a simple, kind-hearted fellow, said that we were all born of woman; that we were born and that we must all die; that it was a great pity, and made his heart bleed, to see a man come down in life after he has been high up; and that we had to face a cruel fact—although it was almost beyond belief—that a man's own relations often caused the man's downfall which, with his own eyes, he had seen done.

'Gambling' Fred was here, looking over the daily paper with 'Red Nosed Scotty'. They are both short sighted, and, unfortunately, have but one pair of spectacles between them, which is now being used by 'Scotty'. Suddenly the red nosed man sees the name of a horse. 'There you are,' he cries exultingly; 'there's a sure winner.' 'Where?' asks his fellow gambler, taking the spectacles and adjusting them on his own nose. 'How can I show you now?' asks the red nosed gambler, in a fretful voice, 'haven't you got the specs on?' At last matters are arranged to the satisfaction of both, and Fred approaches his friend 'Yanks' for the loan of sixpence, to back his horse. But 'Yanks' unceremoniously tells his friend to go to hell. At this the gambler sulks all the evening and unfortunately the next day his favoured horse wins. On this transaction the gambler would have been ten shillings in pocket. After this another horse won, which Fred, in his penniless state, professes to have favoured. He would have backed this horse with the ten shillings won from the other race, and would now have been five pounds in pocket. 'Yes,' says the gambler, pointing to his friend 'Yanks'—'that man has done me out of many a golden pound.'

Poor old 'Scotty' Bill was here, a seller of fly papers; who disturbed the kitchen all day, because of the scarcity of flies, as though the lodgers were to blame. 'We are having damn strange summers of late years,' he said, 'different from my younger days; for there is now scarcely a fly to he seen.'

Here dwelt 'Hoppy' the bootblack, who had a rival in business on the opposite corner. He was certainly the dirtiest man I have ever seen going in and out of a house, but he earned good money, and often came home drunk to this lodging house in a cab, causing a great sensation among the poorer lodgers. His rival did less trade, and could afford to do less, a lodger remarked, seeing that his mother kept a flourishing cats' meat shop. When I have passed near these rival bootblacks, I have often wondered how the thousands of people walked daily between them without being singed, not to mention scorched, by their baneful glances, which were fired at each other across the way.

Here too had 'Irish' Tim come; a very small man with a sarcastic tongue; an out-of-date printer broken on the wheels of new machinery. Did you not want to be subjected to the ridicule of the kitchen it was necessary when expressing an opinion, to look this man straight and sternly in the face, and to speak with the utmost deliberation. He always sat at the same table, and in the same seat, if not already occupied; and his particular table was known as the House of Parliament, owing to the number of arguments conducted there, of which he was the leader. He passed judgment on public men, and although he rarely had a good word for any one, I must say, to Tim's credit, that he never lost an opportunity to stroke the cat. I believe Tim had just a little friendly feeling for simple, eccentric and impulsive Bob; whom he could scorn and contradict without being threatened or bullied in return. Bob was an idealist, a dreamer with a strong imagination; and it was Tim's delight to beat this dreamer back to the thorny paths of his daily life, speaking in the name of common sense.

Bob was full of the wonders of Nature, marvelled much at the undertakings of men, to make railways to cross mountains and bridges to span canyons; and was deeply interested in the early growth of things, ere they were manufactured into a form that every person could recognise. He was a most brilliant conversationalist, and was interestingly dramatic in his readings. He was a good companion for others, but, as I soon discovered to my disappointment, seldom had a comfortable moment when alone with himself. I had a small bedroom to myself, and unfortunately the near cubicle to mine was Bob's. Bob who, probably five minutes before, had been in the kitchen laughing, or reading with childish delight of the gorgeous pageantry of a coming play or a pantomime, or had been seriously wondering at some new discovery, would scarcely set foot in his own quiet room ere he was clutched by a devil. I have become accustomed to foul language from one man to another, but his bold way of directly addressing his blasphemy to his Maker, stiffened the laughter on my lips, and shocked me, inspite of an indifferent faith. This unusually clever man—a genius, if this world ever had one —disappointed at his circumstances, after an indulgence of his ideal, would sit on his bed and try to throttle himself, night after night; and then would smother his face in his bed clothes, and invariably end his mad fit by sobbing. When he reached this pitiful state, this simple, impulsive and childlike man, I felt like standing to his side before the outraged face of his Maker, so great was my pity for him.

Many others were here, whom I was to become better acquainted with—such as the 'Major', 'Australian' Bill, 'Never Sweet', 'Cinders, and 'The Snob', who was sent to prison so often through having an over-liking for other people's pockets; and who, when questioned as to his absence, always said he had been to see his youngest brother. All of these were here, with many others of note.

For the 'Blacksmith' was here, who, every time he saw me preparing to go out, thought I must be on a begging expedition, and he trusted that I would find the ladies kindly disposed. On thanking him for this kind wish, he confided his intention of visiting Deptford, saying that he had given that part of the city a long rest.

'Boozy' Bob was here. 'Drunken Dave' and 'Brummy Tom'; three small men with a large capacity for taking ale. All these men were quiet or at least not objectionable, and none of them could disturb me in my room. The sleep of the house was disturbed more from without than from any cause within. Cats—by day the most docile of God's creatures, every one of them in the night enlisting under the devil's banner—took the place by storm after the human voice had ceased. But perhaps the one who accounted for more than two thirds of my sleepless nights, was a woman, an outsider living in an adjacent block. It was her custom to come home drunk early in the morning, singing and swearing. 'Little Punch', a sickly consumptive, who had lived in this neighbourhood of Southwark all his life, had no difficulty in recognising the voice of Mrs. Kelly. So whenever I enquired as to the origin of a disturbance, the name of Mrs. Kelly was the beginning and the end of it. Mrs. Kelly was not satisfied with a single fight; she occasionally instigated a riot. On the night of that memorable day when Southwark, and in particular the Borough, was visited by royalty, this was the lady that murdered sleep. The police always appeared tolerant with her, and more so on this occasion. As a general rule it is people that live in private houses who have to complain of the presence of a common lodging house, of being disturbed by its low-class inmates; but this lodging house, with beds for nearly two hundred men, was kept as quiet as a large mansion with its one small family and half a score of servants. In its kitchen was a continual din up till twelve o'clock at night; but this did not disturb the sleepers in other parts of the house. Seldom would a loud voice be heard inside; but it was nothing unusual to hear at night the fighting and swearing of men and women, and the screaming of children. This could be expected without fail on Saturday nights and the close of holidays. These horrible and inhuman cries so affected me on one Saturday evening, when, for the sake of the study, I had retired early to bed, that I could neither think, sleep nor lie quiet, and felt compelled to get up and return to the kitchen. This I did, and found thirty or forty men assembled there, most of them more or less drunk, but none of them appeared quarrelsome. Of course it was impossible to sit long here before I was surrounded by them; and sat fearing to breathe deep enough to inhale the fumes of drink which came from both their mouths and their clothes; and being in good favour with these hopeless fellows, was continually invited good naturedly to shake hands with them. Instead of going back to my room, I left the place and entered a public house for the first time in three months. Brummy Tom was there, with another fish porter of his acquaintance. 'Have a drink with me,' he said, 'I have often thought to ask you, but thought you were a teetotaller and would refuse.' 'Brumm' I said, rather bitterly, 'a teetotaller who lives in a common lodging house is to be heartily despised, for he shows himself to be satisfied with his conditions.' With Brummy Tom and his friend for companions, I took a number of long sleeping draughts, and just after twelve o'clock that night was fast asleep in bed. The following morning some of the lodgers were telling of murder cries heard just after midnight, but I praised the power of Bacchus that I had not heard them.

It was always a mystery to me that these men respected me and never failed in civility in their dealings with me, for I did everything that these men dislike. I wore a white collar, which they at once take to be a challenge that you are their superior. Few other men in the house, except they were fighting men, could have produced a toothbrush without being sneered at. True it induced Brown to ask the question whether I felt any actual benefit from cleaning my teeth; that he had heard so many different opinions that he did not know what or what not to believe, saying that he had often watched me, and wondered at so unusual a custom. They all detested the 'Masher', because he was earning more than a pound a week on a good paper stand, and was also in receipt of a good pension; and they all cried shame on him for living in a common lodging house. This man, to my discomfort, showed so much inclination to confide in me, pointing out the different lodgers who owed him money, and calling them low vagabonds and ungrateful scamps, in a voice that was not meant to be a whisper, that I was almost afraid of losing their good will in listening to such words, without saying something on their behalf. Again I was almost a teetotaller, and that was the worst charge of all. In spite of all this, I do not believe that I made one enemy, and am certain that I never received other than kindness and civility from the lodgers of the Farmhouse.

CHAPTER XXVI

RAIN AND POVERTY

The greatest enemy to the man who has to carry on his body all his wardrobe, is rain. As long as the sun shines he is indifferent, but if he is caught in a wet condition after sunset he is to be pitied. He does not fear any ill consequences to health from being wet through, as does his more fortunate brother, but he does not like the uncomfortable sensation of shivering and not being able to keep warm. This unsettled feeling is often made worse by an empty stomach. In fact a full stomach is his one safeguard against the cold, and he cares not then if the rain and the wind penetrate his clothes. No seaman ever searched the heavens for a dark speck, or astronomer for a new light, as does this homeless man for a sign of rain. To escape from the coming deluge he seeks shelter in the public library, which is the only free shelter available; and there he sits for hours staring at one page, not a word of which he has read or, for that matter, intends to read. If he cannot at once get a seat, he stands before a paper and performs that almost impossible feat of standing upright fast asleep so as to deceive the attendants, and respectable people who are waiting a chance to see that very paper. To be able to do this requires many unsuccessful efforts, which fail on account of hard breathing, nodding and stumbling against the paper stand; but success has at last been attained, and there he stands fast asleep and apparently absorbed in a most interesting paragraph. He attains such perfection in this one act that he has been known to stand like a marble statue before a large sheet of costly plate glass, what time sleep had overpowered him in the act of admiring a baker's art. The homeless man must always remember one thing, that though he may sit on wooden seats and stone parapets, eat in public and go in rags, he must not, on any account, sleep. Working men only are allowed that privilege and those who can afford to remain idle. No policeman would think of indulging in a short nap until he made sure that there was no vagrant sleeping on his beat. And what respectable householder could rest in bed knowing that a tramp was sleeping in his doorway? If necessity is the mother of invention, sleep must certainly be necessary to a human being, or the tramp, according to his many chances of experiments, would he the first to prove the contrary. So much for the very lowest men.

But there are others who, in that they have a shelter at night, scorn the name of being called homeless men. These men live in common lodging houses, and are well satisfied with a place to sleep and enough food to keep body and soul together. Most of these men earn their living, such as it is, in the open air, and they earn so little that they are seldom prepared for a rainy day. Therefore, when comes this rainy morn, and the poor fellow rises penniless from his bed, it is then that you see a little seriousness come over him; for he cannot expose his wares to spoil in the rain and, did they not spoil, who would be foolish enough to tarry in bad weather to make an idle purchase? The rain would spoil his paper-toys, his memorandum-books, or his laces and collar studs. In truth, as long as the rain continues his occupation is gone. The paper seller can take his stand regardless of weather, and earn enough for the day thereof, at the expense of a wet skin. Sometimes he is fortunate enough to be stationed near some shelter, but sometimes his stand happens to be outside an aristocratic club or hotel, and he dare not enter its porch, not even if the devil was at his heels.

Then there is the 'downrighter', the man who makes no pretence to selling, but boldly asks people for the price of his bed and board. On a rainy day he has to make sudden bursts between the heaviest showers and forage the surrounding streets, which, being near a lodging house, are invariably poor and unprofitable, whereas his richest pastures are in the suburbs or better still the outskirts of them. The bad weather is, of course, a blessing to those distant housekeepers, however hard it is on the 'downrighter', for it comes as the Sabbath day to their bells and knockers.

Then there are the market men who work two or three early hours in the morning, when the majority of people are asleep. These men are returning in their wet clothes between eight and nine o'clock and their day's work is done. Often they have no change of clothing, therefore it is not unusual for two men to be standing at the same fire, the one drying his wet socks and the other toasting his dry bread, with the articles in question almost embracing one another on the most friendly terms.

It is on this rainy day that one sees those little kindnesses which are only seen among the very poor: one who has not sufficient for himself assisting some other who has nothing. One man who has made eighteen pence at the market, returns, pays fourpence for his bed, buys food, and then in addition to paying for another man's bed, invites yet another to dine with him and in the end gives his last copper to another. One, who happens to have done well the previous day, gives here and there until he is himself penniless. The consequence of all this is that whereas you saw in the morning dull and anxious faces, at midday you see more than half of the lodgers cooking, their beds already paid for. All worry is at an end, and they are whistling, humming songs, or chaffing one another.

It is on this rainy day when they are made prisoners without spare money to pay into the beer house, that they mend and wash their clothes, repair their boots, and have abundant time to cook vegetables. It is a day for Irish stews and savoury broths.

It was on one of these days, when the kitchen was so crowded, that I unfortunately attempted to make pancakes. I knew that such an unusual experiment could not fail to cause a sensation which I did not desire, so I placed myself in a dark corner and quietly and without being observed, made the flour into paste, exactly as I had seen another lodger do some time previous. The flour had been in my possession ever since that occasion, but my courage had up to the present failed. Three or four men were now at the stove, and a number of others were idly walking up and down. I had made half a basin of paste, and this was to make one big thick fat pancake. But how was I to get it into the frying pan without attracting notice? I covered the basin with a saucer, placed the frying pan on the stove, with butter therein, and waited my chance. I had taken the precaution of having in readiness a large plate. At last my chance came, for two cooks were having high words as to whether cabbage should be put into cold or boiling water. Others joined in this argument, so without receiving notice, I dropped the paste into the frying pan and quickly covered it with a large plate. So far, so good: my only difficulty now would be to turn it; for after it was cooked I could carry the pan and its covered contents to the dark corner where I intended to dine; and where, although men might see me eat, none would be the wiser as to what I was eating. Five minutes had passed and no doubt its one side was cooked. The argument was still in full swing, for each man stoutly maintained his opinions, and almost every man who took part cited his mother or sister as an authority, except one, who proudly mentioned a French chef in an Australian gold diggings. Now was my chance. I cast one furtive glance around, rose the hot plate with a stocking, which I had been washing, made one quick turn of the wrist, spun the pancake in the air, caught it neatly and promptly, clapped the plate over it - the whole process done, I believe, in less than ten seconds. The difficulty was now over and I breathed relief I went to my dining corner and sat down, intending to fetch the pancake in five minutes time.

Three minutes perhaps I had been seated when I heard a loud voice cry—'Whose pancake is this burning on the stove?' How I did detest that man: he was always shouting through the kitchen—'Whose stew is this boiling over?' or 'Whose tea is stewing on the fire?' The man always seemed to be poking his nose into other people's business. I did not think it worth while drawing every one's attention by answering him, but made my way as quietly as possible towards the stove. Alas! the idiot, not thinking that I was the owner of the pancake, and was then on my way to attend to it, shouted the second time, louder and it seemed to me, too impatiently—'Whose pancake is this?' If I was vexed when I heard that second enquiry, imagine how I felt when every lodger in the kitchen, not seeing or hearing from the pancake's lawful claimant, began to shout in angry voices 'Whose pancake is that burning on the fire?' My own patience was now exhausted. 'The pancake is mine,' I said, 'and what about it? What is all this fuss about? It is the first pancake I have ever attempted to make and by heavens! if it is to cause such a stir as this, it will be the last.' But while I was making this speech another voice, which froze the blood in my veins, cried angrily—'Whose pancake is this?' It was a woman's voice, it was the Mrs. of the house; and I knew that something more serious was happening than the burning of a pancake—I was burning her frying pan. If I dallied in respect to my pancakes, I must certainly not make further delay in saving the frying pan. To her I at once apologised, but I gave that meddler a look that for ever again kept him silent as to what belonged to me. Such are the doings in a lodging house, vexatious enough at the time, but amusing to recall.

CHAPTER XXVII

FALSE HOPES

The Farmhouse was under the management of an Irishman and his wife. He with a generous heart that always kept him poor, for he often assisted lodgers towards paying for their beds, who, I am sorry to say, were sometimes ungrateful in return. She, more circumspect, but kind hearted and motherly where she thought the case to be a deserving one.

With regards to literary ambition I always kept my own counsel, confiding in one man only—'Cronje'; a man to be relied on, whose sympathetic ears were always open to receive either good or bad news.

I must have been in this house something like twelve months, when I took a sudden notion to send some work to a literary man, asking him for his opinion of the same. In a few days I received a letter stating that want of time prevented him from passing judgment on my work, which he regretted he would have to return unread. This did not offend me in the least, although I was greatly disappointed, for I knew that a man in his position could have little time to spare, and no doubt was pestered with correspondence of a like nature. But, unfortunately, the MS. returned in an ill condition, having been roughly handled through the post, and arrived at the Farmhouse with the ends of the envelope in tatters. When I received this ragged and disreputable parcel from the Manager, I knew that the cat was out of the bag, and that the secret which I had guarded so jealously was now the property of another, but I made no confession, thinking that he would broach the subject, which he did on the following morning. On enquiring if the parcel I had received on the day previous was a manuscript, I lost no time in telling him everything. The upshot of this was that he persuaded me to send some work to a publisher, and if that gentleman thought the book worth publication, he, the Manager, had no doubt that one of the many rich people who were connected with the Farmhouse Mission could be induced to assist me. Hearing this I was sorry that I had not confided in him of my own accord, for I had often seen these rich people coming and going, looking, perhaps for deserving cases.

With these golden projects before me, I again set to work, and, in less than a month, the MS. was ready and in the hands of a publisher. That gentleman wrote in a few days saying that he thought there was literary merit, and that the cost of production would be thirty pounds. The publisher's name was well known, and the Manager was quite satisfied as to its being a genuine offer from an old and respectable firm. Quite contented in my own mind, my part having been performed without difficulty, I gladly allowed this man to take possession of this correspondence, and a few specimen books of verse, which the publisher had sent with it, and, having full trust in the man's goodness and influence, made myself comfortable, and settled down in a fool's paradise. I have never had cause to doubt his goodness, but he certainly overrated his power to influence the philanthropists on the behalf of a lodger.

Several weeks passed, and I had received no encouraging news. No mention had been made of my affairs, and I gave myself over to the influence of the coke fire. After going out in the morning for two or three hours, I would return at midday, often earlier, and sit hopelessly before this fire for ten or eleven hours, after which I would retire to my room. What a miserable time was this: the kitchen, foul with the breath of fifty or sixty men, and the fumes of the coke fire, took all the energy out of a man, and it was a hard fight to keep awake. It has taken the play out of the kitten, and this small animal lies stretched out, overcome by its fumes, without the least fear of being trodden on. Sometimes, when I endeavoured to concentrate my mind, with an idea of writing something, it was necessary to feign a sleep, so that these kind hearted fellows might not disturb me with their civilities. On these occasions it was not unusual for me to fall into a real sleep. And, when I awoke, it sickened me to think of this waste of time; for I was spending in bed more hours than were necessary for my health, and it was a most cruel waste of time to be sleeping in the day. This fire exerted a strange influence over us. In the morning we were loath to leave it, and we all returned to it as soon as possible. Even the books and magazines in the libraries could not seduce me longer than an hour. There was one seat at the corner of a table, which I have heard called 'the dead man's seat'. It was within two yards of this great fire, which was never allowed to suffer from want of coke. It was impossible to retain this seat long and keep awake. Of course, a man could hardly expect to keep this seat day after day for a long winter, and to be alive in the spring of the year. This was the case with a printer, who, unfortunately, had only three days' work a week. The amount he earned was sufficient for his wants, so, in his four idle days, he would sit on this seat, eating, reading, but more often sleeping, until before the end of the winter, he was carried away a dying man. Some of these lodgers claim to be able to recognize in the public streets any strangers who are suffering from this coke fever.

Weeks passed and then months, and I still heard nothing about my book. The Manager had failed, of that I at last became certain. I avoided him as much as possible, because of the confidence I had reposed in him. It was certainly very awkward for the both of us, and I felt much sympathy on his account. When he was near I felt extremely uncomfortable, and I am sure he felt none too easy in my presence.

Spring at last came, and I broke away from the lodging house fire, to indulge in the more pure rays of the sun. I began to absent myself from the house longer every day, until I at last began to regret that there was any necessity to return to it at all. The happiness and stir of Nature, at this time of the year, began to fill me with her own energy. I was in my room, one of these bright mornings, and was looking in the mirror, adjusting my scarf—the mirror and bed being the whole furniture. In this mirror I looked long enough to see a white hair on the side of my head. Thinking this to be hardly true at my time of life, I shifted the glass to a better light, thinking it must have played me false; but sure enough, here it was—a single hair, as white as snow. Yes, I thought, with some bitterness, this comes of waiting to be fulfilled the promises of other people; and you will never rise if you do not make some effort of your own. Thinking of this white hair, I left the house, wondering what I could do to help myself. And, this particular morning, an idea occurred to me, so simple, so reasonable, and so easily to be accomplished, that it filled me with surprise that such a plan had not presented itself before. I had an income of eight shillings per week; then what was to prevent me from borrowing forty or fifty pounds, even though I paid for it a little more than usual interest? Again I was full of hope and happiness, for I could see nothing to prevent the accomplishment of this. My eight shillings were being received in sums of two pounds every five weeks. Two shillings a week were forwarded home, and I lived abstemiously on the remainder. My five weeks' money was due on the following week, so I at once began making preparations for a trip home. When this money arrived I determined to lose no time in executing these plans, for I had visions of being a white-headed man, if I remained under these hopeless conditions for another year or two. The money came on Saturday night, when it was due, and everything being prepared, I was that very night on my way to Paddington Station, after having told the manager that I was going home for a week, and that I would forward him my rent, if I remained longer than that time. Full of this idea I arrived at home.

The following Monday I invaded the offices of my old granny's lawyer, and telling him I wished to set up in business, consulted him as to the best way of borrowing the money, some forty or fifty pounds being necessary. He saw nothing to prevent this from being done, but strongly advised me not to do so; 'at any rate,' he said, 'see your trustee, ask him if he can lend you the amount, and, if he cannot see his way clear to do so, let me know!' In half all hour I was with the trustee. That gentleman had not the amount on hand, but had plans of his own which, if I strictly adhered to, would be more to my advantage in the long run.

'It is now June,' he said, 'and if you allow your income to stand until the beginning of the New Year, you will then have ten pounds saved to your account, and I give you my promise to advance another twenty pounds without a question of interest, making the amount thirty pounds!' Now it happened that three weeks before I left London, I had sent a work to a printer and publisher, who had priced two hundred and fifty copies at nineteen pounds; so that I knew well that thirty pounds would be ample to meet all expenses. But how was I to live for the next six months? Determined to make any sacrifice to attain this end, I closed with the trustee's offer, and, getting an advance from him of one pound, intended to return at once to London, but was persuaded to remain at home for another three weeks. At the end of this time I paid my fare back to London, and again took possession of my room, for which I had forwarded the rent during my absence. In less than four days after my return, I was very near penniless, and saw no other prospect than to start on another half year's wandering.

How foolish all this was! Why did I not start my travels from home, instead of wasting money on a return fare to London? Why did I pay three weeks' rent for the sake of

233

returning to a room for as many days? Well, I had a faint hope that the Manager might, at last, after six months, have succeeded in his attempt.

I told the Manager that I was going on the road for a month or two, but mentioned no purpose, for I was now resolved to act for myself

'You will always find room at the Farmhouse,' he said; 'do not doubt that.'

Trying to appear as cheerful as possible, for I knew this man was also disappointed, I left him, determined never to set foot in that house again until I could dispense with the services of others. At this time I had two silver shillings and some odd coppers, and would soon need assistance as a man, without any question as to my work as an author.

Again I was leaving London, not knowing how much I would have to suffer. One idea consoled me not a little; that I would not require money for a bed for at least three months to come; that the nights, though cold, would not be so dangerous as to kill. Whatever the consequences might be, even if this rough life threatened to injure my health permanently, I was firmly resolved to sacrifice the next six months for whatever might follow them.

CHAPTER XXVIII

ON TRAMP AGAIN

Now followed a strange experience, an experience for which there is no name; for I managed to exist, and yet had neither the courage to beg or sell. Certainly at times I was desperately inclined to steal; but chance left nothing for my eyes to covet, and I passed harmlessly on. When I suffered most from lack of rest, or bodily sustenance—as my actual experience became darker, the thoughts of the future became brighter, as the stars shine to correspond with the night's shade.

I travelled alone, in spite of the civilities of other tramps who desired company, so as to allow no strange voice to disturb my dreams. Some of these men had an idea that I was mad, because I could give them little information as to the towns and villages through which I had that very day passed. They inquired as to the comforts and conditions of a town's workhouse, of which I knew nothing, for I had not entered it. They inquired as to its best lodging-house, of which I was again ignorant, having slept in the open air. They inquired how far I had come that day, which I could not immediately tell them, and they were curious to know how far I was going, which I did not know. The strangest part of this experience was that I received help from people without having made a glance of appeal, and without having opened my mouth. When I asked for water, tea or milk was often brought, and food invariably followed. I began to look on this as a short life of sacrifice, killing a few worthless hours so as to enjoy thousands of better ones; and I blessed every morning that ushered in a new day, and worshipped every sabbath night that closed another week.

After tramping from town to town, from shire to shire, in two months I was in Devonshire, on my way to Plymouth. I felt continually attracted to these large centres of commerce, owing, I suppose, to feeling the necessity of having an object in view; but was generally starved out of them in a very short time. A gentleman on horseback, whom I met near Totnes, saved me from suffering from want, for a couple of days, at least, when I would reach Plymouth. This gentleman drew his horse to a halt, so that he might inquire my destination. He seemed to be much surprised when I told him it was the town of Plymouth.

'Ah, well' he said, glancing towards the ground, 'there is only one foot to get sore, if that is any consolation to you; perhaps this will help you a little on the way,' dropping into my hands three silver shillings.

Without having this case in mind, I certainly fared better in Devonshire than in other counties, and found its people more like the prosperous settlers in new lands. In spite of this, my roughest experience was in this county, owing to the inclemency of the weather, and the difficulty of finding shelter. One night I had gone into the fields, and, getting together a dozen or more wheatsheaves, proceeded to build a house with them, making a dry floor on the damp earth, with walls to shelter from the wind, and a roof to shelter from the dew, leaving just space enough at one end to admit my body. I had been in here comfortable and warm for some time, when it began to rain. In half an hour the rain leaked in large drops through the roof, and in less than an hour these drops had become streams. There was nothing to do but to remain, for it was now too dark to seek shelter. For ten hours it rained incessantly, and I was literally wet to the skin, and no drier than a person immersed in water—not wet to the skin as people commonly express it when they are damp after a few showers. I was nothing daunted, looking on this as one of the many hard experiences that I was compelled to undergo. The next morning I chose a secluded spot in the open air, so as to lie down where the sun, coming out warm and strong, would dry me while I slept. Two or three times have I suffered in this way, but have never felt any ill effects after.

My worst experience of this kind was in the adjoining county of Somerset, at the end of September, when I was again making my way back to London. But it was not the blowing of the wind, or the patter of the rain; not the rustle of the leaves on the swaying branches; not the discomforts of having wet clothes, and being without sign of a barn or empty house in which to shelter; it was none of these that took the courage out of me, it was a wild laugh, harsh, and apparently in savage mockery. I had skirted what appeared to be a park, for something like two miles, and was weary

237

to see the end of it. This at last seemed to come, for I could see through the trees a large open field wherein were wheat sheaves, stacked in their threes, and in their usual rows. Now, had this been a field right up to the roadside, I would most certainly have had no compunction in spending the night there, being tired of carrying such a distance my wet and heavy clothes. As it was, I paused, not feeling inclined to proceed further on my journey, and yet not half liking to cross that narrow strip of park, thinking it might contain game that would be well looked after, making trespassing a serious offence.

When in this irresolute state of mind, I caught sight of a white gate, and a small footpath leading to the field. Night seemed to be coming on at the rate of a darker shade to the minute, and I knew well that in another quarter of an hour it would be difficult to distinguish a house from a barn. Seeing this, I summoned courage, opened the gate, and made my way quickly along the path that led to the wheat sheaves. Standing amidst these I waited silently, listening for any that might be in that locality. Satisfied that there were not, I picked up a sheaf, and was about to lay it flat, when I heard a loud startling laugh, coming from the direction of the road. Dropping the sheaf at once, I bent low, not for a moment doubting but what someone had seen me from the road, and was taking a heartless delight in letting me know his discovery. Although I regretted this, thinking he would inform others, and I would surely be disturbed before morning, perhaps that very hour—I determined to travel no further that night, if I could help it, and proceeded to make my bed, under the impression that he had passed on. I stood up in full, but had scarcely done so, when my appearance was greeted by several long shouts of derisive laughter. Now, a homeless man has no time to be superstitious, he fears the living and not the dead. If he is sleepy he is not particular about feeling in the darkness of cellars or vaults; and, if he were sleeping on a grave, and was awakened by a voice crying —'Arise from off this grave', he would at once think it the voice of a grave digger, or the keeper of the cemetery, rather than the ghostly owner of the same. Therefore, I had not the least idea but what this was the voice of a human being, although it sounded uncanny and strange. I moved again, and again heard that loud peal of laughter. This voice evidently only mocked when I moved, for when I stood still, not a sound was to be heard. This time I gave up all thoughts of making a bed, and being now filled with fear, picked up the thick stick with which I travelled, and stood on the defensive, every moment expecting to see a mad-man burst from under the trees and in three leaps and a bound be at my side.

These movements seemed to cause some merriment, but the laughter again ceased when I stood watching and waiting, and puzzled how to act. Rest was now out of the question, and I made up my mind to leave that accursed place instantly. With this intention I made my way towards the gate. I had scarcely moved in that direction, when the laughing began, this time continuing for a long time, as though jeering its last at my defeat. When I reached the gate, and passed through to the open road, my courage returned, and I looked with some bitterness to see the figure of some country lout hurrying into the darkness, after succeeding in robbing me of my sleep; but, to my surprise, I heard no one, and could see no figure on the road before or behind. It was now that superstition took hold of me, and I got off with all possible speed, often looking back to see if I was pursued; and I did not stop until a human settlement lay between me and that accursed park.

Often have I thought of that night. It is natural to suppose that a thoughtless ploughman, or farm labourer, would have stood at the roadside and laughed or shouted once or twice, and then passed on, but it is scarcely probable that he would have remained there to carry his joke so far. Granted that he had had the courage to laugh so many times, taunting one at a distance, where was his courage now that he had run away, or still stood concealed behind the trees? The voice sounded human, but still seemed wild and a little unnatural. After much consideration the only conclusion I could put to the affair was that the voice came from a bird in the trees; an escaped pet bird that could imitate the human voice. This solution of the mystery did not altogether satisfy me, for I have never had cause to believe that any bird could so perfectly imitate the human voice. Superstition must have thoroughly possessed me for the once in my life, or I should not have walked all night, after the painful exertion of the day.

If I settled towards night time in any place where a bird came hopping restlessly from branch to branch, making a series of short cries of fear, to let me know that I was lying too close to its nest, I would without hesitation shift my position, often to my own discomfort; but at the same time, people could pass to and fro to my indifference.

I would never beg, unless forced to the last extremity, for I feared the strange fascination that arises from success, after a man has once lost his shame. On one occasion I saw

240

a well dressed couple wheeling their bicycles up an incline, which was too steep to ride. Evidently they were lovers, for they seemed to he in no hurry to reach the top of the hill and end their conversation by riding. As I drew near the lady produced her purse, and, placing something in her companion's hand, motioned over her shoulder in my direction. On which the gentleman nodded, and immediately glanced back towards me. Now, these people could not very well make the first overtures, for the simple reason that they know not whether a man is in want, or is a poor, but proud and respectable inhabitant of one of the adjacent villages. I preferred to impress them with the latter opinion, for, when I reached them, I put on an extra spurt, and was soon beyond their hearing. No, I would never make a good beggar, for here was money in readiness, to come at the sound of my voice, or to be drawn by the simple side glance of my eye. When I was some distance away, I looked back, and saw the lady looking rather disappointed, receiving back her coin. Her companion was laughing, no doubt consoling her by saying that I was hardly likely to be in actual need, or I would have asked for assistance, and probably my home was somewhere near. The truth of the matter was that at this time I had not a copper to bless myself with.

Days, weeks, and months went on, and it was now the month of October. It was now that I began to find the necessity of having a bed every night, having been satisfied up till then with a bed once or perhaps twice a week, according to the coppers received. I was back again in Swindon, having been there sometime previous, when on my way to Devonshire. The first three months of sacrifice were over, and I was very little the worse for it; but the next three months required different means, to correspond with the difference in the time of year. Shelter was necessary every night, and to meet these stern demands, I needed something to sell, so as to be sure of coppers for this purpose. With this idea, I bought two dozen laces with the last three coppers I had, and re-opened business as a hawker. The success with which I met in this town astonished, me, owing, I believe, to its being a working man's town, and not filled with half-pay officers and would-be aristocrats that cannot afford, but still feel it their duty, to live in fine villas in the locality of a royal residence. The poor, sympathetic people seemed to understand a man's wants. Business was often transacted without the utterance of words. Taking a pair of laces, they would give a copper, and, smiling their sympathy, close the door. Often one would pay for these useless things and not take them. The kindness of these people so filled me with gratitude, that I found it impossible to continue selling after I had received enough to supply the day's wants, which would often be in less than half an hour. I remained here for two weeks, being able to allow myself half an ounce of tobacco and a halfpenny paper every day. The only thing that worried me in this town was the persistence of an old beggar in the lodging house. Night after night, this man would advise me to go out and stand pad. This was, he explained, that a man, who is afflicted with the loss of an arm, a hand or a leg, blind, paralysed or lame, should stand or sit in a public place in the town, holding in his hand matches, laces or any other cheap trifle, so that he might invite the charity of passers by. This old man could not understand why this was not done, seeing that it required no eloquence—the very act and the affliction speaking for themselves—and was so successful a dodge that even able-bodied men could often pick up a shilling or two in this way. At last I became so impressed with this old man's eloquence, that I left the lodging house three times in one night with a firm resolution to stand pad, and three times I returned without having done so. On the last occasion I did make a little attempt, but foolishly took up a position where no one could see me.

Before I left Swindon I wrote to a friend of mine in Canada, requesting him to forward me a pound to London, as soon as possible, which would be returned to him at the beginning of the new year. I did this so that I might have a couple of weeks at the end of December to prepare my MS. and to be ready for business as soon as that time arrived. It was now the latter end of October, and this pound could not reach London far short of a month. Thinking I was not likely again to suffer for want of a bed or food, after this success in Swindon, I bought a good stock of laces and left that town, with the intention of working the towns on the outskirts of London, so that when ready to enter I would be within a day's march. Unfortunately, after leaving Swindon, success deserted me, which was certainly more my fault than that of the people, for I made very little appeal to them. Arriving at Maidenhead, I had the bare price of my bed, with a dry bread supper and breakfast. My laces were being exhausted, and I was without means to replenish them. From town to town I walked around London, sometimes making sixpence, and always less than a shilling a day; and this small amount had to purchase bed, food, and occasionally a couple of dozen laces. The monotony of this existence was broken a little at Guildford, where I was arrested on suspicion of

243

crime. A plain clothes officer happened to be in the office of the lodging house, who, when he set eyes upon me, requested a few moments' conversation, at the same time leading the way out into the yard. He then came to a halt under a lamp, and, taking from his pocket some papers, began to read, often raising his eyes to scrutinise my person. 'Yes,' he said, at last, 'no doubt you are the man I want, for you answer his description.' 'I suppose,' was my answer, 'it is a case of arrest?' 'It is,' he said, 'and you must accompany me to the station.' On my way to that place he asked many a question of what I had done with my overcoat, and as to the whereabouts of my wife. It had been several years since I had owned the former, and the latter I had never possessed; but this man could not be convinced of either. 'Which way have you come?' he asked. To which I mentioned one or two shires. At this he pricked up his ears, and asked if I had been in a certain town in one of those shires, which I had, and saw no reason to say otherwise. Unfortunately this was the town where the guilty man had operated. The detective was certainly not very smart when he took this confession as evidence of guilt, for the guilty man would have mentioned that particular town as one of the last places to visit. I certainly answered to the description of the man wanted, with exception of not having a blotchy face, which had been characteristic of the guilty man. But on my face they saw no blotches, nor signs of any having been there in the past. Of course, I was discharged in an hour, and returned to the lodging house for the night. The following day I happened to be in Dorking, and was walking through that town, when I heard quick steps behind me, and a voice cry - 'Halt: I want you.' Turning my head I saw it was a police officer.

This man at once took possession of me, saying that he fortunately had been looking through the police station window, when he saw me passing, and that I answered to the description of a man wanted—'for that affair at Cheltenham,' I added. 'Ha,' he said, his face lighting with pleasure, 'how well you know.' We returned quietly to the police station, and when I confronted his superior officer, I asked that person if I was to be arrested in every town through which I passed; telling my experience the night before at Guildford. After one or two questions, and a careful reading of the description paper, also an examination of my pedlar's certificate, he told me I was at liberty to go my way, at the same time saying that no man with any sense would have arrested me. After this I was not again troubled by police officers, owing, perhaps, to their having arrested the guilty man.

CHAPTER XXIX

A DAY'S COMPANION

I had many a strange experience in those days, especially one with an old man, who must have been between seventy and eighty years of age. He accosted me through the hedges and, looking in that direction, I saw him in the act of filling a quart can with blackberries, aided by a thick long stick with a crooked end. 'Wait a moment,' said be, 'for I also am going Bedford way.' I was nothing loth to wait, for I was a stranger in that part of the country, and required information as to which was the best cheap lodging house for the night. I knew that in a town of the size of Bedford there must be more than one common lodging house, and one must be better than another, if only in the extra smile of a landlady, regardless of clean blankets or cooking accommodation.

For this reason I waited, and, in less than three minutes, the old man joined me. His answer to my first question was disappointing, for it seemed that the number of lodging houses which Bedford could boast were all public houses, and there was not one private house that catered for beggars. This was a real disappointment, for I knew that whosoever made tea at such a place, did so under the ill favoured glance of a landlady or landlord, perhaps both, who sold beer ready made. In fact the facilities for making tea, cooking, or even washing one's shirt, were extremely limited at such a place, which made it very undesirable for a poor beggar like myself, who had great difficulty in begging sufficient for his bed and board, and did not wish to be reminded of beer.

'Surely,' I said, 'there must be in a town the size of Bedford one private lodging house, at least, to accommodate tramps.'

'Well,' said he, 'as a tramp I have been going in and out of that town for over thirty years, and I never heard of such a place. You can make enquiries, and I should like to know different,' he continued, rather sarcastically that I had doubted his knowledge. 'The two best houses are the "Boot" and the "Cock", but seeing that the former takes in women, the latter I think would be the best for us. Are you going to do business on the road?' he enquired. 'Not today,' I answered him, 'for I have enough for my bed, and an extra few coppers for food.' 'All right,' said he, 'we will travel together, and if I do a little business on the way it won't interfere with you, and we have plenty of time to reach the lodging house before dark.' Having no objection to this proposal we jogged pleasantly along.

We were now descending a steep incline and my companion, seeing a man coming in the opposite direction, walking beside a bicycle, lost no time in confronting that gentleman and pushing the blackberries under his nose. 'No,' said the man, gruffly, 'do you think I am going to

247

carry those things? but here's a copper for you.' Well, thought I, this man will never sell his berries if he does not show more discretion and offer them to more likely customers.

Just after this we met a lady and gentleman, both well dressed and apparently well to do. Touching his cap to these people my companion soon had his blackberries within a few inches of their eyes, at the same time using all his persuasive powers to induce them to make a purchase. In this he failed, as was to be expected, but continued to walk step by step with them for several yards, until the gentleman hastily put his hand in his pocket and gave the old fellow sixpence, the smallest change that he had.

Several others were stopped after this, and although my fellow traveller failed to sell his perishable goods, a number of people assisted him with coppers. In one instance I thought he surely could not be of sound mind, for he had seen a party of ladies and gentlemen seating themselves in a motor car, and was hurrying with all speed in that direction. In this case he failed at getting a hearing, for before he was half way towards them, the party had seated themselves and the car was moving rapidly away. My companion's lips trembled with vexation at seeing this.

'Wait a moment,' said he, crossing the road to a baker's shop—'I am going to exchange these berries for buns.' Waiting outside I was soon joined again by this strange old fellow who then carried in his left hand four buns, his right hand still being in possession of the blackberries.

'You will never sell them,' I said, 'if you do not offer them at more likely places. See, there is a shop with fruit and vegetables: try there.' 'Why,' he answered with a grin, 'how do you think I could make a living if I sold them? The market value of these berries is about one farthing, and it takes sixteen farthings to pay for my feather (bed) not reckoning scrand, (food) and a glass or two of skimish (drink). In fact,' said he, 'my day's work is done, and I am quite satisfied with the result.' Saying which he tumbled the blackberries into the gutter and placed the can—which he used for making tea—into a large self-made inside pocket. On getting a better view of them, I remarked that no person could buy such berries, for they were about the worst assortment I had ever seen in my life. 'It would not pay to make them very enticing,' said he, 'or they would find a too ready sale.' 'But what do you do when the season is over?' I asked, 'for you cannot pick blackberries all the year round.' 'Oh,' he answered, 'I have other ways of making a living. If I can get a good audience in a public house, I can often make a day's living in a quarter of an hour, with several drinks in the bargain.' 'What, by singing or dancing?' I asked. 'No,' said he, 'but by reciting. Listen to this.' With that he began to recite a long poem, line after line, until I began to hope his memory would fail him. What a memory it was! Hundreds of lines without a break. When he came to the most dramatic parts he paused for action, and I knew that he was heedless of the approach of night, and had forgotten that Bedford was still afar off. There was now no stopping him; poem after poem he recited, and he introduced his subjects with little speeches that were so different from his ordinary conversation, that it was apparent that he had committed them also to memory for the benefit of a fit audience. If he was so zealous after a weary day's walk, and without stimulants, what would he be under the influence of several glasses of strong ale? I shuddered to think of it.

We were now about a mile from Bedford, and my companion had for the last hour been reciting; as for myself I was travelling alone, for I had forgotten him. Sometimes to my confusion he would startle me by a sudden question, but seeing that he made no pause for an answer, I soon understood that no answer was required of me, for that he was still reciting.

As we entered the outskirts of Bedford, my companion found it necessary, owing to increase of traffic, to raise his voice, which he continued to do until at last the traffic became so very great that he could not make himself heard. I had not heard his voice for the last five minutes, when he suddenly clutched my shoulder and demanded what I thought of that. 'You have a wonderful memory,' I said. 'Oh,' said he, 'that is nothing; I could entertain you for several days in like manner, with fresh matter each day. Here we are at the Cock. I like your company and, if you are travelling my way tomorrow, let us go together. It is not every man that I would travel with two days in succession.' And, thought I, it is not every man would travel in your company two days in succession. 'Which way are you going?' I asked him. 'Towards Northampton,' said he. 'Alas,' I answered, 'my direction is altogether different.'

We now entered the Cock, and after calling for two glasses of ale, enquired as to accommodation for travellers, which we were informed was good, there being plenty of room. Sometimes, if ale is not called for, they are disinclined to letting beds, especially in the winter, when they find so little difficulty in filling the house.

On entering the kitchen we found it occupied by a number of men, some of whom recognised my fellow traveller, and spoke to him. But, strange to say, although this man had proved so garrulous with one for a companion, with the many he had very little to say, and sat in a corner all through the evening smoking in silence, and paying no heed to others either by tongue, eye, or ear. Once or twice I saw his lips move, when filling his pipe, or knocking out its ashes, and I thought that he was perhaps rehearsing and training his memory for the following day, in case he would be again fortunate in picking up with an easy fool like myself. For, no doubt, the poor old fellow had been often commanded to desist from reciting, and ordered to hell by impatient and unsympathetic men whom he had at first mistaken for quiet and good natured companions. I had not by a look or a word sought to offend him, but one day of his company was certainly enough.

CHAPTER XXX

THE FORTUNE

It is not unusual to read of cases where men who have descended to the lowest forms of labour—aye, even become tramps—being sought and found as heirs to fortunes, left often by people who either had no power to will otherwise, or whom death had taken unawares. Therefore, when one fine morning a cab drove up to a beer-house, which was also a tramps' lodging house, and a well dressed gentleman entered and enquired of the landlord for a man named James Macquire—the landlord at once pronounced him to be a solicitor in quest of a lost heir. 'Sir,' said he, 'we do not take the names of our lodgers, but several are now in the kitchen. James Macquire, you said?' On receiving answer in the affirmation the landlord at once visited the lodgers' kitchen, and standing at the door enquired in a very respectable manner if there was any gentleman present by the name of Macquire, whose christian name was James. At which a delicate looking man, who had arrived the previous night, sprang quickly to his feet and said in a surprised voice—'That is my name.' 'Well,' said the landlord, 'a gentleman wishes to see you at once; he came here in a cab, and, for your sake, I trust my surmises are right.'

With the exception of having on a good clean white shirt, the man Macquire was ill clad, and he looked ruefully at his clothes, and then at the landlord. 'Please ask the gentleman to wait,' said he, and, going to the tap, began to wash his hands and face, after which he carefully combed his hair.

The strange gentleman was seated quietly in the bar when the man Macquire presented himself, and the landlord was engaged in washing glasses and dusting decanters. 'Mr. James Macquire?' asked the gentleman, rising and addressing the ill-clad one in a respectful manner, which the landlord could not help but notice. 'That is my name,' answered Macquire, with some dignity. 'Do you know anything of Mr. Frederick Macquire, of Doggery Hall?' asked the gentleman. 'I do,' said the ill-clad one; and, after a long pause, and seeming to give the information with much reluctance, he added—'Mr. Frederick Macquire, of Doggery Hall, is my uncle.' Several other questions were asked and answered. 'That will do, thank you,' said the gentleman; 'will you please call at the King's Head and see me at seven p.m.? You have been advertised for since the death of Mr. Frederick Macquire, some weeks ago. Good morning,' he said, shaking James Macquire by the hand in a highly respectful manner, as the landlord could not fail to see, totally regardless of the man's rags.

The ill-clad one stood at the bar speechless, apparently absorbed in deep thought. 'What will you have to drink?' asked the landlord kindly. 'Whisky,' answered Macquire, in a faint voice. After drinking this, and another, he seemed to recover his composure, and said to the landlord—'I am at present, as you must know, penniless, and you would greatly oblige me by the loan of a few shillings, say half a sovereign until I draw a couple of hundred pounds in advance. Whatever I receive from you, you shall have a receipt, and, although nothing is said about interest, the amount owing will be doubled, aye trebled, you may rest assured of that, for I never forget a kindness.' 'You had better take a sovereign,' said the landlord, 'and, of course, the Mrs. will supply any meals you may need, and drink is at your disposal.' 'Thank you,' said Macquire, in a choking voice— 'let me have acouple of pots of your best ale for the poor fellows in the kitchen.'

What a surprise for the poor lodgers when they were asked to drink Macquire's health! On being told of his good fortune, they one and all cheered and congratulated him. But the easy way in which this man Macquire threw his weight about the kitchen and, for that matter, the whole house, was extraordinary.

Now it happened that there were at this house two stonemasons who, although heavy drinkers, had been working steady for a week or more, for their job was drawing to a close, and they knew not how many idle weeks might follow. These men were at breakfast and, being repeatedly offered drink, grew careless and resolved to quit work there and then and draw their money, which amounted to three pounds ten shillings between them. Macquire favoured this resolution and, said he, 'Before your money is spent, I shall have a couple of hundred pounds at my disposal.' The landlord was present at the passing of this resolution and, though he said nothing, apparently favoured it, for he laughed pleasantly.

In less than half an hour Macquire and the two stonemasons were back in the lodging house kitchen, and drinking ale as fast as they possibly could. In a number of cases the former received money from his new friends to buy the beer, but, according to after developments he must have pocketed this money and had the beer entered to his account, in addition to that which he fetched of his own accord. However, when evening came Macquire, though seemingly possessed of business faculties, was not in a bodily condition to keep his lawyer's appointment. As he himself confessed—'he was drunk in the legs, but sober in the brain.' What an evening we had! Not one man in the house retired sober, and the kindness of the ill-clad one brought tears into a number of eyes, for he made the stonemasons spend their money freely, and he made the landlord fetch pot after pot, and all he did in the way of payment was to utter that name, grown strangely powerful—James Macquire.

Now when the next morning came there seemed to be a suspicion that all was not right. For, as soon as James Macquire put in an appearance, one of the stonemasons abruptly asked when he intended to see the lawyer. At this moment the landlord entered, and, though he had not heard the question, he too, would like to know when Macquire intended seeing his lawyer. 'Don't bother me,' said Macquire, 'you see what a state I am in, trembling after drink?' 'I'll soon put you right,' said the landlord, leaving the kitchen, and entering the bar.

The stone masons offered their future benefactor a drink of beer, which he waved aside, saying that he must first have a short drink to steady his stomach. 'You don't mind giving me a saucerful of your tea?' said Macquire to me, for I was then at breakfast. 'With pleasure,' said I, and, filling the saucer, pushed it towards him. 'Thank you,' said he, after drinking it—'that saucer of tea has cost me a sovereign!' 'Nonsense,' said I, inwardly pleased, 'it is of no value whatever.' 'Have you any tobacco?' he asked. At this question one of the stonemasons, in fear that Macquire would promise me more money, sprang forward with tobacco. 'I am not asking you for tobacco,' said Macquire slowly—'but am asking this gentleman.' This was said in such a way as could not give offence; as much as to say that he already knew that the stonemason's heart was good, but that he felt disposed to test mine and, if he found it generous, he would not forget me when he came into his estate. Not setting great value on a pipeful of tobacco, I offered him my pouch to help himself. After he had filled his pipe, he said, in an abrupt manner, as he was walking towards the bar— 'Please remember, friend, I am five pounds in your debt.' 'What a fine fellow he is,' said the stonemason to me; 'for the few kindnesses we did him yesterday, he has promised me and my pal twenty pounds each out of his first advance, and larger sums to follow.'

At this moment the postman entered with a letter addressed to James Macquire Esq. If the landlord, or any one else, had the least suspicion earlier in the morning, it certainly vanished at the sight of this letter. Macquire opened the letter and, after reading it, passed it to the landlord. That gentleman's face beamed with satisfaction, although it was but an ordinary note saying that the lawyer had expected Macquire the night previous, and trusted that he would keep the appointment at the same hour on the following day, by which time the lawyer would be able to advance him some money. 'That's something like business,' said Macquire, to which every one agreed, the landlord and the stonemasons showing the most approval.

'Now,' said James Macquire to the landlord, 'you had better let me have some money.' 'What for?' asked that gentleman; 'you can have anything that you require, as I told you before.' 'Just for my own satisfaction,' said Macquire. 'I am going to walkout for a while, so as to keep myself sober for business.' 'You can't go out in those rags,' said the landlord—'you had better take my best suit.'

In ten minutes or less the ill-clad one was standing at the bar in the landlord's best suit of clothes after which the said landlord gave him all the money available, amounting to thirty shillings. 'How much am I in your debt?' asked Macquire. 'Oh, about three pounds,' was the answer. 'We will call it fifty pounds,' cried Macquire and, drinking his whisky, he left the house, followed closely by the faithful stonemasons.

In half an hour the stonemasons were back, having lost their companion in the market place, and were at the bar awaiting him, thinking he might have already returned. Yes, and they could wait, for that was the last of Macquire, and, to the surprise and mortification of the landlord and the two stonemasons, the house received no more visits or letters from lawyers.

CHAPTER XXXI

SOME WAYS OF MAKING A LIVING

No doubt laces are the best stock to carry, for a gross of them can be had for eighteen pence, sometimes less, which, sold at a penny a pair, realises six shillings; and, counting the number of pennies that are tendered free in pity for the man's circumstances, who must be cunning enough to show only two or three pairs at a time - he has nothing to complain of in the end. Although he sometimes meets a lady who persists in regarding him as a trader and bargains for two pairs for three halfpence, and ultimately carries them off in triumph—in spite of his whine of not being able to make bed and board out of them—in spite of these rare instances, he must confess that in the end he has received eight or nine shillings for an outlay of eighteen pence, and, what is more, an abundance of free food. Then, again, laces are light, they are easy to carry and can be stored in one coat-pocket. Another great advantage is that although a man may get wet through, or roll on his laces in the grass, he does not spoil his living. In fact, if they become crumpled and twisted and their tags rusty, he makes them his testimony that he was wet through, being out all night, which story rarely fails in coppers and he still retains his laces.

But with all these advantages of a light and profitable stock, there are two men who scorn to carry even these and will not on any account make any pretence at selling. These two men are the gridler and the downrighter. The former sings hymns in the streets, and he makes his living by the sound of his voice. Professional singers are paid according to the richness, sweetness, and compass of their voices, but the gridler's profit increases as his vocal powers decline. The more shaky and harsh his voice becomes, the greater his reward. With a tongue like a rasp he smoothes the roughness off hard hearts. With a voice like an old hen he ushers in the golden egg. With a base mixture of treble, contralto and bass, he produces good metal which falls from top storey windows, or is thrown from front doors, to drop at his feet with the true ring. Then, if the voice be immaterial, where lies the art of gridling? No more or less than in the selection of hymns, which must be simple and pathetic and familiar to all. Let the gridler supply the words sufficiently to be understood, and the simple air with variations—a good gridler often misses parts of the air itself for breathing spells and in stooping for coppers—let him supply the words, I say, and his hearers will supply the feeling. For instance, if a gridler has sung an old well known hymn fifty or sixty times a day for ten or fifteen years, he cannot reasonably be expected to be affected by the words. It would be extremely thoughtless to request of such a one an encore without giving a promise of further reward. In fact this man is really so weary of song that if there is any merry making at the lodging house, he is the one man who will not sing, not even under the influence of drink; and, what is more, no man would invite him for, being a gridler and earning his living by song, we know well that his voice is spoilt, and that he cannot sing. The gridler considers himself to be at the top of the begging profession, for his stock never gets low, nor requires replenishing; and his voice is only a little weak thing of no weight, the notes of which are born into the world from his throat, and was never roused from sleep in the depths of his chest. There is no strain or effort in giving these notes to the world—despite the gridler's affectations—and he neither grows pale nor red with the exertion.

But the downrighter not only scorns grinders, pedlars, etc., but he even despises the gridler for being a hard worker. 'I', says he, 'do not carry laces, needles, matches, or anything else; and I do not advertise my presence to the police by singing in the streets. If people are not in the front of the house, I seek them at the back, where a gridler's voice may not reach them. I am not satisfied with getting a penny for a farthing pair of laces—I get the whole penny for nothing. People never mistake me for a trader, for I exhibit no wares, and tell them straightforward that I am begging the price of my supper and bed.'

The fact of the matter is that all these men have different ways of making a living, and each man thinks his own way the best and fears to make new experiments, such an opinion being good for the trade of begging. Sometimes, owing to the vigilance of the police, and their strict laws, the gridler has to resort to downright begging, but his heart is not in the business, and he is for that reason unsuccessful. He longs to get in some quiet side street where he can chant slowly his well known hymns. But everything is in favour of the more silent downrighter; who allows nothing to escape him, neither stores, private or public houses, nor pedestrians. All he is required to do is to keep himself looking something like a working man, and he receives more charity in the alehouse by a straightforward appeal as an unemployed workman, than another who wastes his time in giving a song and a dance. People often hurry past when they hear a man singing, or see one approaching with matches or laces, but the downrighter claims their attention before they suspect his business.

When I met Long John at Oxford, we had much talk of the merits of different parts of a beggar's profession. He, it seemed, had carried laces; he had also gridled sacred hymns in the streets, and sung sporting songs in the alehouses; he had even exerted himself as a dancer, 'but,' said he, 'I must confess, after all, that as a downrighter my profits are larger, at the expenditure of far less energy.'

In the course of conversation Long John informed me that he also was travelling London way, and if I was agreeable we would start together on the following morning. 'And,' said he, in a whisper, so that other lodgers might not hear— 'there is a house on our way that is good for a shilling each. He is a very rich man and has been an officer in the army. He pretends to be prejudiced against old soldiers, and when they appeal to him, he first abuses them, after which he drills them and, after abusing them again, rewards each with a two shilling piece. Do you know the drills?' 'No,' I answered, 'I have never been in the army.' 'That is a great pity' said Long John, 'for we lose a shilling each. However, we will not say that we are old soldiers, for fear of losing all, and be satisfied with the two shillings between us.' So it was agreed.

In less than two hours we were at the gentleman's lodge. Passing boldly through the gates we followed the drive until we saw before us a fine large mansion. Reaching the front door we rang the bell, which was soon answered by a servant. To our enquiries as to whether the master was in the servant replied in the negative, but intimated that the mistress was. Of course, this made not the least difference, as many a tramp knew, except that had we been old soldiers the lady not being able to test us by drills would therefore not have given more than the civilian's shilling. Now, almost unfortunately for us, the downrighter, knowing that the lady would not drill us, and thinking that there might be a possibility of getting the master's double pay to old soldiers, without danger of drill or cross examination—suddenly made up his mind to say that we were two old soldiers. For, thought he, if it does no good, it cannot do any harm. Therefore, when the lady appeared smiling at the door Long John, being spokesman, told a straightforward tale of hardship, and added that we had both served our country on the battlefield as soldiers. He had scarcely mentioned the word soldiers when a loud authoritative voice behind us cried—'Shoulder Arms!' I was leaning heavily on a thick stick when this command was given, but lost my balance and almost fell to the ground. We both turned our faces toward the speaker and saw a tall military looking gentleman scrutinising us with two very sharp eyes. Giving us but very little time to compose ourselves he shouted again—'Present Arms'! This second command was no more obeyed than the first. Long John blew his nose, and I stood at ease on my staff, as though I did not care whether the dogs were set upon us or we were to be lodged in jail. After another uncomfortable pause the retired officer said, looking at us severely—'Two old soldiers, indeed! You are two impostors and scoundrels! Perhaps you understand this command'— and in a voice fiercer and louder than ever he cried 'Quick March!' Long John and I, although not old soldiers, certainly understood this command, for we started down the drive at a good pace, with the military looking gentleman following. When we reached the public road, he gave another command —'Halt!' But this was another of those commands which we did not understand. However, on its being repeated less sternly we obeyed. 'Here,' said he, 'you are not two old soldiers, but you may not be altogether scoundrels; and I never turn men away without giving them some assistance.' Saying which he gave us a shilling each. But what a narrow escape we had of being turned penniless away, all through Long John's greed and folly!

CHAPTER XXXII

AT LAST

In spite of these occasional successes with Long John and others, I was often at my wits' ends to procure food and shelter. This always happened when I travelled alone. I was now heartily sick of this wandering from town to town, and every day seemed to get more unfortunate; until the first day in December, when, forced by extreme want, I resolved to enter the city at once, knowing that a pound was already there waiting my pleasure. That night I was back in the Farmhouse; and what a genial spirit seemed to animate the old coke fire! Not at all like the death dealer, the waster of time, who robbed a human being of his energy and a kitten of its play. Oh no; for this one night we were the best of friends, and sunny smiles passed between us until bedtime.

I had been away five months, and would still have to suffer owing to this early return; knowing that I would not have courage to sell in the streets of London, and that I would be compelled to eke out a living on five shillings a week, until the beginning of the new year—this being a half crown for lodgings, and the same for food.

I was very well satisfied with myself at this time, with the prospect of the new year before me; and at once began to get my work ready for the press. When all original composition was done, and it was necessary to make ready a copy for the printer, even at this time I was confronted with a foolish hindrance. One library in Lambeth, which at one time had a table with pens, ink and blotting pads for the convenience of visitors, had had these things removed; but seeing no sign to the contrary, I still thought I would be allowed to take possession of a corner of this table and write, providing I supplied my own material. So, this library was chosen for my week's writing, but I was warned off at the commencement. Thoroughly incensed at this fresh and paltry hindrance, I sought a library where I knew my work could be continued without interference, even if the writing of it took some years. This library was not so convenient as the other, being some distance away, but there I at last succeeded in performing my task.

Now came the new year when, independent of others, I would be enabled to assist myself. If I failed in making success, the disappointment would be mine only, and if I succeeded, there would be none other to thank but myself. On receiving this money, in the first week in January, I lost no time in seeing the printer and arranging for an edition of two hundred and fifty copies, the cost to be nineteen pounds. This amount certainly did not cover expenses, and here began the series of kindnesses which, after a few more disappointments, were to follow. This printer placed the MS. in the hands of a good reader, and that gentleman was put to considerable trouble, being baffled and interested in turns. The last two lines of a poem entitled 'The hill side park' are entirely his, both in thought and expression. I mention this because two or three correspondents liked the poem in question, and one thought the last two lines the best; so, I take this opportunity to clear my conscience. There was nothing to complain of, both printer and reader being at great pains and patience to make the work better than it was. Naturally, I thought if there was any interest shown, it would not be in the author's personality, but in the work itself,—and for this reason, gave the Farmhouse, a common lodging house, as my address. I was under the impression that people would uninterestedly think the Farmhouse to be a small printing establishment, or a small publishing concern of which they had not heard; to which they would forward their orders, and business would be transacted without their being any the wiser. In the first week in March I received my first printed copy.

The printer had sent thirty copies or more to the various papers, and I was now waiting the result, which at last came in the shape of two very slim reviews from the North; a Yorkshire paper saying that the work had rhymes that were neither intricate nor original, and a Scotch paper saying that the work was perfect in craftsmanship rather than inspired. This was very disappointing, more so to know that others, who were powerless to assist me were interesting themselves on my behalf. Although I still had confidence that the work contained some good things, I began to think that there must be some glaring faults which made the book, as a whole, impossible to review. This first thought became my first belief when other notices did not follow.

Weeks and weeks went by and, having now started to drink, and losing control of my will in this disappointment, I had come down to my last ten shillings, and had a good seven months to go before my money was again due. First of all I had serious thoughts of destroying this work—the whole two hundred and odd copies, which were under lock and key in my room, and to then set to work carefully on new matter, and, when my income was again due, to again mortgage it in another attempt. Being very impulsive, this no doubt would have been there and then commenced, had I not been confronted with the difficulty of doing so. There was only one way of doing this properly, and that was by fire, which would require privacy. My room was the only place where I could do this without being seen, but that contained neither stove nor grate; and, even if it had, two hundred books would take a number of sleepless nights to render into ashes. I thought with some bitterness of having to go on tramp again, and it was in one of these bitter moments that I swore a great oath that these copies, good or bad, should maintain me until the end of the year. For I would distribute the books here and there, sending them to successful people, and they would probably pay for their copies, perhaps not so much for what merit they might think the work contained, as for the sake of circumstances. This idea no sooner possessed me than I began preparing for its execution. For this purpose I obtained stamps and envelopes, and six copies were at once posted. The result was seen in a couple of days—three letters, two containing the price of the book, and the third from the Charity Organisation, the latter writing on behalf of a gentleman who had become interested, and would like to come to my assistance.

Remembering these people in the past, through my former experience with them, I had no great hopes at the present time, in spite of the kind hearted interest of the gentleman in question. However, I called on them the next morning, and after the usual long wait in a side room—which, I believe is not through any great stress of business, but so as to bring one's heart down to the freezing point of abject misery, and to extinguish one by one his many hopes—after this weary waiting, I received an interview.

There is not sufficient venom in my disposition to allow me to describe this meeting in words fit and bitter for its need. This life is too short to enable me to recover from my astonishment, which will fill me for a good many years to come. The questions and answers which had passed between us on our former interview—two years previous, were now before them. But they questioned again in the same strain, and my answers corresponded with those of the past, for I told no lies. Apparently they had no chance here, so they came at once to the business in hand. 'You have written to a gentleman, asking for his assistance?' Not liking this way of explaining my conduct, I said—'No, not exactly that, but have been trying to sell him some work that I had done.' It seemed that they knew nothing of this work—or that it better suited their purpose to appear ignorant—so it was necessary to give them the full particulars. 'Was not the book a success?' they asked. Not caring to admit failure, and still thinking the work worthy of a little success, I answered—'Not yet, but it is too early to judge it as a failure.' Then I gave it in confidence that a gentleman, well known in Southwark, and who often wrote articles on literary subjects, had promised to review it in one of the evening papers, which might lead to other notices. 'What is the name of this gentleman?' The name was at once mentioned, for there was no reason that I knew of, to, withhold it. But instead of this name doing me good, as I then expected, it probably made this case of mine more unfavourable; for I have been told since that this gentleman had more than once attacked the ways and methods of this organisation, both on the public platform and through the press. Not knowing this, at that time, I thought it extremely fortunate to be enabled to mention the favour of such a well known local man.

All went smoothly for a while—although I could plainly see that these people did not recognise the writing of books as work, and were plainly disgusted at the folly of sacrificing an income to that end. Their next question confirmed this opinion—'Do you ever do anything for a living?' I mentioned that I had tramped the country as a hawker, during the previous summer, but had suffered through want of courage, could not make anything like a living, and was often in want and without shelter. There was a rather long pause, and the Charity Organisation rose slowly to their feet, and said, 'Mr. Davies, do you really expect this gentleman, who has written to us, to maintain you? Is there anything the matter with you?' What was the matter with me did not seem to escape many people, and it was most certainly noted by the smallest toddler that played in the street, but the Charity Organisation did not think proper to recognise any other than an able man, strong in the use of all his limbs. 'No,' said these people, 'you must do the same as you did last summer'; which, in other words was—go on tramp, starve, and be shelterless as you were before. And then in the deep silence which followed, for I was speechless with indignation, a voice soft and low, but emphatic and significant, said—'We strongly advise you to do this, but you really must not write any more begging letters. Mr. Davies, we do not consider ourselves justified in putting your case before the committee.' That ended the interview, and I left them with the one sarcastic remark, which I could not keep unsaid, 'that I had not come there with any great hopes of receiving benefit, and that I was not leaving greatly disappointed at this result.'

These people passed judgment in a few minutes, and were so confident that they did not think it worth while to call at the Farmhouse for the opinion of a man who had known me for a considerable time. No doubt they had made another mistake. For, some time before this, an old pensioner, an old lodger of the Farmhouse, had interviewed these people, telling them a story of poverty, and of starving wife and children. The story was a fabrication from beginning to end, yet they assisted this man on his bare word to the extent of ten shillings, so as to enable him to lie about the Farmhouse drunk for several days. Then, some days after this, the Charity Organisation called at the Farmhouse to see the manager, and to make enquiries of this man whom they had so mysteriously befriended. 'What,' cried that gentleman, 'You have assisted this drunken fellow on his bare word, and when I send cases to you, that I know are deserving, you sternly refuse to entertain them.' Perhaps it was this instance, fresh in their minds, which gave them an idea that no good could come out of the Farmhouse. Yet, as far as my experience goes, the object of these people was not so much to do good, but to prevent good from being done; for here, for the second time, they stepped between me and one who might have rendered me some aid.

What I found the most distasteful part of their system was the way in which they conceal the name of a would-be benefactor. I had sent six books, three to men and three to women. One man had replied with a kind encouraging letter and the price of the book enclosed, and one of the two others had written to the Organisation, but, on no account, would they mention his name. Now, when these people answer a letter of enquiry, they have no other option than to say one of two things— either that the applicant is an impostor, and deserves no notice, or that the case is genuine and deserving consideration. They, of course, answered in the former strain, withholding the gentleman's name, so as to leave no opportunity to vindicate one's character.

The interference of these people put me on my mettle, and I was determined not to follow their advice and tramp through another hard winter. I had something like three shillings, at the time of this interview; so, buying two shillings' worth of stamps, I posted a dozen books that very night, being still warm with resentment. The result of these were four kind letters, each containing the price of the book. Only one or two were returned to me, whether purchased or not, which was done at my own wish. Before I again became penniless, off went another dozen. In this way I disposed of some sixty copies, with more or less success; some of these well known people receiving the book as an unacknowledged gift, and others quickly forwarding the price of the same. The strangest part of this experience was this: that people, from whom I expected sympathy, having seen their names so often mentioned as champions of unfortunate cases, received the book as a gift; whist others, from whom I had less hope, because they appeared sarcastic and unfeeling in their writings, returned the price of the work. The Manager was astonished at my receiving no answer from two or three well known people whom he had recommended. At last, after disposing of sixty copies in this way, two well known writers corresponded with me, one of whom I saw personally, and they both promised to do something, through the press. Relying on these promises, I sent away no more copies, being enabled to wait a week or two owing to the kindness of a playwriter, an Irishman, as to whose mental qualification the world is divided, but whose heart is unquestionably great. Private recognition was certainly not long forthcoming, which was soon followed by a notice in a leading daily paper, and in a literary paper of the same week. These led to others, to interviews and a kindness that more than made amends for past indifference. It was all like a dream. In my most conceited moments I had not expected such an amount of praise, and they gathered in favour as they came, until one wave came stronger than the others and threw me breathless of all conceit, for I felt myself unworthy of it, and of the wonderful sea on which I had embarked. Sleep was out of the question, and new work was impossible.

What surprised me agreeably was the reticence of my fellow lodgers, who all knew, but mentioned nothing in my hearing that was in any way disconcerting. They were, perhaps, a little less familiar, but showed not the least disrespect in their reserve, as would most certainly have been the case if I had succeeded to a peerage or an immense fortune. The lines on Irish Tim, which were several times quoted, were a continual worry to me, thinking some of the more waggish lodgers would bring them to his notice. Poor Tim, no doubt. would have sulked, resenting this publicity, but, if the truth were known, I would as soon do Tim a good turn as any other man in the Farmhouse. Boozy Bob, I suppose, had been shown his name in print; but Bob thought it a great honour to be called Boozy; so, when he stood drunk before me, with his face beaming with smiles of gratitude for making use of his name, at the same time saying—'Good evening, Mr. Davies, how are you?'—I at once understood the meaning of this unusual civility, and we both fell a-laughing, but nothing more was said. What a lot of decent honest fellows these were: 'You must not be surprised,' said a gentleman to me, at that time, 'to meet less sincere men than these in other walks of life.' I shall consider myself fortunate in not doing so.

CHAPTER XXXIII

SUCCESS

However much cause I may have at some future date to complain of severe criticism, I have certainly no complaint up to the present against any connected with the making of books. Some half a dozen lines of work, were submitted to publishers, and three times I received letters with a view to publication, which, of course, failed through the want of friends to assist me. Knowing how rough and unequal the work was, and that critics could find—if so inclined—plenty to justify extreme severity, has undeceived me as to my former unreasonable opinion, that critics were more prone to cavil than to praise. I would like it to be understood that I say this without bidding for any future indulgence; for I am thankful to any man who will show me my faults, and am always open to advice.

As I have said, the first notice appeared in a leading daily paper, a full column in which I saw myself described, a rough sketch of the ups and downs of my life, in short telling sentences, with quotations from my work. The effect of this was almost instantaneous, for correspondence immediately followed. Letters came by every post. Of course, all my thoughts had been concentrated on the reading world, so that I was much surprised when two young men came to the house and requested a photo for an illustrated paper. I could not oblige them at that moment, but with a heart overflowing with gratitude was persuaded to accompany them at once to the nearest photographer, now that interest was at its high point. 'Now,' said one of these young men, when I was on my way with them, delighted with this mission—'now, if you could give me a few lines on the war in the East, to go with your photograph, it would be of much greater interest to the public.' Not caring to blow the froth off my mind in this indifferent manner, and feeling too conscientious to take advantage of public interest by writing in such haste, which, to tell the truth, appeared a difficult task—I quickly turned the subject to other matters, thinking he would soon forget this request. But it was of no use; for, every other step or two, he wanted to be informed whether I was concentrating my mind on the war. At last, being under the impression that my natural reserve and feeble attempts at conversation would lead him to believe that something was being done in that direction, I made a great effort to become voluble, and, I believe, succeeded until the photograph was taken. When I left him, his last question was—'What about the war?'

The next morning, after the last mentioned episode, being Sunday, I was enjoying a stroll through the city, which is so very quiet on this one morning of the week; and was thinking of nothing else but my own affairs, more especially of the photo that was soon to appear. The street was forsaken, with the exception—yes, there they were: two men with a camera, and both of them looking my way, anxiously awaiting my approach. 'This,' I said to myself, 'is fame with a vengeance.' I felt a little mortification at being expected to undergo this operation in the public streets. One of these photographers quickly stepped forward to meet me, and, smiling blandly, requested me kindly to stand for a moment where I was. It certainly shocked and mortified me more to learn that they desired to photograph an old fashioned dwelling of brick and mortar, and that they considered my presence as no adornment to the front.

A few days after this first review, a critic of fine literature, who had interested himself privately on my behalf, sent a notice to a weekly literary paper; and it was the respect due to this man's name that drew the attention of some other papers of good standing, for their representatives mentioned this man's name with every respect, knowing, at the same time, that he would not waste his hours on what was absolutely worthless.

What kind hearted correspondents I had, and what offers they made, what questions they asked! and all of them received grateful answers—with one exception. This gentleman who did not require a book, presumably being more interested in the strange conditions under which I had lived and worked, offered me a pleasant home in the country, where I could cultivate my talents surrounded with a little more comfort and quieter scenes. The letter was long, delightful, poetical, and worked warmly on my imagination, sentence for sentence; until the last sentence came like a douche of cold water on a warm body—'Of course,' finished

276

this gentleman, 'it is necessary to supply me with strict references as to honesty and respectability.' Where was I to get these. after having failed to get a library form signed, which would entitle me to borrow books? No doubt the manager of the Farmhouse would have willingly done the latter, as was afterwards done by him, but I was then under the impression that the keeper of a lodging house was ineligible for such a purpose, knowing this to have been the case elsewhere. Where could I obtain these references, seeing that I knew no one who would take the responsibility of doing such a petty kindness as signing a library form? This gentleman's letter, I need scarcely say, remained unanswered, for which, I believe, none will blame me.

Several other letters were received, which I found extremely difficult to answer. One addressed me familiarly in rhyme, beginning 'Dear brother poet, brother Will'; and went on to propose that we two should take a firm stand together, side by side, to the everlasting benefit of poetry and posterity.

Another had written verse, and would be glad to find a publisher, and another could, and would, do me many a good turn, if I felt inclined to correct his work, and to add lines here and there as needed. Not for a moment would I hold these people to ridicule, but it brought to mind that I was without a publisher for my own work, and I believed, in all sincerity, that better work than mine might go begging, as it often had.

In the main my correspondents were kind, sympathetic and sensible, making genuine offers of assistance, for which I thanked them with all my heart, but thought myself now beyond the necessity of accepting them.

As a matter of fact, no one man in a common lodging house is supposed to be regarded with any special favour. The common kitchen is his library, his dining room and his parlour, and better accommodation cannot be expected at the low price of four pence per night. We are all equal, without a question of what a man's past may have been, or what his future is likely to realise. Any man who puts on superior airs is invariably subjected to this sarcastic enquiry —'How much do you pay?' or the incontrovertible remark that one man's fourpence is as good as another's. The Manager has to use great tact in not indulging in too long a conversation with one particular man, and a lodger must not jeopardise his popularity by an overwhelming anxiety to exchange civilities, or to repose confidence in those who are in authority; for these lodgers are in general distrustful and suspicious. If a fish porter—a good number of these men were here—was warned after any misconduct, he would turn to one of his pals and say—'Billingsgate, I see, is not favoured in this place.' And if a paper-seller—of which there were about an equal number—was called to account in the same way, his remark would be that had he been a fish porter the misconduct would have been overlooked. Such was the state of feeling in the Farmhouse, although the caretaker, time after time, almost daily, reiterated the remark that one man was as good as another, and that at no distinction was made between the two classes. Knowing this state of feeling, and the childlike distrust and jealousy of these honest fellows, it was no wonder that I felt a little awkward at the change of circumstances; for, after all I was still a lodger, and paying no more than them for the same conveniences. In spite of this, I don't believe I suffered the least in popularity when the Manager, determined that I should not suffer any longer for want of privacy to pursue my aim, threw open his own private rooms for my convenience. And, every time I took advantage of his kindness, the Manager's wife would take advantage of this by supplying a hot dinner or tea, as the hour might be, so that my studies might not be interrupted, or food postponed through in anxiety to perform a certain task.

The Manager was astonished at my success, and, after he had read several notices, it certainly must have made him bitter against those whom he had approached on my behalf. 'Yes.' he said, 'I must confess to failure, in your case, and I am left wondering as to what kind of cases these people consider worthy of assistance.' The man, being in a subordinate position, dare not openly speak his thoughts, or appear to force the hands of those rich visitors, but he certainly lost no opportunity in showing some honest Irish blood in his references to the Charity Organisation. 'Miss So and So has been here,' said he, one morning; 'and I lost no time in relating your experience with the Charity Organisation. She was very much offended and shocked, and she has now gone there to seek some explanation.' 'As for that,' I answered, knowing these people had all the power to make good their own case, and that I would not be called upon to sift the false from the true—'As for that, this lady will return satisfied, as you will see.' The Manager did not altogether believe this, saying that he thought the lady in question was not a blind believer in anything, and had an unusual amount of common sense. She certainly did return satisfied, saying that she thought they were justified in their conduct, to a certain extent. On being questioned by the

Manager, who claimed it justice that the truth should be known, she said that she dare not make public the sayings and doings of the Society.

I am now giving my experiences honestly and truthfully, and thought for thought, if not word for word, as they happened. As a man whose ambition above an other things is to impress every one favourably, I have come to the conclusion that my work has been praised far more than its worth, owing to having met the writers of some of those articles, and impressing them in a simple, honest way. I am writing these experiences with a full knowledge of human nature, knowing that many people will remark: 'Take no heed of that man, for he has not a good word for anyone or anything'; but, as far as my knowledge and experience goes it is the truth, and, if that seems false and sensational, it is no fault of mine. Certainly I have led a worthless, wandering and lazy life, with, in my early days, a strong dislike to continued labour, and incapacitated from the same in later years. No person seemed inclined to start me on the road to fame, but, as soon as I had made an audacious step or two, I was taken up, passed quickly on from stage to stage, and given free rides farther than I expected.

CHAPTER XXXIV

A HOUSE TO LET

Apparently the ill luck which had pursued me so close in the past, would not let me escape without another scratch. In my pleasant walks in my native town, my eye happened to fall on a beautiful house, untenanted in a neighbourhood so quiet that every other house seemed to be the same. The very name, Woodland Road, was an address for a poet. It was a four storied villa, standing on the top of a hilly road, from where one could see on a clear mistless day the meeting of the Severn and the Bristol Channel; and, looking in another direction, could see the whole town without hearing one of its many voices. Unfortunately, I coveted this house as a tenant, thinking to get more pleasure in one glance from its top window on a bright summer's morning than from the perusal of many books. Even now, in Winter, it presented a warm, comfortable appearance, with its evergreens and its ivied walls. A tall spreading rose bush stood facing its lowest window, and I imagined the bashful red roses looking in at me, as though I would not come out of doors to please them. There were primrose leaves green on the rockery, and one yellow flower still good, withered and bent, in this last week of November. There was also an apple tree and a pear tree, so that the front of the house was both a park and an orchard. Blackbirds, robins, and thrushes visited the grounds daily, and I believe that this house was their nearest approach to town. It only wanted a few touches of Spring, and here were shady nooks, and leafy boughs for birds to sing unseeing and unseen. Thinking that this beautiful place would not remain untenanted for long, I at once made application, being recommended by my old master of the days of my apprenticeship. Had I known that the house was always empty and untenanted, and that people came and went at short notice, I should certainly not have been in such a hurry to take possession, in spite of its natural beauties. It was neither haunted by ghosts nor animal noises, but by the landlady, who lived in the next house. This lady I did not see, nor have I seen her up to the present time, one of my family having taken the place in my name. Probably if I had transacted business personally, and had had an opportunity of seeing this landlady's face, I had not coveted the house, and, according to a right judgment of human nature, would have saved myself the money and disappointment that was to follow. However, the house became mine, and I received the key which was to let me possess this house and its interesting grounds.

I idled a week about town descanting with great pleasure on the beauties of my future home; but I was somewhat taken by surprise at the unfavourable reception with which my news was received. 'Who is the landlady?' asked one.

'Mrs. S.' I answered; 'she lives next door.' 'It is very unfortunate,' said this person, 'that the landlady lives next door.' 'Everyone can please themselves,' said another, 'but as for myself, I would never dream of living next door to my landlady.' 'What!' cried another, 'the landlady lives next door? What a great pity to be sure.' Although the last named depreciator was the respectable wife of a retired tradesman, and had given her own landlady satisfaction for a number of years; in spite of this, I was highly amused at these remarks, taking the uncharitable view that these people were really not so respectable as they seemed, and would not be allowed to live under the watchful eyes of a particular person. My landlady, I thought, be she ever so watchful, dare not interfere without some cause; and, as the house must needs be kept very quiet for my own purpose of study, noises that are not allowed to reach me in the same house, surely will not be able to reach the house next door.

The eventful day arrived, and I gathered together my small family, one from her limited possession of two small rooms, being very pleased to have me with her, which could not otherwise have been. At last we were in full possession, and at once proceeded to arrange furniture, and to make the house comfortable. On the second day I began to work in earnest, having been unsettled and indisposed for several weeks. When I came downstairs to dinner, on this second day, I was informed that the landlady had already been there to say that she objected to us keeping animals. On being told there was not the least intention of doing the same, she said that she certainly thought such was our intention, seeing that we were in possession of wood, and that she strongly objected to any other than that which could be kept indoors. The wood, which had caused all this suspicion, was simply a clothes prop and three shelves which had not yet been removed from where they were first placed. I laughed heartily at this unwarranted interference, but the feminine portion of the family strongly resented it.

The third day I continued my work, the others again working on the comfort of this large house; one being outside trimming the evergreens, and taking a general pride in our half orchard and half park. Ditto the third day, and so on day after day, until the rent became due. This was the first time for me to take a personal hand in my affairs, and, when the agent called, I thought it more business like to put in an appearance, for the first rent day, at least, seeing that the house was in my name, after which others might attend to it. I paid the rent, 9s. 6d.—the house, as I havesaid, was a fine large villa, and was really worth fifteen or sixteen shillings a week; and this small amount demanded for it, was a mystery at which any sensible person would have sniffed. This agent then gave me a book, with the rent entered to my account. After this he handed me a letter, which, said he, was sent from the office. Not dreaming of its contents, I there and then opened this letter, and to my astonishment saw that it was a notice to quit within one week of that date, at the orders of Messrs. H. and B., her solicitors. This notice was a severe blow, for, up till then, the place had been unsettled, and we had only been enjoying the expectation of future comfort. 'Who, or what does this lady object to?' I asked the agent, with some bitterness. 'I need absolute quiet for my work, and the amount I have done in the past week proves that I have had it. What then has disturbed my landlady, that has not interfered with my work? To make a person suffer the expense, and worse, the worry of moving twice in a few days, should not be done without due consideration, and some definite reason.' But the agent knew or pretended to know nothing of the affair, and he left me at the door, feeling more shame and mortification that I have ever felt before. There was nothing else to do but to pack up again as soon as possible and to seek fresh quarters, which, after great difficulty, were found.

To think that I have lived thirty five years, and not to have known the folly and ill policy of living next door to one's landlady! But this particular landlady is eccentric, can afford to be independent, and I verily believe she would not sell a house for even twice its worth if she thought the would-be purchaser to be a man incapable of taking charge of property. Her house is more often unoccupied than let, as I have since been told, for the most respectable people cannot live near her. Apparently this is the case, for the house was still empty several weeks after I had quit, in spite of its unreasonably low rent and the beauty of its surroundings.

A robin came to the back door every morning and was fed. Perhaps this time wasted on the robin might have been better employed in winning the good graces of the landlady.

What a pity such an eccentric person should have such power to receive people as tenants for a few days, and then to dismiss them without warning or giving any definite reason. And what a harvest her idiosyncrasies must be to her solicitors. They even followed me up and demanded another week's rent, after the expense of moving to the top of a high hill and down again, which, up to the present, I have not paid. A lawyer would certainly be a lucky man to be allowed control over the interests of half a dozen such clients, and he could dress his wife and daughters in silk, and thoroughly educate his sons on his makings. I have been told that she is a deeply religious woman. Therefore, although she said in her own heart—'on no account can these people live in a villa of mine,' she must have prayed that room would be reserved for us in the many mansions above.

This chapter should justify itself for the sake of the worldly wisdom contained in the simple words—'Never live in a house next door to your landlady or landlord'; which deserves to become a proverb. Many people might not consider this warning necessary, but the hint may be useful to poor travellers like myself who, sick of wandering, would settle down to the peace and quiet of after days.

Such has been my life, rolling unseen and unnoted, like a dark planet among the bright, and at last emitting a few rays of its own to show its whereabouts, which were kindly received by many and objected to by a few, among the latter being my late landlady.

Perhaps I am deceived as to the worth or worthlessness of certain people, but I have given my experience of them without exaggeration, describing as near as memory makes it possible, things exactly as they occurred. I have made no effort to conceal my gratitude for those who have befriended me, and I have made every effort to conceal bitterness against enemies. If I have not succeeded in the latter it is with regret, but if I have failed in the former, for that I am more truly and deeply sorry. If I have appeared ignorant of certain matters I claim exception from sin through a lack of prejudice which is, after all, the only ignorance that can be honestly named with sin.

These have been my experiences; and if I have not omitted to mention trouble of my own making, for which no one but myself was to blame, why should I omit the mention of others, whom I blame for hours more bitter? People are not to be blamed for their doubts, but that they make no effort to arrive at the truth. However much people of a higher standing may doubt the veracity of certain matters. I have the one consolation to know that many a poor man, who is without talent or means to make his experiences public, knows what I have written to be the truth. It is but a poor consolation, for such a one is the sufferer, and not the supporter, and he is powerless in the hands of a stronger body.

A NOTE

The Poet Davies, William

> I am the Poet Davies, William,
> I sin without a blush or blink:
> I am a man that lives to eat;
> I am a man that lives to drink.
>
> W.H.Davies, 'I am the Poet Davies, William'

William Henry Davies was born in Newport, Monmouthshire, in 1871, and it is here that *The Autobiography of a Super-Tramp* opens (p. 1). Davies died, at the age of sixty-nine, in the Gloucestershire village of Nailsworth, where he had settled in later life and which he remarked was near to, but still outside, Wales. A life that begins in the South Eastern county of Wales, and quickly moves out to a wider world beyond, ends in a South Western county of England, looking back towards home turf. *The Autobiography of a Super-Tramp* is a book structured by Davies's wanderlust, and it is this sense of movement and mobility, despite the encumbrance of a maimed leg, which affords Davies's super-tramp persona a unique if disquieting perspective on the societies around which he moves.

The turn of the twentieth century saw the publication of a number of works which celebrated the Welsh homestead as a locus of national identity, of belonging and affiliation, of shared tradition and historical continuity. For example, Owen M. Edwards's *Cartrefi Cymru* ('The Homes of Wales', 1896), Davies's friend Edward Thomas's *Beautiful Wales* (1905), and *Teulu Bach Nantoer* ('The Little Family of Nantoer', 1913) by 'Moelona' (Elisabeth Mary Jones) all in various ways posit the domestic hearth as the focal-point of national character.[i] Set against this context, Davies's work, including *The Autobiography of a Super-Tramp*, is quite literally a departure. His first collection, *The Soul's Destroyer*, is the book which he struggled to bring into print – a struggle described in the latter sections of *Super-Tramp*. The title poem opens in a London slum before moving back to Wales; warning against the perils of alcoholism, the Soul's Destroyer of the title, the poem recasts the Welsh homestead not as a site of harmony and rootedness, but rather as a space of drunkenness and domestic abuse. In *The Autobiography of a Super-Tramp*, the Welsh matriarch, Davies's god-fearing and theatre-despising grandmother, is left behind and home is a place to which there can be no return. Instead, the text shows how the 'incorrigible Super-tramp' (to quote from George Bernard Shaw's preface) finds himself time and again in marginalised or liminal positions: criss-crossing the Atlantic; on the banks of rivers and canals; on top of or underneath railway carriages, or indeed on the wrong side of the tracks; feverish and hallucinating in swampland; in doss-houses and tramp colonies. A sense of the pull and push of modernity finds Davies orbiting the city, 'on the outskirts of London, walking it round in a circle; sometimes ten miles from its mighty heart, or as far distant as twenty miles; but without the courage to approach nearer, or to break away from it altogether' (p. 209). From these mobile and marginal vantage points, the super-tramp offers a unique perspective on the emergent modern world.

Over the course of his career Davies would attempt other kinds of life writing or autobiography inflected by his time on the road; aside from *The Autobiography of a Super-Tramp*, he published the volumes *Beggars* (1909), *The True Traveller* (1912), *A Poet's Pilgrimage* (1918), *Later Days* (1925), and *The Adventures of Johnny Walker, Tramp* (1926). Nonetheless, as Davies's biographers have noted, it is problematic to think of them as round unvarnished accounts of his life on the road. In print as well as in the flesh, he seems to cover his tracks, and though their basis lies in the author's lived experience, his accounts of life on the road are unreliable and self-mythologising. There are several indications of how *The Autobiography of a Super-Tramp* is a work of myth-making. There is, for example, the title, suggested by George Bernard Shaw. Shaw's play *Man and Superman* had first been performed – minus the Third Act, 'Don Juan in Hell' – in 1905, and he had been an early champion of Davies's work and the author of the preface to *The Autobiography of a Super-Tramp*. Shaw's own title derived from Friedrich Nietzsche's figure of the *Übermensch*, or 'Super-Man', described in *Thus Spoke Zarathustra* (1883). The super-man is a figure of some conjecture among Nietzsche's readers, but is generally regarded as an extraordinary and superior individual whose outlook and morality transcend that of his society. While portraying himself as the super-tramp distances Davies from the more earthy and illicit sections of the text, the prefix also carries with it the suggestion that it is not the super-man but the figure of the tramp who, unexpectedly, is able to transcend or circumvent the values and conventional codes of his society.

America: 'an ideal place for tramps'

The super-tramp's comment on modernity, and the societies in which he finds himself, are frequently associated with his mobility – the way he moves and the places to which he moves. On first impressions, the tramp threatens and challenges the prevailing ideas of a society predicated upon stability, rootedness and commitment. Yet, simultaneously and particularly in the American context, the movements and mobilities of the tramp are in many ways entirely compatible with the independence, resourcefulness and enterprise which underpin a modern industrial capitalist order. The *New York Times* was quick to identify this as a feature of the book, remarking that in *The Autobiography of a Super-Tramp* Davies

> is perhaps more friendly to the United States and its people than any English [sic] author who ever visited us.
> He found the people generous and the climate pleasant; he considers the United States an ideal place for tramps.

And this is higher praise than many British novelists of our day would give us.[ii]

These words are taken from the *New York Times*'s 1917 review of the first American edition of *The Autobiography of a Super-Tramp*. It would take until the report of Davies's death in September 1940 for the paper to correctly identify his nationality, describing him as 'William H. Davies: Welsh Hobo Poet'.[iii] Despite its initial misattribution, the reviewer makes a perceptive observation in pointing to the inter-relationship between the United States and the figure of the tramp. The *New York Times* is drawn to the book not only for what Davies recounts of his own picaresque adventures around the country, but also for what the *Autobiography* relates and reveals about America itself: the tramp moves differently, and sees differently, and because of this is able to offer a new perspective on his host society.

In this regard it is unsurprising to see that the *New York Times* approves Davies's notion that America is the 'ideal place for tramps'. There is more to this than the simple question of hospitality and welcome; it points to a much more significant connection between the United States and the figure of the tramp, or hobo. The tramp is in many ways a peculiarly American figure. The aftermath of the Civil War in 1865 returned many thousands of men to society who had in their soldiering days acquired a host of skills which made them well-adapted to life on the road: mobility, resourcefulness, independence, a streetwise savvy in the ability to find food and shelter. 'Tramp' as a category of identity comes into being at this post-war moment; shifting from a verb meaning a long, tiresome march (such as those undertaken by columns of soldiers), 'tramp' becomes a noun referring to an itinerant or vagrant person.

Given that the category of tramp and the American nation are twinned at birth, it is no coincidence that Davies's first experiences as a tramp are on the road in the United States. Following the death of his grandmother in Newport, and malcontent after 'a month or two of restlessness' at home with his mother and her new husband, Davies's wanderlust takes hold: 'full of hope and expectation' (p. 18) he embarks for America. Arrived at Liverpool and awaiting his first Atlantic crossing, Davies remarks how he is struck by the 'extraordinary description' he is given, citing on the one hand the modernity of America's skyscrapers and engineering triumphs, and on the other the rural beauty of her prairies and countryside. Its vastness and variety clearly appeal to the aspiring tramp: 'the loneliness of its prairies and deserts; engineering triumphs over high mountains; and how the glorious South was flushed with roses what time the North could not save a blade of green from the snow; all this happening under the one wide spreading flag' (pp. 19-20). Davies himself is witness to the coming of the modern America he finds so alluring: in Chapter Thirteen, 'The Canal', he describes witnessing the building of the Chicago Sanitary and Ship Canal, a major engineering project providing that city with trade links and sanitation. There, on the banks, alongside the 'riff-raff of America and the scum of Europe' (p. 100), stands the super-tramp, just alongside the outgoing excreta and the incoming wealth: it seems a particularly apposite indication of the position of the tramp in the landscape of modernity.

A similarly impressive feature of the infrastructure which enabled the collapsing of time and space, and the movement of people and goods around the country, was the American railway, and the tramp is to be found here too. No doubt Davies had the railways in mind when he mentioned the 'engineering triumphs over high mountains'; it truly was the begetting force which characterised the new mobility – economic and geographical – in American society. As with the Chicago canal, the tramp again occupies an ambiguous position: he is mobile not because he is ensconced in the carriages, riding on board. Instead, Davies's super-tramp 'rides the rods' underneath the boxcar, or 'rides the bumpers' above. In what is likely the most famous episode in the text – Chapter Nineteen, 'A Voice in the Dark' – Davies demonstrates that the coming of mechanised, industrial capitalism is ruthless and dangerous as well as exhilarating, always evading the tramp's grasp or, worse, maiming him as it passes 'swiftly on into the darkness' (p. 158). (The violent potential of mechanised industrial capitalism is similarly foisted on to the body of the tramp for comic effect in Charlie Chaplin's 1936 masterpiece, *Modern Times*, as the Little Tramp is pulled literally into the cogs of the machine.)

Davies is witness to other forms of violence on the road. His journey through the Southern States of America brings him face to face with inter-racial violence between white and black Americans, and on these occasions, the ugliness of his response is startling. Indeed, his racism is all the more shocking given his shrewdness elsewhere in observing social inequalities and the hypocrisy of individuals and institutions in positions of social authority. Davies is attuned to the difficulties and contradictions of America after slavery: he notes the 'strange contrast' between black Americans of different generations, with the elders remembering being slaves in their youth while those of the younger generation are cowed in a 'half defiant gloom [...] still in some respects slaves to the white men' (p. 117). Later, Davies recounts the economic paradoxes of a situation in which black people felt themselves materially worse off as free men.

Yet when Davies's attention shifts from these economic and material perspectives, his response becomes baser. He finds the black men he encounters on the road 'insulting and arrogant', lacking the 'truer courage' of white men (p. 110). His account of the lynching in Chapter Fifteen is an appalling description of the brutal execution of a black prisoner forcibly extracted from jail and shot while hanging from a tree. Confessing that the scene 'dried in me the milk of human kindness', Davies notes with approval how the vigilantes conducted their heinous act while at the same time showing contempt for the 'cowardice' of the terrified prisoner. Davies's biographer Lawrence Normand has noted how he seems to have accepted at face value the racist stereotypes of black Americans so current in the Southern States in the early twentieth century.[iv] Davies fails to query the way in which the press is instrumental in generating negative stereotypes and prejudicial discourses. In a later book, *A Poet's Pilgrimage* (1918), he describes hearing a verse from an American 'coon song' (a popular racist genre promulgating images of black identity as libidinal or minstrel-like) sung in a Newport tavern. Later in the *Autobiography* he is similarly fascinated by the grim memento mori of the shrivelled heart of a black man lynched for supposed child murder.

Davies is not the only writer of the twentieth century to find himself uncomfortably fascinated by the question of racial and ethnic otherness, and to reveal a morbid curiosity in the 'savage' or the 'primitive'. Joseph Conrad's *Heart of Darkness* (1899) indicated that colonial narratives of expansion and progress were only a thin veneer to a barbarism that lurked beneath, and that the 'modern' and the 'primitive' were barely distinguishable. The paintings of Henri Matisse and Pablo Picasso and the music of Igor Stravinsky similarly share a fascination with primitivism as an at-once compelling and repellent counterpoint to European civilization. Furthermore, like Conrad, Matisse, Picasso and Stravinsky (in a list that could extend to include a whole swath of eminent modernist artists), W.H. Davies's super-tramp is an exile, a transient, dislocated figure stranded outside his home culture. As a consequence, he is forced to confront a crisis of identity – the problems of belonging and not belonging – no doubt heightened by a life on the road. *The Autobiography of a Super-Tramp* is a document of a unique encounter with modernity in all its forms; however, on this point it clearly lacks the discourse and the vocabulary to account for racial and ethnic difference. A difficult consequence of the book's wanderlust, therefore, is the nastiness of its responses to new experiences on new horizons.

'A wooden leg – or was it a cloven hoof?'

Gwyn Jones's seminal critical interpretation of 'Anglo-Welsh literature', *The First Forty Years*, finds little space for W.H. Davies. He notes with tongue in cheek that Davies had a 'nice' side made up of poems which celebrated 'cows and flowers and *hiraeth* for the sweet days that have been, with a lot of Welsh place-names in them'. Meanwhile, 'on the occasions when he wasn't nice, well, he was half-English, wasn't he? and had a wooden leg – or was it a cloven hoof? into the bargain'.[v] However ironically, Jones links Davies's Welshness to his quainter voice – bucolic, pastoral, safe. The more dangerous aspects are distanced, attributable to his 'half-English' status.

Caradoc Evans, ever the contrarian, took a different view. In an article in the *Western Mail* in January 1916 he described Davies as 'this Welsh poet who sings of the heart of the drunkard and the soul of little children, of the temptation of Nature and the aspiration of lost women.'[vi] He went on to note that 'Wales is unkind to a tramp who cannot speak Welsh; and he cannot' (and by 1916 Evans had some experience of Welsh unkindness in response to the debased rendering of the Welsh language in his 1915 collection of stories, *My People*). For Evans, at least, it is precisely those dangerous aspects of Davies's writing which make him a true poet; he is an early champion of Davies's credentials as an important Welsh writer. *The Autobiography of a Super-Tramp* suggests Wales's literary genius is not to be found within her borders, but instead in a down-at-heel London doss house, or else out on the open road.

Tomos Owen

Notes

[i] Katie Gramich has told this story; see her 'Narrating the Nation: Telling Stories of Wales', *North American Journal of Welsh Studies*, 6.1 (Winter 2011), available at <http://welshstudiesjournal.org/index>.

[ii] 'Noted English Poet Studies America as a Tramp', *New York Times*, 18 March 1917, p. SM5.

[iii] 'William H. Davies: Welsh Hobo Poet', *New York Times*, 27 September 1940, p. 30.

[iv] See Lawrence Normand, *W.H. Davies* (Bridgend: Seren, 2003), pp. 64-6.

[v] Gwyn Jones, *The First Forty Years: Some Notes on Anglo-Welsh Literature* (Cardiff: University of Wales Press, 1957), pp. 7-8. Emphasis in original.

[vi] Caradoc Evans, 'Tramp and Poet: How Fame Came to a Newport Man: Adventurous Career', *Western Mail*, 15 January 1916, p. 7.

Trevor Fishlock is a writer and broadcaster, former correspondent of *The Times* in India and New York and *The Daily Telegraph* correspondent in Moscow. He won the International Reporter of the Year prize in the British Press Awards. He is the author of books on Wales, India, Russia, America and 19th century exploration. He has written and presented more than 150 television programmes on life and history in Wales.

Tomos Owen is a lecturer in English Literature at Cardiff University. He has published on several aspects of London-Welsh literary culture of the early twentieth century, including the work of Arthur Machen and Caradoc Evans. He has also published on depictions of rioting in Welsh writing, and is the editor of two anthologies of creative writing for Parthian.

LIBRARY OF WALES

The Library of Wales is a Welsh Government project designed to ensure that all of the rich and extensive literature of Wales which has been written in English will now be made available to readers in and beyond Wales. Sustaining this wider literary heritage is understood by the Welsh Government to be a key component in creating and disseminating an ongoing sense of modern Welsh culture and history for the future Wales which is now emerging from contemporary society. Through these texts, until now unavailable or out-of-print or merely forgotten, the Library of Wales will bring back into play the voices and actions of the human experience that has made us, in all our complexity, a Welsh people.

The Library of Wales will include prose as well as poetry, essays as well as fiction, anthologies as well as memoirs, drama as well as journalism. It will complement the names and texts that are already in the public domain and seek to include the best of Welsh writing in English, as well as to showcase what has been unjustly neglected. No boundaries will limit the ambition of the Library of Wales to open up the borders that have denied some of our best writers a presence in a future Wales. The Library of Wales has been created with that Wales in mind: a young country not afraid to remember what it might yet become.

Dai Smith

LIBRARY OF WALES

FUNDED BY

Noddir gan
Lywodraeth Cymru
Sponsored by
Welsh Government

CYNGOR LLYFRAU CYMRU
BOOKS COUNCIL of WALES